Ecocriticism on the Edge

ALSO AVAILABLE FROM BLOOMSBURY

Ecocriticism on the Edge

The Anthropocene as a threshold concept

TIMOTHY CLARK

Bloomsbury Academic
An imprint of Bloomsbury Publishing Plc

B L O O M S B U R Y
LONDON · NEW DELHI · NEW YORK · SYDNEY

Bloomsbury Academic
An imprint of Bloomsbury Publishing Plc

50 Bedford Square	1385 Broadway
London	New York
WC1B 3DP	NY 10018
UK	USA

www.bloomsbury.com

**BLOOMSBURY and the Diana logo are trademarks of
Bloomsbury Publishing Plc**

First published 2015

© Timothy Clark, 2015

British Library Cataloguing-in-Publication Data
A catalogue record for this book is available from the British Library.

ISBN: HB: 978-1-4725-0648-1
PB: 978-1-4725-0573-6
ePDF: 978-1-4725-0670-2
ePub: 978-1-4742-4630-9

Library of Congress Cataloging-in-Publication Data
A catalog record for this book is available from the Library of Congress.

Typeset by Newgen Knowledge Works (P) Ltd., Chennai, India
Printed and bound in India

In memory of my wonderful mother
Mary Florence Clark, née Cook
10th July 1931–2nd June 2014

CONTENTS

LIST OF ILLUSTRATIONS

ACKNOWLEDGEMENTS

Parts of this book have appeared elsewhere in an earlier form. Material has been reworked from the following essays: 'The Challenge of the Meta-Contextual: Henry Lawson's "Telling Mrs Baker" (1901) and Some Animal Questions for Australia', in *Oxford Literary Review* 29 (2007); 'Some Climate Change Ironies: Deconstruction: Environmental Politics and the Closure of Ecocriticism', in *Oxford Literary Review* 32.1 (July 2010); 'Derangements of Scale', in *Telemorphosis: Essays in Critical Climate Change*, Vol. 1, ed. Tom Cohen and Henry Sussman (Ann Arbor, MI: Open Humanities Press, 2012); 'What on World Is the Earth?: The Anthropocene and Fictions of the World', in *Oxford Literary Review* 35 (2013), 5–24; 'Phenomenology', in *The Oxford Handbook to Ecocriticism*, ed. Greg Garrard (Oxford: Oxford University Press, 2014).

Adam Trexler generously provided me with some exact page references to his excellent *Anthropocene Fictions (2015)* while it was still in proofs, a study I had read and quoted in mss before publication.

Work on this book was made possible through generous periods of research leave granted to me at Durham University, and then by the preservation of solitude. Thanks are due to Dr Matthew Griffiths for his close feedback on earlier versions of the manuscript, both as a copy-editor and an accomplished ecocritic.

PREFACE

Many kinds of environmental destruction provoke calls for protest, action or remediation on the spot, at a local or national scale: excessive logging in ancient forests, the pollution of rivers through sewage discharge or the spillage of chemicals, urban sprawl, the hunting and deliberate extermination of wildlife in a particular area, road building . . . These are all issues with very obvious and visibly destructive effects and they prompt clearly defined kinds of emotional response and protest.

However, the twenty-first century has seen an increased awareness of forms of environmental destruction that cannot immediately be seen, localized or, by some, even acknowledged. Phenomena such as ocean acidification, climate change, the general effects of incremental forms of ecological degradation across the planet, global overpopulation and resource depletion do not present any obvious or perceptible target for concern or protest at any one place, or often any immediate antagonist perceptible at the normal human scale. The largely benumbed recognition of this reality has become one feature of life in the so-called Anthropocene, to use the currently still informal term for the epoch at which largely unplanned human impacts on the planet's basic ecological systems have passed a dangerous, if imponderable, threshold. One major new effort at work in contemporary literary and artistic practice and criticism is to find some way of usefully or authentically engaging such crucial but elusive concerns, precisely when it is acknowledged that they resist representation at the kinds of scale on which most thinking, culture, art and politics operate.

The past few years have seen increasingly forceful studies of both climate change denial and the way the Anthropocene evades normal categories of attention and, as a result, a new variant of so-called ecocriticism has become necessary. This book aims to gauge that shift, using specific literary texts, whether they have an environmental focus or not, to explore the critical issues in their full difficulty and relative unresolvedness. The literary texts used, mainly short stories, were not chosen primarily in order to make some case for their individual importance or that of their authors, but mainly insofar as each helped stage or test the environmental implications and assumption of given modes of reading and interpretation. This involves tracing closely the way in which received or mainstream modes of reading and criticism, even when socially 'progressive' in some respects, are now, despite themselves, being changed into what are effectively implicit forms of denial as the world alters around them.

The Anthropocene is both frightening and intellectually liberating: the uncertainty and incalculable complexity of the issues, especially in forecasting likely future climates or the effects of human action or inaction, impel the resulting discussions in opposing directions. The first is the sense of being overwhelmed, of paralysis, even despair – how can you engage issues that are implicated in multiple events and behaviours and natural processes across the whole planet? To deny this is to evade the nature and urgency of the situation. Secondly, however, the very uncertainties can be intellectually liberating. The breakdowns of inherited demarcations of thought can still become a means of disclosure and revision, tempering the sense of alarm with a host of new insights.

CHAPTER ONE

The Anthropocene – questions of definition

Considering that it has yet to be officially recognized by geologists, the context of its original coining, the proliferation of the term 'Anthropocene' over the past five years has been striking. Features in magazines with titles such as 'Welcome to the Anthropocene' are no longer news. The term, though often used vaguely and now in danger of becoming hackneyed, is clearly filling a need – though a need to name what exactly?

The term was first coined by atmospheric scientists as a name for the geological epoch that the Earth entered with the industrial revolution, around 1800. It is characterized by the unprecedented fact that humanity has come to play a decisive, if still largely incalculable, role in the planet's ecology and geology, that 'Human activities have become so pervasive and profound that they rival the great forces of nature and are pushing the Earth as a whole into planetary *terra incognita*'.[1]

The original coiners of the term dated the Anthropocene from the industrial revolution and the invention of the steam engine. Others, however, have argued that extensive agriculture and forest-clearing may already have significantly affected the Earth system and marked a new epoch thousands of years ago.[2] The force of the term, however, applies mostly to the 'Great Acceleration' since 1945 in which human impacts on the entire biosphere have achieved an unprecedented and arguably dangerous intensity. For geoscientists seeking to broadcast the fears inspired by their research, the coinage 'Anthropocene' is primarily 'a politically savvy way of presenting to nonscientists the sheer magnitude of global biophysical change' (Noel Castree).[3]

The term has rapidly become adopted in the humanities in a sense beyond the strictly geological. Its force is mainly as a loose, shorthand term for all the new contexts and demands – cultural, ethical, aesthetic, philosophical and political – of environmental issues that are truly planetary in scale, notably climate change, ocean acidification, effects of overpopulation, deforestation, soil-erosion, overfishing and the general and accelerating degradation of ecosystems. This is broadly how it is used in this study.

For Tom Cohen, 2011 marks or will mark in future retrospect, the rough date at which the irreversible nature of global warming was widely recognized, with the '"anthropocene era" naming itself as if from without',[4] while Timothy Morton stresses that one defining feature of this situation, which he also terms the Anthropocene, is precisely the impossibility of a secure overview. His book *Hyperobjects* (2013) describes the Anthropocene as 'the daunting, indeed horrifying, coincidence of human history and terrestrial geology',[5] with the dawning realization of 'a new phase of history in which nonhumans are no longer excluded or merely decorative features of . . . social, psychic, and philosophical space' (12). This is the time of the human realization of what he nicknames 'hyperobjects', that is 'things that are massively distributed in time and space relative to humans, and which defy overview and resist understanding' (1).[6]

For Tobias Menely and Margaret Ronda, the 'Anthropocene' names the moment at which expanding global capitalism, with its increasingly destructive side effects of pollution, deforestation, and immiseration, reaches a threshold of self-destruction, but also of self-deception, as the accelerating conversion of all natural entities into forms of human capital becomes more and more patently in denial of ecological realities and limits.[7] Ulrich Beck's arguments are similar, as he describes modernity entering a newly uncertain, reflexive stage, the age of 'unintended consequences'.[8]

Slavoj Žižek argues that anthropogenic climate change is only a 'pseudo-problem' masking the deeper question of international capitalism.[9] However, it is not now enough to identify modern capitalism as the exclusive agent of environmental violence. Aside from the fact that socialist systems of government have also had appalling environmental records, the processes culminating in the Anthropocene include events that predate the advent of capitalism, primarily the invention of agriculture, deforestation and the eradication over centuries of large mammals in all continents beyond Africa as humanity expanded across the globe. Morton traces environmentally destructive attitudes back to the effects of the psychic space of inhabitation made possible by agriculture in the Neolithic: 'agriculture turns reality into domination-ready chunks of parcelled out space waiting to be filled and ploughed by humans'.[10] As Dipesh Chakravarty writes: 'the current crisis has brought into view certain other conditions for the existence of life in the human form that have no intrinsic connections to the logics of capitalist, nationalist or socialist identities'.[11] If the deep history of agriculture forms one unavoidable context for thinking in environmental ways about capitalist, communist or other modes of political organization, then to critique capital may remain supremely important, but is also insufficient. 'All progressive political thought, including postcolonial criticism, will have to register this profound change in the human condition' (Chakravarty).[12]

The term 'Anthropocene' is also a catchphrase, used as both intellectual shortcut and expanded question mark to refer to the novel situation we are in. The word is increasingly also a piece of academic rhetoric (e.g. is it cynical to observe that 2011, Cohen's supposed date for recognition of the Anthropocene, is also that of the publication of the book in which he writes that? Or that his co-author Claire Colebrook is already using the impossible term 'post-Anthropocene'?).[13] The term, already rather free from the constraints of geological terminology, may remain useful so long as its various but related uses retain a self-critical, even self-deconstructive force, even marking the term's own equivocality as symptomatic of the kinds of blurring of would-be sharp conceptual, rhetorical, material and disciplinary borders in a newly recognized planetary context.

The overview effect

More than a decade before the term 'Anthropocene' was even coined, Michel Serres's *The Natural Contract* (first published in 1990) offered one of the earliest considerations of the deeper implications of humanity having become a geological force. In effect, Serres set out some basic stakes for the concept:

> On planet Earth, henceforth, action comes not so much from man as an individual or subject, the ancient warrior-hero of philosophy and old-style historical consciousness, not so much from the canonized combat of master and slave . . . not so much from the groups analyzed by the old social sciences – assemblies, parties, nations, armies, tiny villages – no, the decisive actions are now, massively, those of enormous and dense tectonic plates of humanity.[14]

Serres's book had called for a 'natural contract' to supplement the hypothetical 'social contract' that underlies human beings living together in ordered groups. This would acknowledge and address the violence humanity has waged against the Earth itself. Serres's essay poises itself on a moment of simultaneous supreme danger to humanity and the Earth, and the possibility of humanity as steward and 'mother' of the Earth, taking on a kind of cosmic role.

Nevertheless, for all its prescience, Serres's final section on the image of the whole Earth from space was also an instance of the kind of dangerous fantasy that the Anthropocene may represent, testimony to just how elusive and unpreconceivable its challenges may be. First, Serres celebrates a moment of totalization, a culmination of the human project:

> Seen from above, from this new high place, Earth contains all our ancestors, indistinguishably mingled: the universal tomb of universal history. What funeral service do all these vapour plumes herald? And since, from up here, no-one perceives borders, which are abstract in any case, we can speak for the first time of Adam and Eve, our first common parents, and thus of brotherhood. One humanity at last. (121)

The act of engaging with the Earth as a whole is taken as that of an achieved humanity in the singular. This is 'the universal-subject, humanity, in solidarity at last, in contemplating the object-universe' (122). It is the realization, or at least anticipation, of a unified human agent, reconceiving it and its possibilities in the prospect of the planet below it, like the image of the star-baby at the end of Stanley Kubrick's *2001: A Space Odyssey* (USA, 1968).

Serres concedes that this moment of (imagined) transcendence is also a moment of realized dependence and finitude:

> Flying high enough to see her whole, we find ourselves tethered to her by the totality of our knowledge, the sum of our technologies, the collection of our communications; by torrents of signals, by the complete set of imaginable umbilical cords, living and artificial, visible and invisible, concrete or purely formal. (122)

Nevertheless, for Serres this is not a chastening realization of human finitude, but the achievement of knowledge as self-transcendence ('we pull on these cords to the point that we comprehend them all' (122)). He anticipates here contemporary arguments that the Anthropocene, in its very danger, could also represent the hope for a new form of humanism, one tied to a collective self-recognition of the human as 'steward' of the planet, envisaging the Earth as a vast garden-city sustained by various geo-engineering schemes. Likewise for Erle Ellis, writing in an anthology celebrating a supposedly 'postenviromental' liberalism, the Anthropocene can mark 'the beginning of a new geological epoch ripe with human-directed opportunity'.[15]

Yet Serres is writing metaphorically of something he has never seen. In fact, no-one has immediate access to the world as a planet: what we have is a complex set of data from various recording stations at various points on the surface or above, and a history of such data or comparable information, all needing to be synthesized, interpreted and debated. So, many of the intellectual challenges and dangers of overload that accompany the thought of the Anthropocene are already and at once embedded in the perplexing and multiple conception of the 'Anthropocene' itself, as no sort of unitary or easily perceived object but the correlate of numerous observations, and sometimes conflicting theories in many different disciplines, of paleoclimatological reconstructions, atmospheric modelling and so on.

Bruno Latour also argues against the too-hasty appropriation of the whole Earth image by forms of environmental moralism:

> it is useless for the ecologically motivated activist to try shaming the ordinary citizen for *not* thinking globally enough, for not having a feel for the Earth as such. No-one sees the Earth globally and no-one sees an ecological system from nowhere.[16]

In sum, Serres's essay is an exercise in anthropocentric illusion. At times, the prose resembles a rousing head-teacher's pep-talk to a young humanity ready to leave school and take on the cosmos. Serres's otherwise prescient account of the Anthropocene in the early 1990s is still entangled in the human self-conceptions it is actually bringing to a close. For the major irony of the Anthropocene is that, though named as that era in the planet's natural history in which humanity becomes a decisive geological and climatological force, it manifests itself to us primarily through the domain of 'natural' becoming, as it were, dangerously out of bounds, in extreme or unprecedented weather events, ecosystems becoming simplified or trashed, die-back or collapse.[17]

'We are as Gods? No, for we have created the power but not the mind'[18]

In their *The Techno-Human Condition* (2011), Braden R. Allenby and Daniel Sarewitz present an image of the current human world that is almost an inverse of that given by Serres. Acknowledging the Anthropocene as 'a world in which human activity increasingly affects global systems, including the climate and the hydrological, carbon, and nitrogen cycles of the anthropogenic Earth' (10), they argue that 'the world we are making through our own choices and inventions is a world that neutralizes and even mocks our existing commitments to rationality, comprehension, and a meaningful link between action and consequence' (64–5).

Why is this? Their subject is technological complexity and the dysfunctions that arise out of the human inability to think beyond certain levels of complexity. Allenby and Sarewitz contrast three levels of complexity in the relation of our species to technics (a relation essential for any definition of what human beings are). A Level I relation is, crudely, that of the traditional notion of technology as a simple tool. An aeroplane, for instance, is a complex piece of engineering. Nevertheless, considered as a means of getting quickly from A to B, it sets up a simple relation of instrumentality – we use it for a predetermined end, merely fast transport. However, if passenger planes are often late, delayed or part of an unreliable service, it is because they are actually now embedded in higher-level technical networks, systems of social and technical control, with additional complications in their own security and pricing systems, relations to the law and so on. These are all far more complex than the aeroplane itself as a tool, and liable to unexpected failure. They form what Allenby and Daniel Sarewitz term a Level II system. Whereas in a Level I system there are simple and visible relations of cause and effect – the tool, unless broken, does what we employ it for – at Level II we are presented with a 'a complex socio-technological system, infinitely less predictable and more complicated than the jet airplane itself' (38).

For Allenby and Sarewitz, many environmental problems could be described as the unintended effects of interference between events at different levels of complexity. What may be simply convenient at Level I (individual car use) may become disastrous at other levels:

> So are automobiles the institutionalization of environmental evil, or an expression of personal freedom? Both effects derive from a link between the Level I functionality that attracts people to use cars in the first place and Level II complexity; but the question is incoherent, for it conflates two different views of the technology system, two different sets of effects, and two unrelated questions of values. (46)

A Level III system represents a yet higher level of complexity, incalculability and ramification. Allenby and Sarewitz's example is again the automobile. Cars, trucks and so on are part of a socio-technological network of the kind already described at Level II, but their effects on society, infrastructure, psychology, health etc. have become incalculable. That is, a proliferation of emergent effects has long exceeded the possibilities of human foresight or planning:

> cars in networks create emergent behaviors that, at least temporarily, subvert the usefulness of the car as an artifact. (We call one such emergent behavior a traffic jam). But as the basis of a technology constellation that fuelled a stage of economic evolution in the West, the automobile did far more: it co-evolved with significant changes in environmental and resource systems; with mass-market consumer capitalism; with individual credit; with behavioral and aesthetic subcultures and stereotypes; with oil spills; with opportunities for, and a sense

of, extraordinary human freedom, especially for women who were otherwise trapped in their houses by social and economic patterns. We'll call this Level III. (39)

Events at Level III broadly correspond to Morton's notion of the hyperobject, entities whose physical and temporal scale and complexity overwhelm both traditional conceptions of what a thing is and what 'understanding' it could mean. However, Allenby and Sarewitz's conceptualizing of issues in terms of three contrasting levels of complexity allows a more specific sense of how Level III entities arise and exceed the terms of thinking applicable at lower levels.

Allenby and Sarewitz also offer the example of vaccines:

If one thinks of a vaccine as a means of reducing levels of infection, it looks like a Level I technology; if one thinks of it as a means of improving economic growth, it looks like a Level II technology; if one thinks of it as a part of long-term demographic trends and subsequent political and social evolution in a developing country, it looks like a Level III technology. (40)

The challenge is that Level III effects represent complex emergent properties that defy our ability to model, predict or even understand them, a problem already all too familiar to scientists attempting to model human influence on the future climate. Ignorance of the effects of complexity may account for why it is that 25 years of measures to address climate change have been so patently inadequate, as dangerous emissions continue to grow, with the climate now altering in a manner that exceeds some of the worst-case scenarios of the 2007 report of Intergovernmental Panel on Climate Change, especially in relation to the loss of sea ice.[19] The relative failure of such measures as the 1997 Kyoto Protocol to limit carbon emissions stems from the absurdity of reducing climate change to the simplistic Level I issues of carbon emissions and 'footprints' (Allenby and Sarewitz, 112; see also 170). This stance also results in a crude green moralism that, however helpful in a trivial sense, evades the complexity of the causes of climate change. Allenby and Sarewitz write:

The campaign to create a moral universe predicated on carbon footprint, which began with initiatives against sport-utility vehicles, is now extending across society as a whole. Climate-change science and climate-change policy are rapidly becoming carbon fundamentalism, a simplistic but comprehensive structure of moral valuation that can be applied to virtually any individual or institution. (124)

One provisional way to characterize the Anthropocene, in the broader sense of a cultural threshold used in this study, is that more and more events and problems are emerging at Level III, rendering obsolete modes of thought that are confined to Levels I and II, even if those still describe the kinds of thinking almost all people try to live by. 'How can human intentionality and rationality – those paragons of the Enlightenment project – be meaningfully expressed when accelerating technological evolution and complexity make a mockery of conventional notions of comprehensibility?' (85). Allenby and Sarewitz omit detailed or deeply considered reference to the complex natural and Earth systems in which technological activity is embedded, something which would further deepen the challenge to human understanding. Also omitted is overpopulation, a factor that must increasingly be acknowledged as transforming events or entities at lower levels of complexity into Level III forms of incalculability and entrapment. The third-level status of this particular issue is already apparent in the fact that even beginning to discuss it means entering at once a confusing and very often heated controversy over definitions, causes, rights, and responsibilities and, for some, even whether it exists at all.

The Anthropocene blurs and even scrambles some crucial categories by which people have made sense of the world and their lives. It puts in crisis the lines between culture and nature, fact and value, and between the human and the geological or meteorological. As a bewildering and often destructive contamination of human aims and natural causality, the Anthropocene manifests itself in innumerable possible hairline cracks in the familiar life-world, at the local and personal scale of each individual life. Something planetary is breaking through, entailing a politicization of what may once have seemed insignificant, as familiar day-to-day practices incite an engaged 'green' political awareness. For example, someone's routinely driving a car may be condemned as an act of more significance, on the planetary scale, than their voting habits. The opinions that a critic may air at a conference may seem of less significance than the fact of having taken a flight to reach it, tacitly endorsing the existence of the airline industry. The planetary scale of the Anthropocene compels us to think and act as if already citizens of a world polity, even while it increasingly undermines the conditions of co-operation for any would-be cosmopolitan citizenship. In some countries at least, acknowledging the very existence or not of global warming has become, absurdly, a matter of political allegiance.

If criticism and politics to date have had such difficulty finding adequate strategies to engage with climate change, the most prominent feature of the Anthropocene, it is perhaps because there is no simple or unitary object *directly* to confront, or delimit, let alone to 'fix' or to 'tackle'. There is no 'it', only a kind of dissolution into innumerable issues. So it may be that ecocriticism has found it hard to deal with climate change as a sustained and direct object of analysis because the issue is one that refuses to stay put, dispersing as soon as you look at it into multiple questions, disciplines and topics, most of them at once outside the sphere of literary studies, others outside the humanities altogether, and many of them (for instance, the size of one's family) only counting as 'environmental' at all through variously hypothetical contextual and scale effects.

Allenby and Sarewitz's argument suggests a true sense of the scope of the challenges an environmental criticism must take up. Consider, for instance, the bewildering number of things that might be considered as significant 'environmental' issues relating to resource and energy use, to waste production, or to the perpetuation of social and economic systems with environmentally destructive effects. A list could include: day-to-day Western assumptions about lifestyle, the political systems of numerous countries, the fuel efficiency of modern cars and heating systems, population trends and sexual habits, definitions of the good life, the nature of money and exchange, the aspirations of the poor, the politics of national sovereignty, the impersonal demands of 'advanced' infrastructures that imprison their inhabitants in a kind of 'energy slavery' (William Ophuls),[20] the size of households, the melting threshold of arctic tundra, the exact nature of innumerable other unknown or badly understood biological, meteorological and chemical processes and so on. Each issue in itself is made more problematic by scale effects that may render each of significance only in relation to the others together, now, in the past and over an indefinite future. In sum, it is not surprising that attempts to address climate change within the closed frameworks of consumer democracy, with their panaceas of improving fuel efficiency and of informed consumer choice ('ecological modernization'), should define the issue simplistically in terms of quantifiable gas emissions, nor that the measures should be so limited in effect.

For Allenby and Sarewitz, the current world is becoming one that is almost the inverse of Michel Serres's fantasy of an empowering totalization of human knowledge as it envelops the Earth. Serres's exultant humanism contrasts with their more dystopian reading of the present as forming a kind of cognitive boundary or 'tipping point' for an unmanageable complexity, beyond which there seems nothing but paralysis: 'Any framework or model that can be understood, and that is based on a coherent worldview, is by definition at best only a partial truth. One could almost say "If you understand it, it isn't true; and if it is true, you can't understand it"' (186). This is pithy, provocative, but also perhaps a little glib and surely fatalistic, as though, in the face of all these alarming future scenarios triggered by human action, there was absolutely nothing anyone could do.

The air of excessive resignation in Allenby and Sarewitz's account can seem morally evasive. Might they even risk being seen as closet apologists for global capitalism, if only in so far as they see technical and economic systems as having become as unanswerable as a force of nature, without alternatives? The clarity of their own conceptualization of three different levels of complexity is in itself an example that an emergent phenomenon, such as the effects of widespread automobile use, need not elude some sort of understanding, even if they are not amenable to full prediction.

Sarewitz and Allenby's diagnosis of forms of Level III paralysis concerns the Anthropocene in terms of a bafflingly vast loss of comprehension. However, this still seems too sweeping a conclusion. A refinement of their argument would be to take the Anthropocene as naming an arena of tragic, opaque and sometimes irreconcilable dilemmas, within a context of increasingly constricted possibility, readability and scope for action.

Take the famous UN definition of 'sustainable development': 'sustainable development is development that meets the needs of the present without compromising the ability of future generations to meet their own needs' (The World Commission on Environment and Development, 1987).[21] The UN's subsequent detailed and far more encompassing studies of 'sustainability', most recently 'Global Environmental Outlook' 5 (2012), reaffirm how deeply an increasing proportion of the world's growing population of 7 billion already lives in a manner that exceeds the carrying capacity of the planet.[22] While it would be easy to describe the Anthropocene as entailing a divisive threshold at which meeting the needs of the present and meeting the needs of the future become incompatible, the later UN document still sets out in detail how transition to a sustainable planet would require 'navigating a wide range of highly complex and interrelated issues simultaneously' (450), political, social, governmental, technical, demographic, economic and ethical. For the regional field of ecocriticism, this suggests a practice that would try to loosen the sense of paralysis described by Allenby and Sarewitz and work through the conflicting, even contradictory demands of various environmental questions, if only to make their dilemmas explicit. In the narrow university context, such massive tensions translate themselves into intractable questions of legitimacy. These pit students' reasonable expectations of a degree that will render them employable against the undeniable problem that current destructive systems of production and the governments that support them can only be seen as increasingly illegitimate.

Many of the tensions and intellectual fragilities of ecocriticism come from the drive to reconcile increasingly incompatible claims under one diagnostic framework, despite a context that must render them more and more at odds with one another. Critics can be watched playing claims off against each other like the famous guessing game of rock, scissors and paper.[23] Thus, urgent demands to recognize that cultural and political systems are dependent on nature are met by ripostes from thinkers concerned with social justice that concepts of 'nature' are always cultural constructs and often serve the ends of more privileged groups, while others stress the material constraints on any would-be progressive politics in a vast and ever-expanding human population; the need to preserve or create national parks is held to clash with the rights of that land's indigenous human inhabitants, while, in turn, such 'postcolonial' ethics is attacked for being almost uniformly anthropocentric; the need to stress the extreme dangers of global warming is met by arguments that too apocalyptic an environmental rhetoric defeats itself as mode of political influence, while others argue that global capitalist society is structurally deaf to environmental influence in any case, except in forms of systemic self-deception . . . and so the controversies cycle on.

This study will approach the intellectual challenges of the Anthropocene and its unreadability in terms of the inevitable question of scale. As a concept transferred from geology, the Anthropocene enacts the demand to think of human life at much broader scales of space and time, something which alters significantly the way that many once familiar issues appear. Perhaps too big to see or even to think straight (a 'hyperobject', certainly) the Anthropocene challenges us to think counter-intuitive relations of scale, effect, perception, knowledge, representation and calculability. In its context of overpopulation, global pollution, the degradation of oceans and other forms of action at a distance, together with the latent action of unknown natural 'tipping points', the mere fact of two lives existing together – anywhere on the Earth – can now raise new and imponderable ethical and cognitive questions about their relation, quite separate from the issues of cultural identity, politics, recognition and so forth, that have engaged most criticism hitherto, with its agendas of human understanding and mutual recognition. I may have no access to the singular world (including the culture and values etc.) of another person, but I am in them in a minimal sense, affecting their lives indirectly, and leave obscure, if unidentifiable, traces and hairline cracks there (some people, of course – most Western Europeans and North Americans for instance – more destructively than others).

In other ways, however, the scale of the Anthropocene entails a disconcerting *de-politicization*. The would-be progressive understanding of recent centuries of human history as the advance of human freedoms through various peoples' struggle for rights comes also to be seen, less heroically, as a phenomenon of natural history, namely of a species experiencing a boom in numbers, possibilities, and in some cases at least, in liberties and security, through the discovery of vast resources of fossil fuels. With the realization of this, 'Modernity's "promise" now appears threatening and unsustainable'.[24] A recent call for papers for a conference on feminism and the Anthropocene confronts directly another de-politicizing implication of the Anthropocene. The question for the conference was: what does feminism have to say 'to the claim that humans now act as a geological force in ways that are *independent of or indifferent to social, cultural, or political will or intent?*' (emphasis added).[25]

The Anthropocene also manifests itself in new kinds of psychic affects and a destabilization of norms as to the serious and the trivial. Global environmental issues such as climate change entail the implication of the broadest effects in the smallest day-to-day phenomena, juxtaposing the trivial and the catastrophic in ways that can be deranging or paralyzing – for what can *I* do? The Anthropocene and its attendant disasters also play into some very peculiar forms of social pathology. Harald Walzer writes of social and intellectual responses to climate change: 'In the history of science there has probably been no comparable situation in which a scenario of such change in large parts of the world, based on solid scientific evidence, has been regarded with such equanimity by social or cultural theorists'.[26] The Australian journalist and cultural critic Philip Adams describes a public meeting on the serious dangers of global warming: 'it was a religious event. People were not concerned about greenhouse gases coming from rice paddies or cattle, they wanted to hear about the evil automobile and the evil power factory'. Likewise, 'the more the scientists predicted a catastrophe, the more the audiences seemed to like it'.[27]

THE TRAGIC ENVIRONMENTAL LEVIATHAN

One definitive feature of the Anthropocene is the emergence of the human species per se as a different form of 'transpersonal agency'. It is an agency that must now, for the first time, be posited 'as operating at the universal level of the human species as a whole – a super-subject beyond all possible subjective experience',[28] or, in Serres's memorable phrase, 'enormous and dense tectonic plates of humanity'.

Dipesh Chakrabarty argues that the Anthropocene entails both 'a new universal history of humanity',[29] and, since 'the whole crisis cannot be reduced to a story of capitalism' over the past 400 years, it also entails a new sense of 'we' as subject of history, one determined not by a particular mode of production but emerging out of a now common sense of danger.

However, elaboration of the Anthropocene as a threshold concept involves acknowledgement of emergent effects whose force is a kind of inertia or potential paralysis in the hoped-for emergence of 'species-being' as a recognized universal human self-image. The newly recognized agent of humanity as a geological force is something indiscernible in any of the individuals or even large groups of which it is composed. It is a power that barely recognizes itself as such and which is not really capable of voluntary action or planning, as it arises from the often unforeseen consequences of the plans and acts of its constituents.

The tragic danger at work with this new agency can be expressed in an image. One of the most famous conceits in political theory is the picture of a giant man used by Thomas Hobbes in his treatise *Leviathan* of 1651 to depict 'Leviathan', the mighty creature, composing many individuals, that makes up that more-than-personal entity, the state. The striking feature of the image is that the gigantic Leviathan is himself depicted as physically comprising a multitude of tiny homunculi, enacting the paradox of his double nature – that he is both composed of a multitude of individuals come together to form a commonwealth, but that the result is a new, powerful single entity that is far more than the sum of its parts, one which produces internal order and security.

For Hobbes, the Leviathan of the state exists partly to overcome what he saw as a brutal state of nature in which individuals would compete without restraint for food, resources and space, rendering life violent and forever insecure. With the emergence of humanity as planetary agent despite itself, however, we are faced with an entity enacting a syndrome almost the reverse of the move from a supposedly (brutal) stateless nature to the ordered restraint of a commonwealth. One can picture the current humanity as a super-Leviathan whose body is made up of lots of smaller Leviathans or human groups. Many would be rational, peaceful and accommodating, or people just trying to get by as best they can. But this time the giant they comprise would not be the force of restraint and order that was the Leviathan in Hobbes. Rather, if characterized in terms of the psychology of an individual, this planetary giant would not seem to have the supposedly definitive human characteristics of foresight and restraint, but it would be a self-destructive and self-deluding figure, more like a psychopath.

FIGURE 1 *From the frontispiece of the 1651 edition of Thomas Hobbes'*
Leviathan.

The cliché of humanity having become a geological force has
implications beyond the fact of human violence against the Earth and
other species. A geological force is also an impersonal one, one that,
like plate tectonics or earthquakes, does not heed entreaties, respect
individual rights or admit of being altered by human decisions. In this
case, however, the geological force at issue is, paradoxically, a total
effect of innumerable human decisions. Nevertheless, it can seem as
imperturbably closed to human direction as is a hurricane or the tilt of
the planet's orbit.

A global imaginary?

The Anthropocene brings to an unavoidable point of stress the
question of the nature of Nature and of the human. It represents,
for the first time, the demand made upon a species consciously
to consider its impact as a totality upon the whole planet, the
advent of a kind of new reflexivity as a species. Individual acts of
generosity, cultural change, economic success, medical progress,
national achievements and so on become something that must be
conceived at this higher, unprecedented level of self-reflection.

But what on earth *is* thinking or acting 'as a species'? As Chrakrabarty writes:

> When [E.O.] Wilson . . . recommends in the interests of our collective future that we achieve self-understanding as a species, the statement does not correspond to any historical way of understanding and connecting pasts with futures through the assumption of there being an element of continuity to human experience . . . Who is the 'we'? We humans never experience ourselves as a species. We can only intellectually comprehend or infer the existence of the human species but never experience it as such.[30]

The aim, nevertheless, is that politics, culture and art should now aid a sort of species-consciousness, so that the worst effects of environmental degradation can be countered by the redemptive force of an increased and shared self-recognition– that the human Leviathan achieves some kind of responsible consciousness. In E. O. Wilson's words:

> Humanity has consumed or transformed enough of Earth's irreplaceable resources to be in better shape than ever before. We are smart enough and now, one hopes, well informed enough to achieve self-understanding as a unified species . . . We will be wise to look on ourselves as a species.[31]

The hope is that the dangers of the Anthropocene will be sufficient to induce such a shift. The programme of ecocriticism itself has been the consolidation of this emergent culture, a metamorphosis in the way 'we' think, understand and read. A crude sort of species-identity has long been implicit in environmental criticism, with its admonitions that 'we' must change drastically the way 'we' think, otherwise basic natural systems will collapse.

The work of the environmental critic then becomes to consider and appreciate work in literature, criticism and the arts that helps articulate this shift towards a new kind of eco-cosmopolitanism capable of uniting people across the world without erasing important cultural and political differences. It is hoped that an emergent culture, coterminous with the species, will make up a collective force strong enough to help counter the day-to-day forces and decisions accelerating the extinction of terrestrial life. For instance, Ursula Heise writes of texts that take on the issue of overpopulation, John Brunner's *Stand on Zanzibar* (1968), David Brin's *Earth* (1990) and John Cage's long poem, 'Overpopulation and Art' (1992):[32] 'Brunner and Cage envision communication technologies and networks as opportunities for local individuals and communities to develop an eco-cosmopolitan awareness and presence [. . .] thereby gaining access to a different category of space that is not envisioned as a scarce and unevenly distributed resource'.[33] For Heise, the texts by Brunner and Cage enact a transformation of our imagined individual relationship to the global population, so we can come to internalize a belonging to a 'virtual' crowd, to the eco-cosmopolitan. Morton's ethics of what he calls the 'ecological thought' – the comprehensive realization of everything being connected to everything else – projects a comparable eco-cosmopolitan stance ('Give us nowhere to stand, and we shall care for the Earth').[34]

However, ecocriticism may need to confront an intractable question. What if the kind of transformed imagination celebrated in this sort of cultural programme, this awareness of interconnection, could not be assumed to be an effective agent of change – in other words, *how far does a change in knowledge and imagination entail a change in environmentally destructive modes of life*?

At stake in this question is what has been described as a founding intellectual tenet of ecocriticism. Hannes Bergthaller sums it up pithily:

> The idea that the roots of the ecological crisis are to be found in a failure of the imagination, and that literary studies – the human imagination being their home turf – therefore have an important role to play understanding and overcoming this crisis, is foundational to most forms of ecocriticism.[35]

This touches the heart of ecocriticism. To trace environmental degradation to mistaken knowledge, a false world view (the supposed sovereignty of the human, or of the male, notions of nature as inert resource, scientific 'abstraction' etc.), remains the main move of much environmental thought. Ecocritics repeatedly refer to the 'social imaginary' or the 'cultural imaginary' as their object of engagement, taking culture in the sense of shared 'symbolic meanings for various domains of experience', including 'actions and beliefs classed as right and wrong' (Jerome Kagan).[36] The work of an ecocritic is seen as one of 'reimagination', to change 'the imaginary' of his or her culture. This is the basis of innumerable social-ecological and ecofeminist programmes, claiming to trace environmental destruction back to primarily *cultural* or *cultural political* factors, and producing readings based on a faith that environmental destruction can be remedied by cultural means, by some future or ongoing transformation in our ability to adequately reimagine individual or group identities and environmental contexts.

Morton expresses a broad critical consensus when he writes

> Art can help us, because it's a place in our culture that deals with intensity, shame, abjection, and loss. It also deals with reality and unreality, being and seeming. If ecology is about radical coexistence, then we must challenge our sense of what is real and what is unreal, what counts as existent and what counts as non-existent. (*The Ecological Thought*, 10)

This is a strong claim, convincing enough as an account of the force of some art for some people. But how plausible is it to describe the environmental problem itself in the way Lawrence Buell and innumerable others do, as at bottom a 'crisis of the imagination, the amelioration of which depends on finding better ways of imaging nature and humanity's relation to it'?[37] The notion of the 'cultural imaginary' already sounds suspiciously super-structural. The recurrent phrase is striking for almost conceding in advance its marginality and weakness as a sphere of agency ('cultural *imaginary*') as compared with primacy of the power of material modes of production, food habits, energy use, reproductive trends and so on (i.e. culture in a far broader, material sense). Of course, most ecocritics are working for changes in those areas of life too: my scepticism relates to the decreasingly convincing commitment that these can be very significantly advanced through the interpretation of cultural artefacts. If the Anthropocene entails living in a space of contracting freedom of movement and increased resistance to overview, then a stronger ecocriticism may emerge from one more directly engaged with its own current limits.

Ursula Heise's *Sense of Place and Sense of Planet* (2008) exemplifies the still-dominant paradigm of the critic as a sort of cultural historian, a practitioner of 'cultural analysis' (13). The critic's task is to offer a kind of descriptive overview, tracing the transformation and genealogy of art forms and discourses (e.g. 'Part of today's anti-globalization rhetoric, with its allegorization of villainous transnational corporations, descends directly from [the] corporate-conspiracy discourse of the 1960s and 1970s' (27)). Underlying such an argument is a commitment, fundamental to most ecocriticism, to the place of literature and art in identity formation, the idea that 'the aesthetic transformation of the real has a particular potential for reshaping the individual and collective ecosocial imaginary'.[38] Again, the 'cultural' or the 'cultural imaginary' is assumed to form a semi-autonomous sphere of effective agency and human self-understanding, to be that which the work of criticism reflects and which it hopes, in turn, to influence. Perhaps, however, future criticism in relation to the environmental crisis will divide between those readings whose methodology, like Heise's, uses or adapts inherited conceptions of the human, the social, cultural etc., and those for whom the environmental crisis questions the seeming self-evidence or coherence of such basic conceptions. It is a matter of what Tom Cohen usefully terms 'a politics of cognition'.[39] Criticism may not be just a matter of helping the construction of an eco-cosmopolitan identity, or of defending texts that make phenomena such as climate change more forcibly apprehensible. It also becomes the reexamination of inherited notions of the human, the cultural and 'identity' in the first place.

A great deal of work in current ecocriticism now consists in (a) coming up with a set of those features that literature or art adequate to the environmental emergency would ideally have, be it texts that work on multiple scales, which challenge notions of the real, accord true agency and worth to the nonhuman, which show how porous human bodies and psyches are to material environmental effects, or which acknowledge counter-intuitive perspectives and resist idealistic notions of human identity, and then (b) homing in on some text, artwork or cultural event, whether old or newly produced, to show it can match some or all of the requirements and is correspondingly 'important'.

This is useful and necessary work, but it does not confront the deeper issue of its initial commitment to a certain conception of the cultural per se. One question central to this book is this: how far is much environmental criticism vulnerable to delusions that the sphere of cultural representations has more centrality and power than in fact it has? Worse, might this exaggerated sense of significant agency in turn produce or perpetuate an illusion all too convenient for the destructive status quo, the belief that endorsing certain symbolic or the imaginary events may be far more crucial or decisive than it really is? To exaggerate the importance of the imaginary is, in itself, to run the risk of consolidating a kind of diversionary side-show, blind to its relative insignificance.[40]

The Anthropocene names a newly recognized context that entails a chastening recognition of the limits of cultural representation as a force of change in human affairs, as compared to the numerous economic, meteorological, geographical and microbiological factors and population dynamics, as well as scale effects, such as the law of large numbers,[41] that arise from trying to think on a planetary scale. The editors of the new book series 'Environmental Cultures' offer a perhaps telling diminuendo of claims when they write that 'cultural criticism can help avert, resolve, mitigate or at least comprehend ecological problems'.[42] My study offers readings which can support only the last claim without reservation, though improved comprehension must be a minimal condition for making the stronger claims more viable.

The kinds of comprehension that do emerge can be illuminating but also alarmingly close to being paralyzing, given the scope and complexity of the issues. Nevertheless, any commitment to a new planet-wide eco-cosmopolitanism cannot be met by an ecocriticism which, in the past, has often been too intellectually, politically and morally simplifying. Later chapters will take up the question of how the Anthropocene may name a kind of threshold at which modes of thinking and practices that were once self-evidently adequate, progressive or merely innocuous become, in this emerging and counter-intuitive context, even latently destructive. Tracing this may also mean a rather more aggressive attitude to other schools of literary criticism than seems currently the case among ecocritics. As well as trying to outline modes of reading that do justice to environmental issues and animal ethics, ecocritics should become more forthright in highlighting the destructive implications and assumptions of given critical schools (whether historicist, formalist, postcolonial or, indeed, many others). Such readings would uncover, for example, the extent to which critics and modes of thought are entrenched in modes of cultural self-understanding that are either inherently destructive or which now become destructive in the Anthropocene.

Summary

A brief overview of how the argument will progress may be useful.

The next chapter takes up the fact that in daily life we lack any immediate sense of the Earth as a finite planet. Environmental damage happening at that scale remains usually counter-intuitive and even invisible. A deeper sense of the nature of these limits to perception is necessary to help conceive the insidious way in which the Anthropocene is turning the normal into a form of unwitting entrapment. These limits can be gauged by consideration of responses to what has already become one of the icons of environmentalism, the image of the whole Earth as taken from space.

The third chapter concerns the way this disruption of scalar norms affects procedures for reading a literary text, in this case a short lyric by Gary Snyder. The focus is on the specific time-honoured notion that to understand a text is to reconstruct its context. Yet 'putting it back in context' is something that must become more problematic when we are forced to consider issues which, in however minute a way, require both planetary and even futural contexts. The odd-seeming nature of this new demand, at once over the top and yet now often unavoidable, is exemplary of the kind of discomposure, even derangement, of norms of judgement and understanding that accompany the thought of Anthropocene.

The next two chapters take up the notion of 'scale framing'. Any context for a reading needs to be limited in some way if it is to be coherent, or merely to end, but the complexities of the Anthropocene highlight the dangers for ecocriticism of premature modes of intellectual containment and even of simplification. The most difficult challenge for critical reevaluations in the Anthropocene is represented by scale effects, that is, phenomena that are invisible at the normal levels of perception but only emerge as one changes the spatial or temporal scale at which the issues are framed. The controversial issue of overpopulation is highlighted, both as an instance of 'scale effects' and as a flash point at which tensions, commitments and forms of moral containment in environmental thinking come under the greatest strain and visibility.

A second chapter on scale framing consists of a close reading of one American text, a short story by Raymond Carver (compared briefly to a narrative by the Nigerian writer Ben Okri). This considers how reading a text at different scales or contexts is a practice that produces *contradictory understandings and evaluations at the same time*. This conflict of scales does not allow one reading to trump the others as the 'correct' one. It highlights those quandaries of judgement that seem set to characterize all kinds of personal, social and political decision-making in the Anthropocene, the choice of the least bad option amid a less than optimal set of choices.

Chapter Six consists of another close reading, taking up John Miller's claim that '[W]e need to rethink ... what we mean by "human" and "animal" because climate change, among other interlinked factors, has made it impossible for these terms to mean what we thought they meant'.[43] The chapter evaluates the way knowledge of the Anthropocene affects rereading of a text of 1901 from Australia. In particular, how does a sense of an expanded, ecological context, which must include a sense of the human as one animal in relation to others, throw into sharp relief the anthropocentric limits of dominant forms of postcolonial criticism and politics?

The readings given in the previous two chapters concerned modes of scale framing that now emerge as unjustified and premature. Yet to reject old modes of framing the issues is to risk an erosion of intellectual and moral boundaries that can feel vertiginous and disorientating. Chapter Seven posits the emergence of a general condition that can be nicknamed 'Anthropocene disorder'. The term is coined to name a sense of the loss of proportion, not in reference to old norms of judgement that need to be restored, but a loss of proportion *tout court*, vertiginously and as yet without a conceived alternative. Recent trends in environmental criticism, such as the so-called material ecocriticism are seen to exemplify 'Anthropocene disorder' in their own instabilities of argument and tone. Ecocritical practice, like environmental politics more widely, swings uncertainly between modes of understanding known to be forms of probably dubious intellectual containment on the one hand, and an alarming complexity of ramifications and unknowns on the other.

Chapter Eight concerns the phenomenon of *denial*, the commonest form of Anthropocene disorder and one set to become more widespread as the changing context transmutes more and more received modes of action, thinking and interpretation into unwitting forms of denial. A reading of a text by Lorrie Moore, juxtaposed with a recent study of climate change denial, is used to highlight the dynamics of the problem.

With the exception of the text by Lorrie Moore and the climate change novels briefly mentioned in Chapter Four, almost all of the works considered in this study have been read in relation to a newly realized planetary context whose breadth and nature would not have been known by their writers at the time. This final chapter, however, takes up consideration of modern novels and works of art that are trying explicitly to engage with the Anthropocene. The question arises, can its new demands be met by new forms of artistic and cultural innovation or, more darkly, are certain limits of the human imagination, artistic representation and the capacity of understanding now being reached?

Notes

1 Will Steffen, Paul J. Crutzen and John R. McNeill, 'The Anthropocene: Are Humans Now Overwhelming the Great Forces of Nature?', *Ambio* 38 (2007), 614–21, 614. For a useful overview of the semantics of the term 'Anthropocene' see Bronislaw Szerszynski, 'The End of the End of Nature: The Anthropocene and the Fate of the Human', *Oxford Literary Review* 34.2 (2012), 'Deconstruction in the Anthropocene', 165–84.

2 See William S. Ruddiman, *Plows, Plagues, and Petroleum: How Humans Took Control of Climate* (Princeton, NJ: Princeton University Press, 2005); Wolfgang Behringer, *A Cultural History of Climate*, trans. Patrick Camiller (Cambridge: Polity, 2010), 209–11. See also William Ruddiman, Steve Vavrus, John Kutzbach and Feng He, 'The Real Debate about Anthropogenic Global Warming', *The Anthropocene Review Blog*, 10 May 2014, http://anthropocenerev. blogspot.co.uk/

3 Noel Castree, 'The Anthropocene and the Environmental Humanities: Extending the Conversation', *Environmental Humanities* 5 (2014), 233–60. See also J. *Zalasiewicz, J.* et al., 'Response to Austin and Holbrook, "Is the Anthropocene an Issue

of Stratigraphy or Pop Culture?'", *GSA Today*, v. 22. http://www.
geosociety.org/gsatoday/comment-reply/pdf/i1052-5173-22-10-e21.
pdf Two new journals have recently appeared, *Anthropocene* (http://
www.journals.elsevier.com/anthropocene) and *Anthropocene
Review*. The latter contains a Hub Bibliography of mainly scientific
literature with 'Anthropocene' in the title, http://anthropocenerev.
blogspot.co.uk/p/hub-bibliography.html

4   Cohen, Claire Colebrook and J. Hillis Miller, *Theory and the
Disappearing Future* (London: Routledge, 2012), 128.

5   *Hyperobjects*: *Philosophy and Ecology after the End of the World*
(Minneapolis, MN: University of Minnesota Press, 2013), 9.

6   The concept of the hyperobject is the correlate of Morton's specific
theory of knowledge and perception (a variety of so-called object-
oriented ontology). However, since the hyperobject is simply what
any object becomes for this philosophy, Morton's specific references
to actual hyperobjects can seem a bit arbitrary, as these include
evolution (18), an atomic bomb (50), London or any vast city
(90–1), the Earth (51), oil and radiation (54), the Florida Everglades
(58), ancient comets (53), spacetime (61), subatomic, atomic and
molecular particles (40–5), 'perhaps economic relations' (100),
'climate' (103), 'capital' (112), 'devotional singing' (169) etc. In
effect, the Anthropocene is taken as the moment at which it is
realized that *all* objects must be seen as breaking out of the frames
in which human thinking has previously confined them, and are
hyperobjects according to the postulate that all things are deeply
connected to all others, are withdrawn from human comprehension
to a degree, but are also uncanny in their (unmanageable) proximity
and their participation in our own being.

7   Tobias Menely and Margaret Ronda, 'Red', in Jeffrey Jerome Cohen
(ed.), *Prismatic Ecology: Ecotheory Beyond Green* (Minneapolis,
MN: University of Minnesota Press, 2013), 22–41.

8   Ulrich Beck, *World Risk Society* (London: Polity, 1999), 119.

9   *Living in the End Times* (London: Verso, 2010), 334.

10 'The Oedipal Logic of Environmental Awareness', *Environmental
Humanities* 1 (2012), 7–21, 16.

11 'The Climate of History: Four Theses', *Critical Inquiry* 35 (2009),
197–222, 217.

12 Chakravarty, 'Postcolonial Studies and the Challenge of Climate
Change', *NLH* 43 (2012), 1–18, 15.

13 'Framing the End of Species: Images without Bodies', *Symplokē*
21.1–2 (2013), 51–63, 61.

14   *The Natural Contract*, trans. Elizabeth MacArthur and William Paulson (Ann Arbor, MI: University of Michigan Press, 1995), 160.

15   'The Planet of No Return: Human Resilience on an Artificial Earth', in Ted Nordhaus and Michael Shellenberger (eds), *Love Your Monsters: Postenvironmentalism and the Anthropocene*, e-book, (NP: The Breakthrough Institute, 2011), location 800.

16   'Waiting for Gaia: Composing the Common World through Arts and Politics', np, www.bruno-latour.fr/sites/default/files/124-GAIA-LONDON-SPEAP_0.pdf

17   Chapter 8 of Claire Colebrook's *Death of the Posthuman: Essays on Extinction*, Vol. 1 (Open Humanities Press, 2014), makes another argument about Serres, with his work on parasitism and pollution suggesting a view that qualifies the humanism of *The Natural Contract*, stressing the emergence of the human itself from impersonal systems of information and parasitic energy transactions.

18   Braden R. Allenby and Daniel Sarewitz, *The Techno-Human Condition* (Cambridge, MA: MIT Press, 2011), 11.

19   See P. Rampal, J. Weiss, C. Dubois and J.-M. Campin, 'IPCC Climate Models Do Not Capture Arctic Sea Ice Drift Acceleration: Consequences in Terms of Projected Sea Ice Thinning and Decline', *Journal of Geophysical Research*, 116 (August 2011). For a survey of papers arguing that the IPCC report of 2007 was too conservative, see the Sceptical Science com article, 'How the IPCC is more likely to underestimate the climate response', http://www.skepticalscience.com/print.php?r=51

20   See Ophuls, *Requiem for Modern Politics: The Tragedy of the Enlightenment and the Challenge of the New Millennium* (Boulder, CO: Westview Press, 1997), 169–74.

21   The World Commission on Environment and Development (*Our Common Future*: Oxford: Oxford University Press, 1987), 43.

22   http://www.unep.org/geo/geo5.asp

23   In this guessing game of chance each of two players simultaneously names one of these three imaginary objects to 'compete' against an opponent's nomination. Each named object 'defeats' one of the other three but is also 'defeated' by the remaining one, making an open-ended sequence of win then lose or vice versa: scissors cut paper, rock blunts scissors, paper enwraps rock. . . .

24   Paul Alberts, 'Responsibility towards Life in the Early Anthropocene', *Anglelaki* 16.4, December 2011, 5–16, 7.

25 Call for papers, 'Anthropocene Feminism', http://c21uwm.com/anthropocene/

26 *Climate Wars: Why People Will Be Killed in the 21st Century* (Cambridge: Polity Press (2012), 27).

27 Philip Luker, quoting Adams, *Philip Adams: The Ideas Man, A Life Revealed* (Melbourne: JoJo Publishing, 2012), chapter 18, location 3127.

28 Thomas H. Ford, 'Aura in the Anthropocene', *Symplokē* 21 (2013), 65–82, 65.

29 'The Climate of History', 221.

30 Ibid., 220.

31 E. O. Wilson, Foreword to Jeffrey Sachs, *Common Wealth: Economics for a Crowded Planet* (New York: Penguin, 2008), vi–xiii, xii.

32 Brunner, *Stand on Zanzibar* (London: Doubleday, 1968); Brin, *Earth* (London: Orbit, 1990); Cage, 'Overpopulation and Art', in Marjorie Perloff and Charles Junkermann (eds), *John Cage: Composed in America* (Chicago: University of Chicago Press, 1994), 14–38.

33 Heise, *Sense of Place and Sense of Planet: The Environmental Imagination of the Global* (Oxford: Oxford University Press, 2008), 90.

34 Timothy Morton, *The Ecological Thought* (Cambridge, MA: Harvard University Press, 2010), 24.

35 'Housebreaking the Human Animal: Humanism and the Problem of Sustainability in Margaret Atwood's *Oryx and Crake* and *The Year of the Flood*', *English Studies* 91 (2010), 728–42, 730.

36 Jerome Kagan, quoted in Helen Small, *The Value of the Humanities* (Oxford: Oxford University Press, 2013), 47.

37 *The Environmental Imagination: Thoreau, Nature Writing and the Formation of American Culture* (Cambridge, MA: Harvard University Press, 1995), 2. Such stress on cultural change may be over-determined by the fact that it seems an attractively non-coercive option, when, in actuality, most environmental measures take the form of increased social regulation and surveillance, an authoritarian trend it may be more difficult to feel comfortable with. Every new headline about a move to 'save' a marine environment, a local wood, or to decrease some source of pollution is either one involving some change in regulation, invariably an increase, or it entails that regulation's further monitoring and enforcement (though

often in fact neglected), to hold back or deflect social and economic pressures that would otherwise be overwhelming.

38   Heise, 'Afterword: Postcolonial Ecocriticism and the Question of Literature', in Bonnie Roos and Alex Hunt (eds), *Postcolonial Green: Environmental Politics and World Narratives* (Charlottesville, VA: University of Virginia Press, 2010), 251–8, 258.

39   'Toxic Assets: de Man's Remains and the Ecocatastrophic Imaginary (an American Fable)', in *Theory and the Disappearing Future*, 89–129, 108.

40   The under-examined nature in ecocriticism of ideals of cultural agency is exemplified in a recent issue of *Green Letters* (Feb. 2014), entitled 'Junk/Composting'. A misleading use of naturalistic metaphor – of human cultural processes as a sort of 'composting' – introduces a set of essays whose strength is marred rather than enhanced by such enframing. For instance we read: 'displayed, repeated, re-read, the idea and visual record of a "Great Pacific Garbage Patch", and related imagery, has been slowly composting in a global cultural sphere, perhaps nourishing changes in consciousness that might be individual, social, even, one day, political'. It is as if the complexities and chances of cultural effects were as inherently efficacious in some slow, pervasive way as the use of fertilizer in the growing of vegetables.

41   The 'law of large numbers' is, 'in statistics, the theorem that, as the number of identically distributed, randomly generated variables increases, their sample mean (average) approaches their theoretical mean' (*Encyclopedia Britannica*, www.britannica.com/EBchecked/topic/330568/law-of-large-numbers).

   To translate this into the example of human-induced CO_2 emissions: the greater the number of people in the world, then the more the proportional effect of any individual's impact is likely to approach the mean.

42   http://asle.org.uk/call-for-proposals-environmental-cultures-book-series/

43   John Miller, 'Biodiversity and the Abyssal Limits of the Human', *Symplokē* 21 (2013), 207–20, 209.

CHAPTER TWO

Imaging and imagining the whole Earth: The terrestrial as norm

The environmental ethics emerging from the Anthropocene entails thinking on scales of space and time often considerably greater than usual. Critics such as Morton or Mitchell Thomashow[1] devote considerable thought to projects and modes of art and literature that can convey environmental realities which stretch our mundane sense of space and time. These projects define much that is exciting and set to become more so in contemporary art and literature. They support the ecocritical agenda of inducing a green cultural shift, against the kinds of short-term thinking and expectations that can accept long-term environmental damage for short-term convenience. However, resistance to this kind of culture shift may come from sources deeper than cultural or social-political factors.

'When we observe the environment, we necessarily do so on only a limited range of scales, therefore our perception of events provides us with only a low-dimensional slice through a high-dimensional cake' (Simon A. Levin).[2] However, one scale forms a kind of norm for us, the usually taken-for-granted scale of our day-to-day existence and perception. We experience phenomena at a (mostly) fairly stable and consistent speed – too slow and our perception would give us an almost static world in which nothing happened – too fast, and everything would blur into indistinctness.

We understand distance, height and breadth in terms of the given dimensionality of our embodied existence. A particular human scale is inherent to the intelligibility of the Earth around us. This is not a merely cultural matter, susceptible of change by cultural means, but a given, unavoidable mode of reading things, imbued with an obviousness and authority that it takes effort to override – one or two cold winters in Britain and millions of people are deriding the very notion of global warming.

The Anthropocene entails the realization of how deeply this scale may be misleading, underling how (worryingly) our 'normal' scales of space and time must be understood as contingent projections of a biology which may be relatively inexorable. This is now manifest in the disjunctions between the scale of planetary environmental realities and of those things that seem immediately to matter to human engagement from one day to another. It also demands consideration of what we mean when we talk about humanity 'changing the Earth' or of our need to realize the finitude of the 'Earth'. The Earth is obviously implicit and assumed in our existence in any conceivable respect, including how we talk and think. It is all-pervasive, assumed but unthematized. The question of the meaning of the Earth is latent even in the simple pervasive confusion about the words 'earth' and 'world'. Does the term name the physical planet or the universe? When we speak of 'the world', the referent is almost always to the specific planet (as in 'the deepest seas in the world'), yet to speak of a person's 'world view' is to imply a view of the cosmos in the broad sense. The idiom, 'what on earth?' seems to hover between one sense and the other, as if they made no difference. Yet, why is the conflation of the terms 'earth' and 'world' so prevalent and so hard to avoid?

 Since late 1968 one defining icon of modernity has been the Apollo photographs of the whole Earth seen from space. The image has already become the obvious emblem of the Anthropocene. Ironically, however, one can argue that it is the very plurality, contradictoriness and evasiveness of interpretations of the image that make it appropriate for this purpose. It has been read as an icon of life's almost unbearable fragility; as the achievement through technology of the age-old dream of a god's-eye view; an instance of the contingent privilege of vision in the human sense of what something 'really' is ('. . . but what does it *look like?*'); a terrifying view of its target from a weapons platform. Questions arise. Does the image convey a new sense of place, or a radical sense of displacement? Why do the photos almost always deploy a conventional sense of up and down? Is this a representation of 'nature' or of 'culture'? Why is the Earth so hypnotically beautiful?

The sight of the Earth was of course anticipated, but it remained and still remains an inexhaustible surprise, an event, like the arrival of even an expected child ('the child that arrives is always unforeseen. It speaks of itself from the *origin* of a different world or from a *different* origin of this one' (Jacques Derrida)).[3] The sight of the whole Earth has been received in heterogeneous ways. Always mediated in image or discourse, its eventhood is always being neutralized – for instance, even the phrase I have used above, 'defining icon of modernity', already suggests the complacent meta-language of a would-be panoramic cultural history. A new reading must try to respond to, and keep open, that peculiar eventhood, its challenge to the seemingly absolute reality of the 'normal' human scale.

The Apollo images have usually been read in terms of humanity's conception of itself, as if the planet were no more than a gigantic mirror in which the human could study its own features. Denis Cosgrove highlights one dominant form of such appropriation. First, there is what he terms 'one earth' discourse, that is, arguments that affirm the image in terms of humanist ideals of the unity of humanity. The image of the whole globe becomes the icon of a supposed or desired cultural unity, a symbol of modernity's ideal of a common humanity (in effect, this usually means Western humanism in triumphal mode). Against this, what Cosgrove calls 'whole earth' discourse highlights the seeming fragility and isolation of the planet itself, an environmentalist awareness of the increasingly destructive power of human technologies. In this respect, Cosgrove's argument ties in with hopes that the Anthropocene represents the possibility of a new, potentially redemptive, form of human identity, based on self-recognition as a species.[4]

Both readings assimilate in given cultural terms (conceptions of a shared humanity, or of the human as the Earth's failing steward and manager) an image whose initial force is to dislocate given frames of meaning-making and scale, something at work for instance in the fact that no immediately obvious trace of humanity appears in the image, beyond the fact itself of the image having been made.

This is even more the case with another famous whole Earth image, that of a minuscule 'pale blue dot' barely discernible within the glare of its star. Writer and astronomer Carl Sagan requested that this image of the very distant Earth be taken, for its cultural value, from a very distant robotic spacecraft turned back towards the sun on a trajectory now carrying it out of the solar system. Sagan writes:

> We succeeded in taking that picture [from deep space], and, if you look at it, you see a dot. That's here. That's home. That's us. On it, everyone you ever heard of, every human being who ever lived, lived out their lives . . . on a mote of dust, suspended in a sunbeam.[5]

This is the planet as the human archive, foundation of all cultural memory, the fragile material matrix of all inscription, self-relation and commemoration. Again, the Earth is read solely as an index of the human ('That's us'), but one now collapsed towards an impossible experience of overload, in which we are forced to imagine everything about human life at once and at the one site – the myriad incommensurable horizons shrinking down upon each other to a point, like water down a plughole.

So the distant planet also becomes a *memento mori*, for images of the whole Earth almost always lead to preaching ('To my mind, there is perhaps no better demonstration of the folly of human conceits . . . it underscores our responsibility to deal more kindly and compassionately with one another').[6]

Serres's *The Natural Contract* (1990), anticipating some of the questions of the Anthropocene, ends with a rhapsodic, meditative section concerning images of the Earth from space. The Earth appears as:

> The largest apple. The most beautiful sphere or turbulent ball. The most ravishing boat, our caravel new and eternal. The fastest shuttle. The most gigantic rocket. The greatest space-ship. The densest forest. The most enormous rock. The most comfortable refuge. The most mobile statue. The complete clod of earth open at our feet, steaming. (121)

Yet it is as if, despite himself, Serres were confirming Yaakov Jerome Garb's point that it is a 'fantasy that we can somehow contain the Earth within our imagination'.[7] In Serres's prose, a summary overview disintegrates into a disjunctive series of exclamatory images, each supplementing the others. His claim that these whole Earth photographs show, for the first time, 'the world as it really is' is surely problematic. All Serres's images celebrating the appearance of the Earth from outside derive their entire representability and conceivability from a specifically human existence on the Earth's surface. In fact, can anyone describe the Earth as a whole and not use terms, concepts and images derived from the specific categories of life on its surface (apple, forest, blue dot)? Of course not. The Earth is not 'one' in the sense of an entity we can see, understand or read as a whole. No matter from how far away or 'high up' it is perceived or imagined, or in what different contexts – of cosmology or physics – it is always something we remain 'inside' and cannot genuinely perceive from elsewhere. It is a transcendental of human existence, and its final determinations are undecidable. The image of the whole Earth opens upon 'abyssal dimensions to which we can never suitably bear witness' (David Wood).[8] *Terrestriality*, defined as that 'normal' prereflective sense of scale inherent to embodied human life on the Earth's surface, forms a kind of transcendental, one that both underlies and exceeds any view that it is merely our social context that determines our understanding of ourselves. Our being-of-the-earth may be something *unvordenklich* ('un-prethinkable') in H.-G. Gadamer's sense, that is that outside of whose terms one cannot think.[9] Consider, for instance, the case of trying to hypothesize an extra-terrestrial philosophy or science: we are at once confronted with the problem of not being able to tell how much of it would be already anthropomorphic and thus terrestrial. Michael A. G. Michaud highlights one unresolved dilemma:

> If mathematics is universal and eternal, claim the Platonists, aliens will understand concepts like prime numbers and pi. The anti-Platonists dismiss this idea as anthropomorphic; alien brains, responding to different environments, would have radically different mathematics.[10]

What, then, distinguishes contemplation of the image of the whole Earth from the impact of a crash course in philosophy or some powerful reminder of the contingency of being alive ('Gosh, why are we here?')? One answer would be that the terrestriality of one's own sensorium is implicated in the effect of the image in profound and inextricable ways. Language about the sight of the Earth as a planet forms a singular kind of catachresis, that is, a knowingly inadequate simile or metaphor used to convey something for which no literal or as yet accepted term exists, stretching to breaking point language derived from the seeming coherence of the world of immediate consciousness. In this respect, the language used by the Apollo astronauts, looking back at the planet as whole, becomes peculiarly interesting. Neil Armstrong wrote: 'It suddenly struck me that that tiny pea, pretty and blue, was the Earth.'[11] Or this is William Anders, who took the famous 'Earthrise' photographs from lunar orbit at Christmas 1968:

> The Earth looked so tiny in the heavens that there were times during the Apollo 8 mission when I had trouble finding it. If you can imagine yourself in a darkened room with only one visible object, a small blue-green sphere about the size of a Christmas-tree ornament, then you begin to grasp what the Earth looks like from space. I think that all of us subconsciously think that the Earth is flat or at least almost infinite. Let me assure you that, rather than a massive giant, it should be thought of as the fragile Christmas-tree ball, which we should handle with care.[12]

There are multiple disjunctions and invaginations of scale here, rendering the speaker and implicitly the reader both very large and very small. The Earth is 'a Christmas-tree ball which we should handle with care', as if we were huge gods holding it in our hands – but standing on what? For the Earth, now as a kind of transcendental, is yet the basis for all that is imagined or perceived in Anders's account, even the slightly archaic phrase 'the heavens', with its evocations of a pre-Copernican cosmos, or the Christmas imagery linking the sight of the Earth with a providential nativity. The Earth is both an object *in* the picture, but also the frame and the ground of picturability. To think of the planet as either a 'massive giant' or a fragile Christmas-tree ball is an exercise in comparative size and scale that derives its intelligibility from our own terrestriality, even as Anders's account must now ironize

FIGURE 2 *Christmas tree ornament.*

the phenomenological 'life-world' in profoundly destabilizing ways. The terrestrial measure constitutive of my world becomes defamiliarized and even deranged when the Earth as a whole is viewed as an object in that world. In Anders's account, a family living room at Christmas, with its tree and decorations, becomes in a sense immediately 'bigger' than the planet in the window of a space capsule, even as, simultaneously, that room and its Christmas-tree ball have never been smaller. When the Earth seems bigger inside than out, then, ultimately, the very notion of size becomes opaque.

In the opening section of *The Infinite Conversation* (1969) Maurice Blanchot writes of how texts for conveying knowledge have, since Aristotle, almost always been committed to a continuity of form in presentation, that is, one thing leading smoothly to or developing from another within a homogenous element of thinkability.[13] The deep presupposition at issue is that reality itself is 'continuous' in that way, that being can admit of synthesis in some overarching conceptual unity, a 'world' as at least a regulative idea. In Armstrong's, Anders's and Serres's accounts of the planetary Earth, all the catachreses paper over a *dis*continuity of perception, language and understanding between referents on the surface of the Earth and the planet considered as a whole. Each image leaps over vast disjunctions in scale.

Implications

What implications emerge here for trying to think the Anthropocene, whose emblem might indeed be the whole Earth image?

For one thing, the image highlights just how far human perception and thinking are bound to the 'normal' scale of embodied experience on the Earth's surface, and that we live with no intuitive or significantly internalized sense of the Earth as a planet. Take the simple sentence, 'Every spring our planet is transformed'. This is the opening statement of a BBC documentary on the nature of soil.[14] Of course the statement is nonsense: spring somewhere is always autumn somewhere else, as the tilt of the planet's axis continually inclines different parts of the globe sunwards in its orbit, while in the tropics the language of the temperate seasons does not apply. The careless statement is an instance of psychic terrestriality at its most parochial.

To contemplate the sight of the whole Earth is to think the disjunction between individual perception and global reality, a disjunction that has now become so consequential in the Anthropocene. The scale at which one speaks of oneself as a person-with-a-world may be constitutively opaque to understanding beyond a now dangerously narrow spatial-temporal window. David Wood writes:

> If my tree is dying, I notice. But the earth slowly dying is not obvious, not something I can see at a glance out of my window . . . There is a gap between what I can see and what may really be happening. The glance is ripe for education.[15]

The phenomenal self-evidence of my singular world is itself a scalar effect unable, so to speak, to see itself as such. So we must take issue with the work of green thinkers such as David Abram who try to defend the immediate life-world of embodied perception as a kind of norm from which we have strayed into forms of destructive scientism and 'abstractions'.

DERANGEMENTS OF LANGUAGE: 'SAVING THE PLANET'

One symptom of a now widespread crisis of scale is a derangement of linguistic and intellectual proportion in the way people often talk about the environment, a breakdown of 'decorum' in the strict sense. Thus a sentence about the possible collapse of civilization can end, no less solemnly, with the injunction never to leave a TV on standby or forget to recycle a cardboard box. A headline in *New Scientist* magazine reads 'To save the planet, chow down on a caterpillar'.[16] An item in the same journal for 3 March 2014 proclaims, 'Captains of industry, listen up. There is a fortune to be made from saving the planet' (7). A motorist who occasionally takes a bus prides herself on helping 'save the planet'. Jonathan Bate claims 'poetry is the place where we save the earth'.[17]

This ubiquitous phrase, used as shorthand for so many environmentally informed actions (even buying a slightly more efficient fridge) condenses in itself a set of mutually implicated but contradictory notions of the Earth, of humanity, of language and of ethics.

1. First, it is a falsehood. Environmental degradation caused by humanity is most probably not a threat to the Earth itself, whatever that could mean, only to the biosphere in its given form. Sally Weintrobe calls the phrase 'debased': it is 'as if Earth depended on us and not the other way round'.[18] It incorporates a deluded conception of human power, feeding a crude sci-fi scenario by evoking, however fleetingly and in an exciting image of redemptive violence, the human as saviour.
2. The phrase, echoing so many predictable plots from space opera, presents a sense of disaster exaggerated to the pitch of fantasy, encasing anything it touches with a sense of unreality, deadening further what is already a cliché. The term empties itself of reality by being both hyperbolic and fictionalized. (Compare the laughable sentence 'It's time to save the sea', a title in the Durham Wildlife Trust's magazine for Winter 2012, 21).
3. The emptiness of the phrase is effectively a mode of denial, a denial, for instance, of what the phrase 'saving the planet' would refer to if taken seriously, something too traumatic to be genuinely imaginable. The peculiar, almost knowing silliness of this ubiquitous phrase highlights the communal quasi-psychosis, as it were, through which much of the media and public opinion meet the challenges of the Anthropocene.

Diagnostics such as Abram's highlight a presumed violence and
negativity inherent in the workings of calculative reason in techno-
science and industrial modes of production. Claire Colebrook offers
a darker version of such a diagnosis, seeing the instrumental violence
of calculative reason as inherent to theoretical thinking as such:

> man is a theoretical animal, a myopically and malevolently self-
> enclosed machine whose world he will always view as present
> for his own edification. . . . If it is possible for thought to bracket
> reality, to suspend the self-evidence of the world, then this both
> enables philosophy in general, and the 'man' of humanism and
> logic (including ecology) who regards the world as the milieu or
> environment for his own life. The self-enclosure and myopia of
> man cannot be considered as an accident.[19]

So the Anthropocene comes to name a dark moment in humanity's
realization of its own nature. There is another element of its danger,
however; one to do less with the violence inherent in reason than
with what might be called a kind of transcendental stupidity inherent
in embodiment. The supposedly immediate 'life-world' of our
unreflective perception is far from being the possible foundation of
secure theorizing that Abram and others would take it for, idealizing
bodily immediacy as some kind of authenticity, 're-achieving a direct
and primitive contact with the world'.[20] It is merely epiphenomenal
and unable to see itself as such. It projects an illusory ground, a surface
realm of human possibility, one that is delusory, latently ecophobic
and even sometimes a form of denial. We inhabit distance, height
and breadth in terms of the given dimensionality of our embodied,
earthly existence. The particular physical scale is inherent to the
intelligibility of things around us, imbued with an obviousness and
authority which it takes an effort to override.

The personal scale of the human body and of its immediate
inherence in things, terrestriality, has seemed to offer a kind of
scalar and ethical norm with which to criticize the fantasies of
techno-science, or the capitalist commodification of nature. It
underlies the localist programmes of much environmentalist
thinking. For instance, in the seminal anthology *The Ecocriticism
Reader* (1996), Neil Evernden endorses the seemingly ecological
ethics implicit in something Northrop Frye writes about art, 'that
the goal of art is to "recapture, in full consciousness, that original
sense of identity with our surroundings"'.[21]

However, it is now such an absorption in the immediate that becomes an object of suspicion. How could anyone, presented with a modern Western breakfast, intuit that the food miles that went into it may circle the globe? The demand now, baldly expressed, would be to realize that while immersed in my own phenomenal field of significances, I am also effectively on the other side of the world.

In sum, meditation on the whole Earth image highlights one of the greatest obstacles to being able to think the Anthropocene: that the familiar 'life-world' that gives us our immediate sense of orientation and of significant context in our lives, and which is even defended by some environmentalist thinkers as a perceptual and cognitive norm to be affirmed against scientism, now becomes epiphenomenal, even a 'phantasm' somewhat in Jacques Derrida's sense. That is, it is something illusory in which one must believe simply by being alive, just as one cannot imagine being dead without, impossibly, also projecting oneself as the imagined witness to that condition. The daily phantasm of the familiar world is both a completely normal experience but also one constituted in an eclipse of the fact that its very familiarity is more truly 'the inconceivable, the contradictory, the unthinkable, the impossible'.[22]

Neil Turnbull speculates: 'Might the planetary earth be the postmodern equivalent of the Cartesian *malin genie* [evil demon] – that which undermines any idea of a fixed and stable "first principle" of knowing and judging?'[23] In this respect, the image of the whole Earth, fragile and impossible fully to conceptualize, remains still an event and impetus to thought. The staleness of the cultural icon of the-Earth-from-space still does not fully occlude a sense of acultural shock. It is one not to be neutralized by forms of reactive humanism, moralistic appropriation or normative vitalism ('Gaia'). Its continuing event of surprise is a testimony to our terrestriality, both its scale and its drama of phantasms, something delusory in which one cannot not believe simply by being alive.

The phantasm of normality: Terrestriality and John Keats's 'To Autumn'

Terrestriality remains a kind of boundary concept, one that defines the elusiveness, intellectual difficulty and counter-intuitive nature of day-to-day life when trying to think the Anthropocene.

What seems as commonsensical as the immediate life-world of our ordinary experience, our given sense of familiarity and even of responsibility, may now be implicated in destructive scenarios we can neither see nor barely calculate. What was once a norm, the 'natural', emerges as a biological contingency that is becoming deeply problematic. If consideration of literary and cultural criticism in the Anthropocene involves the need newly to think on differing and conflicting scales, then the default scale of human terrestriality will have to be kept constantly in mind, often now as an object of suspicion.

Such suspicion may re-inflect readings of even very familiar texts. Take John Keats's ode 'To Autumn', written in 1819.[24] This famous text exemplifies what seems a universal human characteristic, that is to perceive familiar natural processes and their seasonal timing as a basic framework of 'meaning' for life, a background norm providing a relative sense of stability, comprehensibility and, usually, reliability for all human affairs. In this case the mythic and more-than-human figure of 'Autumn' becomes a sensuous representation of seasonal fruition and change.

Readings of 'To Autumn' often see it as a 'poem that seeks to achieve a calm acceptance of time, change, and mortality', of the 'soft-dying day', to quote the poem's last stanza.[25] Eric Gidal reads Keats's work in this way and contrasts it with the kinds of enlightenment utopianism espoused by his contemporaries William Godwin and Percy Bysshe Shelley, for whom a future perfectibility of humanity is imagined in terms of complete control over the climate of the Earth.[26] Jonathan Bate foregrounds the way in which unlike other odes, including those by Keats, 'To Autumn' is not centred on a dramatized human consciousness – an 'I' that would say, as in the other odes, 'I hear' or 'I see' and so on –. but depicts a process unfolding without any foregrounding of human figures, even a perceiver. In this way, he argues, the poem's series of sensuous images can no longer be understood simply as dramatizing changing states of mind or feeling in a central human speaker.

> Season of mists and mellow fruitfulness,
>   Close bosom-friend of the maturing sun;
> Conspiring with him how to load and bless
>   With fruit the vines that round the thatch-eves run;

To bend with apples the moss'd cottage-trees,
  And fill all fruit with ripeness to the core;
  To swell the gourd, and plump the hazel shells
  With a sweet kernel; to set budding more,
And still more, later flowers for the bees,
Until they think warm days will never cease,
  For Summer has o'er-brimm'd their clammy cells.

Bate argues that 'To Autumn' stands out for its concern with natural or material conditions of life, over and above the usual appropriation of them as symbols or cultural embellishments, for instance, there 'are "later flowers for the bees", not bees for the human bee-keepers'. It celebrates the necessary seasonal over-abundance of gnats and swallows.[27] This does not, however, make it a celebration of a whole ecosystem in some non-anthropocentric way, for what the poem depicts is a small farm with its central dwelling and outbuildings, a largely cultivated space.[28] Rather, it can be shown that what Bate reads as the poem's effect of benign impersonality is rather part of its seeming to render perceptible the normativity of the seasonal/natural as a reassuring background for human affairs.

It does this through a deft manipulation of temporal scale. As often noted, the poem's three stanzas depict the progress of the season over a few months, from what is still late summer in the first stanza with its maturing sun, to images of harvest and a cider making in the second and finally, in the third, to the bare fields and darkening skies of incipient winter. The effect of Keats's poem rests significantly on the device of a shifting of scale that allows the illusion of seeing 'Autumn' as a totality, in an assured overview enacted in a speeded time frame and which projects a seeming horizon of significance and purpose for all life within it (what Bate sees as 'an at-homeness-with-all-living-things' (109)). Furthermore, in these three stanzas one condensation of dimensions (several months in miniature) is also projected onto another, for the stanzas also move through just one day's progression of hours, from the mists associated with morning in the first stanza, through the heat of midday in the second to the barred clouds and gnats of evening in the last one. In this way, the slow process of the changing season, an effect of the Earth's axial tilt, is mapped onto the more immediate day/night cycle. Each depicted process seems subtly to correspond to and corroborate the other, as if day and year revolved harmoniously within or around each other. The achieved form of the text as a whole, encapsulating a version of months in the reading experience of a minute, gives to these natural processes the neatness of an aesthetic artefact, almost that of an object one might hold in one's hand. In this way, the motion of these three condensed stanzas is already an implicit analogue of an image of the Earth from space, with life depicted as this circle of hours, day and year. Likewise, autumn's implicit projection of future death is muted by its imprint in a circular trajectory that also entails renewal.

Claude Lévi-Strauss writes that 'the intrinsic value of a small-scale model is that it compensates for the renunciation of sensible dimensions by the acquisition of intelligible dimensions'.[29] Much of the criticism of 'To Autumn' concerns precisely the 'intelligible' content produced by the mode of Keats's miniaturization or compression of time scale. The conception of the living Earth inherent in this celebration of the seasonal is of a self-renewing circle of self-contained change-in-continuity that gives form, structure and purpose to all life that inhabits it – thus the affirmative pathos of dominant readings of this poem as a piece, almost, of secular or naturalized theology. This is to render the phantasmal terrestriality of human perception and sense of scale at their most beguiling and even consolatory.

Contrast this particular mythicization of the human scale with a text that sets out to derange it, Alfred Tennyson's dramatic monologue 'Tithonus' (1860), the lament of a figure who has been granted immortality in order to live with Eos, goddess of the dawn, but only as a perpetual ageing with no end. Tennyson's language deploys the simple technique of just speeding things up:

The woods decay, the woods decay and fall,
The vapours weep their burthen to the ground,
Man comes and tills the field and lies beneath,
And after many a summer dies the swan.[30]

This is both one temperate autumn and many such autumns. 'The woods decay' may mean not just the leaves but also all the trees, the woods themselves, falling, dying and being replaced. (So the swan, an image of long fidelity in love, also dies.) Unlike in Keats's ode, beyond a certain scale the cyclic movement of the seasons turns what would have been perceived as the 'natural' into the quasi-mechanical or orbital. As the poem ends, each reappearance of the Goddess of dawn now appears to Tithonus as the repeated working of a cold and vast if beautiful machine:

> Release me, and restore me to the ground;
> Thou seest all things, thou wilt see my grave:
> Thou wilt renew thy beauty morn by morn;
> I earth in earth forget these empty courts,
> And thee returning on thy silver wheels. (1118)

In shifting from the 'human/terrestrial' to the 'astronomical', all the cultural aura and sense of moral authority invested in the terms 'natural' or 'seasonal' shifts into a sense of the contingencies of orbital geometry. The life of trees and humanity becomes but the giddy and repetitive recycling into each other of energy and matter on the surface of a spinning ball. At this speed, as 'real' as any other, a human life may look as purposeless as the falling rain: 'The vapors weep their burthen to the ground / Man comes and tills the field and lies beneath.' Here, the act of poetic miniaturization – several centuries in the reading experience of seconds – is disconcerting, rather than offering the illusion of a mildly consoling overview as Keats's ode does.

In 'To Autumn' the seemingly accepting image of seasonal evanescence is made possible by affirming an idea of nature as some reassuringly continuous backdrop for human life – for the swallows that depart are also set to return another year, and there is even perhaps the consoling effect of a personal identification with the whole middle-scale process of which one's own extinction will form a part. Yet, as we now realize, this homely sense of permanence, now fragile, was in any case illusory.[31]

So, against the idealization of this text as 'ecological', an antithetical reading is at least equally possible: that the poem's attraction is, above all, a subtle *denial* of death. The whole structure, tone and the sensuous imaginary of the poem, especially as Bate recuperates them, also instantiate Maurice Blanchot's argument that the ultimately illusory *raison d'être* of human thought and culture has always been to appropriate death as a source of meaning, whether by reference to its place in a reassuring meaningful 'nature' or otherwise. This antithetical reading would be less a matter of disagreeing with Bate's points about the aesthetic effect of 'an at-homeness-with-all-living-things' (109), but to see it as supporting an opposed overall conclusion, with the denial of death as perhaps the keystone of faith in human exceptionalism and fantasies of sovereignty.

There is a thin, undecidable line between acceptance of death and denial of the nature of its reality. Critics tend towards using Keats's poem to endorse a sense of 'the ecological' that is more the latter than the former. However, like our being unable to think straight about death, the poignancy of Keats's text is the way it hovers between the senses of the 'natural' (as a supposedly desirable norm) and that of the merely orbital or astronomical as already described. In Tennyson's line, 'Man comes and tills the field and lies beneath', the sense that human life is cyclical gives no consoling sense of perpetual renewal, only of a cycle as impersonal as the Earth's orbit or spinning.

Notes

1   Thomashow, *Bring the Biosphere Home: Learning to Perceive Global Environmental Change* (Cambridge, MA: MIT Press, 2002).

2   Simon A. Levin, 'The Problem and Pattern of Scale in Ecology: The Robert H. MacArthur Award Lecture', *Ecology* 73 (1992), 1943–67, 1945.

3   'The Deconstruction of Actuality', in Martin McQuillan (ed.), *Deconstruction: A Reader* (Edinburgh: Edinburgh University Press, 2000), 527–53, 535.

4   Cosgrove, 'Contested Global Visions: One-World, Whole-Earth and the Apollo Space Photographs', *Annals of the Association of American Geographers* 84 (1994), 270–94, 288.

5   Carl Sagan, *Pale Blue Dot: A Vision of the Human Future in Space* (New York: Random House, 1997), xv.

6   Ibid.

7   Yaakov Jerome Garb, 'Perspective or Escape?: Ecofeminist Musings on Contemporary Earth Imagery', in Irene Diamond and Gloria Ferman Orenstein (eds), *Reweaving the World: The Emergence of Ecofeminism* (San Francisco, CA: Sierra Club, 1990), 264–78, 278.

8 Ted Toadvine, 'Scholar's Session on David Wood' (Society for Phenomenological and Existential Philosophy, Philadelphia, 14 October 2006) http://pages.uoregon.edu/toadvine/Toadvine%20 and%20Wood%20Scholar's%20Session.pdf

9 For the *das Ünvordenkliche* in Gadamer, see my *The Poetics of Singularity: The Counter-Culturalist Turn in Heidegger, Derrida, Blanchot and the Later Gadamer* (Edinburgh: Edinburgh University Press, 2005), 80–1.

10 *Contact with Alien Civilizations: Our Hopes and Fears about Encountering Extra-terrestrials* (New York: Copernicus Books, 2007), 284.

11 From 'Space Quotations: Looking Back at the Earth Quotes', www. spacequotations.com/earth.html

12 Anders, quoted in Denis Cosgrove, 'Contested Global Visions', 284.

13 *The Infinite Conversation,* trans. Susan Hanson (Minneapolis, MN: Minnesota University Press, 1993), 5–6.

14 'Deep Down & Dirty: The Science of Soil', Executive Producer Jacqueline Smith, BBC 4, 17 April, 2014.

15 *The Step Back: Ethics and Politics after Deconstruction* (Albany, NY: SUNY, 2005), 167.

16 14 May 2013, www.newscientist.com/article/dn23536-to-save-the-planet-chow-down-on-a-caterpillar.html

17 *Song of the Earth* (London: Picador, 2000), 283.

18 'Introduction' to Sally Weintrobe (ed.), *Engaging with Climate Change: Psychoanalytic and Interdisciplinary Perspectives* (London: Routledge, 2013), 1–15, 5.

19 Colebrook, 'Not Symbiosis, Not Now: Why Anthropogenic Change Is Not Really Human', *Oxford Literary Review* 34.2, 'Deconstruction in the Anthropocene', 185–210, 193, 197.

20 Maurice Merleau-Ponty, *Phenomenology of Perception*, trans. Colin Smith (London: Routledge and Kegan Paul, 1962), vii.

21 'Beyond Ecology: Self, Place, and the Pathetic Fallacy', in Cheryll Glotfelty and Harold Fromm (eds), *The Ecocriticism Reader: Landmarks in Literary Ecology* (Athens, GA: University of Georgia Press, 1996), 92–104, 98.

22 Derrida, *The Beast and the Sovereign*, Vol. II, trans. Geoffrey Bennington (Chicago, IL: University of Chicago Press, 2012), 148.

23 'The Ontological Consequences of Copernicus: Global Being in the Planetary World', *Theory Culture and Society* 23 (2006), 125–39, 133.

24   Jack Stillinger (ed.), *The Poems of John Keats* (London: Heinemann, 1978), 249.

25   See, for example, Alan Bewell, *Romanticism and Colonial Disease* (Baltimore: Johns Hopkins University Press, 1999), 180.

26   Thus, in Shelley's *Queen's Mab* (1813) the orbital tilt of the Earth's axis is 'corrected' to produce conditions of perpetual spring. Against such hubris, Gidal praises Keats's stance as one 'in which mortality and redemption are the nurturing materials of the airs, waters, and places in which we make our home' ('"O Happy Earth Reality of Heaven!" Melancholy and Utopia in Romantic Climatography', *Journal for Early Modern Cultural Studies* 8.2 (Fall/Winter 2008), 74–101, 97.

27   'The poem not only yokes external and internal marks of biological process (the bending of the apple tree, the swelling of the gourd), it also yokes community and chemistry (bosom-friend and sun), physics and theology (load and bless), biology and aesthetics (a link which we may express through the two halves of the word which describes the closing images of the poem: bird-song') (*Song of the Earth*, 107).

28   The area is treed, but it is not the dense forest it would have been before the Neolithic – it is a cultivated space. The plants in the first stanza are domesticated crops, vines, apples, thatch (from wheat), unspecified 'fruit', hazel-nuts, and bees which, associated with the 'o'er-brimmed', *do* evoke the making of honey. The autumnal process of the first two stanzas is the making of a human 'store', what with the 'granary, the reaped furrow, cider, and meat' ('full-grown-lambs').

29   *The Savage Mind* (Chicago, IL: University of Chicago Press, 1966), 24. Lévi-Strauss makes the point that most pictorial artworks are in fact miniatures (and, if one wants to push the point, one can obviously say that so is a long realist novel like *Middlemarch*, condensing all those lives and years into a reading experience of hours).

30   Christopher Ricks (ed.), *The Poems of Tennyson* (London: Longman, 1968), 1112–18, 1114.

31   As Nigel Clark writes: 'We know now that a wildly fluctuating climate was the norm until the geologically recently past, some 10,000 or so years ago.' Thus Clark goes on: 'this means that almost all the achievements of humankind with which we are familiar and about which we are knowledgeable are stamped with anomalousness and provisionality' ('Volatile Worlds: Confronting Abrupt Climate Change', *Theory Culture and Society* 27 (2010), 31–53, 38).

CHAPTER THREE

Emergent unreadability: Rereading a lyric by Gary Snyder

An 'emergent' event is one whose novelty meets no available, matching or adequate discourse in representation, discussion or judgement. Emergence in the strictly philosophical sense has the following basic definition:

> when a physical system of sufficient complexity is in a suitable configuration new properties 'emerge' in a way that could not have been predicted from physical laws governing less complex or differently configured systems. (Simon Prosser)[1]

The Anthropocene could be called, to all intents and purposes, an effect of radical and unpredictable emergence in the condition of the world, the proliferation of situations at Level III complexity.[2] Its force remains largely unforeseen and its intellectual, ethical and political demands may be deeply counter-intuitive, at odds with current ways of thinking and behaving. For instance, the issue of atmospheric pollution inaugurates the need to think of the open air as a bounded space in which the consequences of actions may accumulate, mutate and re-emerge unexpectedly on the other side of the planet.

In an interview of 1993, Jacques Derrida was asked to elucidate his concept of the 'event', as meaning more than merely the not-anticipated. He argued that

> An event cannot be reduced to the fact of something happening. It may rain this evening or it may not, but that is not an absolute event. *I know what rain is*; so it is not an absolutely different singularity. In such cases what happens is not an arrival.[3] (Emphasis added)

Derrida categorizes rain in the realm of non-events. However, the remark highlights a lingering anthropocentrism in Derrida's predominantly anti-anthropocentric thinking.[4] The Anthropocene entails, among other things, a refusal to be so sure that we do know what rain is. We find ourselves asking of the unfamiliar weather, 'What does it mean?', like a pagan priest fearfully reading the future from the flight of birds. The best-known passages in Bill McKibben's polemic *The End of Nature* (1989) concern precisely a new de-natured sense of disenchantment in the very sound of running water, such as a forest stream flowing quickly after rain.[5]

To recognize the Anthropocene as 'emergent' alters the understanding of what may be environmentally destructive or not. For the encroachment of human activity on more and more of the biosphere is often a result of activities that once straightforwardly enhanced human welfare but which have now crossed a certain threshold in magnitude and impact. In effect, the Anthropocene here names a necessarily vague but insidious border at which what used to be clear human goods begin to flip over into sources of degradation and environmental harm. For instance, the progressive-liberal successes of increased social inclusion, prosperity and consumption arguably also impoverish the lives of innumerable future generations; increased longevity in human populations, aided by improved health services, may also contribute to the planet's next mass extinction event.

How then to write literary criticism in a time of acknowledged mass extinction without just seeming absurd? How far is such writing vulnerable to the claim that we are still denying or negotiating with the Anthropocene by trying to squeeze it into conventional categories? The insidious effect of the Anthropocene, as an emergent phenomenon with drastically revisionist after-effects, is that what most people take for normality must drift towards being a form of environmental denial. To engage with the question of how this transformation also applies to the regional field of literary and cultural criticism, this chapter examines three 'green' readings of a fairly well-known poem by Gary Snyder, the first of his debut collection *Riprap* (1959)[6]

Mid-August at Sourdough Mountain Lookout

Down valley a smoke haze
Three days heat, after five days rain
Pitch glows on the fir-cones
Across rocks and meadows
Swarms of new flies.

I cannot remember things I once read
A few friends, but they are in cities
Drinking cold snow-water from a tin cup
Looking down for miles
Through high still air.

It seems a poem of irenic meditation, celebrating the psychic release of solitude in a nonhuman environment, a space liberated from the pressures of a social identity. This is how most readings of Snyder take it, in terms of a natural therapy and self-discovery on a personal or individual scale. For Timothy Gray the poem is about a process of 'de-education' ('I cannot remember things I once read') of 'the poet hoping to commune with his natural surroundings'.[7] For Tim Dean, the poem celebrates being free 'from the ties of the civilized'. Here the 'I' 'does not order or dominate the landscape in any way' but is situated in the natural realm, as a part of it. The looking is seen as non-purposive, 'not subsumed here to any other measure'.[8]

   Nick Selby, however, argues convincingly that this is a poem about work, to be situated in relation to various American uses of landscape.[9] The speaker's seeing is deeply purposive, for it is surely part of the task of being employed as a fire-watcher, as the young Snyder was in the 1950s.[10] Fire-watching is what Sourdough Mountain Lookout in Washington State was used for, high on a ridge north-east of Mount Ranier (it is also the subject of Philip Whalen's longer poem, 'Sourdough Mountain Lookout' of 1956).[11] In Snyder's lyric, the specific details of the landscape are focused on appearances that, after three days of heat in mid-August, may suggest fire or smoke ('Pitch glows on the fir cones . . . Swarms of new flies'). Contrary to the familiar association of such reveries with leisure, the mountain is a place of work and the trees a potential crop. Selby takes this further by exploring Snyder's poetics as one for which a poem is itself a workplace for examination of the crucial part played in American conceptions of national identity by varying appropriations of the land as icons of true 'Americanness'.

All three ecocritical readings see what Snyder is doing as valuable in loosely 'green' terms, whether this is an exposure to the natural world as a kind of personal therapy, an affirmation and chastening acceptance of human finitude, or as a staging of poetic writing as itself a mode of intellectual work implicitly critical of American cultural appropriations of the landscape. Nevertheless, all may now be questioned as to their assumptions and methods.

Gray's and Dean's readings of Snyder exemplify much early environmental criticism from the 1990s, with its focus on changing individual attitudes to the natural world, or on individual consciousness. They render the poem a seemingly simple instance of a kind of eco-therapy effected by immersion in a remote forest landscape, one that might somehow, if made more general, transform an environmentally irresponsible society.

Selby's reading exemplifies a method that has dominated ecocriticism in this century. By contrast with the methodological individualism of Gray and Dean, this approach tends towards more *social*-ecological arguments, that is, tracing environmental degradation to cultural dysfunction, systemic failures of justice and equity. Literature is read, interpreted and evaluated in relation to the cultural politics of its day, with the critic being particularly attentive in retrospect to the destructive effects of modes of hierarchy, exclusion and exploitation among human beings as these are further reflected in attitudes to the natural world, as mere object of use, of moral indifference and so on. In this respect, Selby contrasts Snyder's conception with the tradition of a US literary nationalism based on the cultural appropriation of landscape, as in R. W. Emerson's argument in 'The Poet' (1844) that 'America' can itself be seen as a great poem whose ample geography '"dazzles the imagination"'.[12] Of another famous passage in Emerson,

Selby writes: 'Whereas Snyder's poetics of work marks a troubled exchange between land and text, Emerson's moment of visionary transcendence signals a spiritual appropriation of the land that turns its gaze away from that very land' (186). Against this, Snyder's poem is affirmed as a kind of counter-construction, one that sets out partly to undo the symbolic appropriation of American landscape, the poem's imagery and structure expressing a cleavage between both land and self (193), and between the actual forest and the land in books: 'I cannot remember things I once read'. For Selby 'America' is the name for a specific form of cultural appropriation of the natural landscape and Snyder's work forms a challenge to it: 'At the moment of its realization in the poem, the narrator's "I" is obliterated, forgotten, even as it reads itself into the land and the text' (185). Similarly, Snyder's later collection *Turtle Island* (New York: New Directions, 1974) contests in its title, which is an aboriginal name for the North American continent, the very naming of America.

Inherited forms of reading and interpretation such as these by Gray, Dean and Selby are now newly at issue in the Anthropocene.

Historical contextualizing

Most mainstream literary critics, it must be said, are oblivious to the Anthropocene and its challenges, and seem to remain content with the role of the critic as a kind of minor cultural historian. Herman Rapaport summarizes the kind of historical contextualization approach still dominant in literary departments:

> Traditional historicism claims that the meaning of a text is established by its historical context, which is seen as a rational totality that norms the text by means of revealing meaning in terms of publicly held understandings that can be found in the historical record.[13]

For instance, a reading of Jane Austen will identify the meaning of a novel with Austen's particular inflection of attitudes and discourses of her day (on status, gender, marriage, decorum and similar matters) as these can be inferred from other documents of the time. The later

'New Historicism', emerging in the 1980s, shared with traditional historicism 'the idea that the author traffics in shared social/cultural meanings' of his or her time and that the critic's job is to reconstruct these (35). Literature is read and interpreted as an historical document to be put back together or reclarified by reference to its original context. Selby's reconstruction of 'Mid-August at Sourdough Mountain Lookout' would be exemplary in this regard.

What is significant or insignificant in the past can change, however, even drastically. An emergent effect of the Anthropocene is to revise strongly notions of what is or is not historically significant. The industrial revolution, to give the most obvious example, remains an event whose full implications are open, and perhaps now more ambivalent than before. Even once trivial-seeming or uncontroversial decisions about infrastructure (such as town planning laws that encourage the use of cars) can take on a kind of retroactive significance unimagined at the time. The literal as well as the cultural climate of the twenty-first century may well alter the way someone reads, say, the motif of automobiles and all they may represent in *The Great Gatsby* (1925). Historicist critics have also been developing new 'eco-historicist' readings which approach texts from the past in relation to their specific climatic conditions, or which reconstruct the experience of life or thought in a specific meteorological context, alert to how human cultures have responded to or created environmental change,[14] such as Ken Hiltner's analysis of controversies over the burning of highly sulphurous coal in seventeenth-century London.[15] In addition, and more controversially, the retrospective light of the Anthropocene casts into new relief developments that many regard as human advances, including social changes such as the rise of the liberal values of individualism, and personal freedom, for these cannot now be disengaged from such environmentally degrading impacts as increased consumption, individual property rights, growing markets and expanded resource use.

So how might this relate specifically to the quoted readings of Snyder's lyric? For one thing, as environmentally literate readers will already have seen, it turns out that the fire-watcher depicted in 'Mid-August at Sourdough Mountain Lookout' would actually be engaged in an environmentally destructive practice in a way unrecognized at the time. To suppress small fires, which are now understood as ecologically benign, is only to encourage conditions for a massive and genuinely destructive fire at a later date, as forest brush and debris builds up. Yet through much of the twentieth century 'fire suppression' was 'a veritable religion of the forest service'.[16] Counter-intuitively, what looks superficially like environmental protection on the small scale actually abets environmental destruction on the regional and even global level, for, in the Anthropocene, deforestation becomes a planetary issue. In *Back on the Fire* (2007) Snyder writes:

> Guarding against forest fires, finally I had found the Right Occupation. I congratulated myself as I stood up there above the clouds memorizing various peaks and watersheds, for finding a job that didn't contribute to the Cold War and the wasteful modern economy. The joke's on me fifty years later as I learn how much the fire suppression ideology was wrong-headed and how it has contributed to our current problems.[17]

Clearly the later understanding of fire casts an ironic light over the reading of Snyder's poem in terms of what comes to seem, retrospectively, a premature green moralism in the readings by Dean and Gray. Their romantic conceptions become unwittingly complicit in environmental degradation. The issue of fire-watching in 'Mid-August at Sourdough Mountain Lookout', that preventing fires is actually increasing the ecological danger, becomes in its small way an allegory of how ecological issues can escape the empirical or common-sense perception of the present moment. Ironically, the kind of 'imagist' poetic that Snyder practices, supposedly capturing the essence or feel of a moment authentically with minimal mediation ('no ideas but in things', as William Carlos Williams put it),[18] emerges in this context as an endorsement of anthropocentric illusion.

Secondly, notions of reading through the reconstruction of an original local context become less certain and adequate in other ways. To name or describe the significant act being represented in the text, we must now respect the break between the retrospective insights of the Anthropocene and the poem's more benign significance in its original context. We now ask: fire prevention, or the opposite; environmental engagement or escapism: and; is to celebrate the transformative solitude celebrated in the poem still of value, or does it just indulge a merely symbolic green politics? What is singular to the text now becomes not what may or may not have been unique to its specific time or space, but what, in the emergent retrospect of the Anthropocene, may now appear as significant or increasingly significant for the first time. Reading cannot pretend to be just some act of retrieval; it also becomes a measure of an intractable break in consciousness and understanding.

The act represented in Snyder's text could also no longer be fully localized in either space or time. A supposedly benign environmental politics at one time actually adds, however minutely, to atmospheric pollution in the longer term. So the speaker's act would not just be happening on the side of Sourdough Mountain but throughout the forest, the local bioregion and, indeed, globally. Such an act could also not be fully sited in the early 1950s, for the potential effects are cumulative over an indeterminate time.

To condemn the fire-watcher's act as now undercut by these far more massive scenarios may well seem 'over the top', 'not fair', and 'unreasonable' and so on, exemplifying the kind of incongruities of scale familiar in environmental slogans ('eat less meat and save the rain forest'). At the same time, such feelings cannot override the conviction that to read at scales that used, familiarly, to 'make sense', now consciously involves an act of intellectual evasion. Such is already the uncertain space and affliction of environmental awareness more generally. Viewed in terms of the deceptive rationality and scale of day-to-day life, environmental activists seem condemned to get everything out of perspective, to veer between a general priggishness about trivialities and an emptily apocalyptic rhetoric. Intellectually, the Anthropocene effects a general crisis of tone and of proportion – what might be nicknamed 'Anthropocene disorder' (see Chapter Seven), a sense of the destructive incongruity of given norms of behaviours and thinking, without, as yet, any clear sense of an alternative.

Spatial containment: Methodological nationalism

Methodological nationalism names the assumption, usually implicit but all-pervading in many critical readings, that the nation-state and its boundaries form a natural or at least self-evidently justified context for discussion of the literary and cultural artefacts that arise within its borders. The nation-state is implicitly identified as the horizon that defines issues of interest, with an insidious tendency even to identify society itself with the nation-state.

Selby reads 'Mid-August at Sourdough Mountain Lookout' as an intelligently thought-out iconoclastic 'rereading' of the 'American' landscape, in debate with other readings from fellow nationals. His revisionist reading of the poem questions the individualist focus found in readings such as those by Dean and Gray, yet contains itself the classic marks of methodological nationalism. It links and interrelates various pronouncements on landscapes within the borders of the United States as being 'Indicatively American', 'quintessentially American', as forming a 'symptomatically American moment', or as '"most American"', and quotes Harold Bloom on a text of Emerson, as 'the most American passage that will ever be written' (186). The word 'American' acts here as a performative term of intellectual closure that seems to accumulate reality simply out of repetition, like a nationalistic 'Amen' – and this is to cite only one page of the article.

Yet to see Snyder's text solely as part of a cultural debate in American self-idealization is disappointingly parochializing and, set to become increasingly fragile and unsatisfactory, given all the broader ways in which the text and its issues can be opened up. In accounts of literature the repetition of 'American' – or some other such national marker – can even project effects of territoriality and exclusiveness that are unwittingly aggressive, supporting the pessimistic view examined in Margaret Atwood's *Oryx and Crake* (2003),[19] where art is seen as unable to transcend territoriality, and even has one function in expressing it. Such intellectual territoriality forecloses the scope for readership of the poem to those who are literate in that particular cultural context. Among other things, it is in latent tension with Snyder's own deep engagement with other national traditions. A more global perspective would, for example, open up such issues as the influence of the Japanese haiku on this sort of modernist poem, Snyder's interest in far Eastern, indigenous American and non-American cultures and in time scales that embrace prehistory. As Mark McGurl poses the issue of further expanding the context: 'If the idea is to plumb the depths of deep time, why not scrap the idea of "American literature" all together?'[20]

Selby's limitation of the pertinent context to a bounded national space, however contested, is now inadequate. Secondly, he never

FIGURE 3 *Conflagration.*

takes up the fact that the speaker in 'Mid-August' did not know what he was doing. The natural world, in this case the ecology of forest systems and fire, has a capricious life of its own, one that does not fit the passive role cast for it either by the US Forest Service or by Selby's representation of Snyder's lyric as simply reminding us that 'landscape is always mediated through acts of reading' (185). The fire-watcher is actually helping destroy the forest by releasing its own latent capacity for violent change. Any representation of Snyder's poem as some confident cultural-political intervention is undermined. As Bruce Braun and Sarah J. Whatmore write: 'What, and where, is the "political" when emergent properties cannot be predicted, when all the actors cannot be known in advance, and when immanent causality necessarily bedevils political calculation?'[21]

Conceptions of nature and the transcorporeal

Dean and Gray offer a notion of nature now widely regarded as obsolete, a norm of change-in-permanence and of homeostasis, a norm in relation to which a human being can regain a sense of authenticity supposedly lost in urban civilization. This offers a largely false image of ecosystems whose appearance of stability may in fact represent a standoff between biological and climatic forces liable to veer rapidly into an altered state. In Selby's reading, on the other hand, no commitment is being made about what nature is. His point is simply its very otherness to the various idealizations and appropriations that mark US cultural history, so that it is easy to envisage him taking the romantic humanist readings of Dean and Gray as another such appropriation. However, the drawback of Selby's method of reading is that it casts the natural world as itself merely passive, as remaining just the unknowable other behind the play of human representations.

Yet, nature is not so much an unknowable in this tidy way as something that is partially knowable, in capricious and potentially misleading or inadequate ways. The notion of nature as the other to culture has been giving way in environmental thought to more blended conceptions of the two as forming one perhaps bafflingly complex entity (as in Donna Haraway's earlier coinage 'natureculture').[22] This is not just out of the recognition that human effects on ecosystems render notions of pristine nature or wilderness merely escapist. Recent concepts such as Timothy Morton's 'the mesh'[23] or Stacy Alaimo's 'transcorporeality'[24] also express the fact that human cultures are always entirely part of natural systems of energy exchange in the biosphere, as subject as any other entity to the laws of physics and biology, even while, on the other hand, concepts of 'nature' have, simultaneously and confusingly, never been separable from human politics. And now both these points become further underlined by the inextricable mess that is the Anthropocene.

Under the heading of 'material ecocriticism', recent developments in ecocriticism seem at first more germane to thinking the Anthropocene. For instance, the influential new concept of 'trans-corporeality' as defined by Stacy Alaimo, seems to fit well the environmental ironies in Snyder's lyric. She writes: 'the human is always intermeshed with the more-than-human world', underlining 'the extent to which the substance of the human is ultimately inseparable from "the environment"' (2), forcing us to trace often invisible lines of interconnection and affect between bodies across space and time. It means a heightened awareness of the degree to which seemingly inert material things are also active agents, implicated in the transmission of often unwanted or unknown environmental effects. For Alaimo, the insights of disability studies into environmentally induced diseases also underline how even the internal, mental life of human beings is inseparable from unseen or unknown environmental causes. In sum, to see 'matter as "interactive becoming"' is to 'infuse a posthumanist environmentalist ethic that refuses to see the delineated shape of the human as distinct from the background of nature, and instead focuses on interfaces, interchanges, and transformative material/discursive practices' (Alaimo, 142). Alaimo deploys this insight in a reading of Muriel Rukeyser's *The Book of the Dead* (1938),[25] a poem of protest against the fatal callousness of a mining company in West Virginia which deliberately exposed its over-exploited migrant workforce to deadly levels of silica. Later chapters take up case studies of people suffering environmental illness due to unusual chemical sensitivity, and, the intellectual and ethical challenges of the new posthuman entities arising out of DNA mutations in Greg Bear's sci-fi novels.[26]

Alaimo's concept of 'trans-corporeality' would seem at first to exemplify well the perceived dissolution of physical and cognitive boundaries that marks the Anthropocene. It entails a suspicion of readings that recuperate all the elements in a text in overly mental or discursive terms and in this way the concept helps resist the tendency to overvalue the realm of cultural representations as the exclusive site of significant agency.[27] Physical entities, such as human bodies, are not just things to be read solely as exemplifying some sort of discourse: they have a certain sense and force separate from those systems of representation and description.

So 'trans-corporeality' seems directly relevant to a putative revisionist reading of 'Mid-August at Sourdough Mountain Lookout'. Nevertheless, Alaimo's conception of the trans-corporeal is also an instance of intellectual containment. The oddity here is that while Alaimo mentions global warming in relation to 'trans-corporeality', the crucial gas, CO_2, is not really considered in her book. The ambiguity of CO_2 as a 'greenhouse gas' is that a certain level of it is necessary for the natural insulation of a planet that would otherwise be drastically colder. CO_2 is not *in itself* polluting. It only becomes so, producing what we experience as damaging interference effects, when a certain hazy threshold is crossed (as it does in the Anthropocene). So trans-corporeality as it relates to this ubiquitous gas, affecting sea-level, ocean acidity and temperature, cannot be as easily categorized or situated as the chemical toxins that concern Alaimo, in her reading of Rukeyeser on silica poisoning for instance. The trans-corporeality at issue in a reading of Snyder alert to global warming is more complex and not so fixable to a relatively local and easily ascertainable sense.[28]

Analogously, though not discussed by Alaimo at all, overpopulation likewise concerns something that would normally be desirable (here more people, there a heat-trapping gas). Unlike toxins or desertification, neither CO_2 nor increasing human numbers are in themselves kinds of environmental harm – up to, that is, a controversial but potent scalar threshold at which their effects can transmogrify in destructive ways.

In effect, with trans-corporeality, Alaimo invents a concept germane to the challenges of the Anthropocene but deploys in such a way as to contain it within the far more manageable bounds of inherited conceptions of local or social wrongs. Now, however, the mess of the Anthropocene also means no longer being so confident that we know where or how to make such containments. To localize trans-corporeal effects at their most visible (toxic substances, environmental diseases) is helpful, but evades the fact that the Anthropocene means that such effects, whether minuscule or violent, are everywhere and that even the past effects (such as earlier greenhouse gas emissions) are now being rendered toxic in ways they were not before.[29]

Biological contexts: The fire ape

At issue in the Anthropocene, by definition, is the relationship of the human to other species and to the finite physical environments of the Earth. This raises new questions about what human beings are, especially as their effects *en masse* now seem so disjoint from their natures individually. For instance: can the question of human destructiveness be contained by arguments about cultural difference – by claims that human beings might be ecologically benign and that only certain now-dominant forms of culture are destructive of the natural world? Alternatively, does one need to think environmental destruction at some sort of species level, as latent in the sort of thing humanity is? Thirdly, with the thought of emergent effects, is it any longer sufficient to talk about 'human nature' at all as a given, when the challenge becomes to think the Anthropocene as a threshold at which humanity becomes a new unprecedented agency en masse, escaping subjective experience of itself.

In this respect, the most telling argument against the limits of our three readings of Snyder concerns something more deeply assumed in each of them. More provocative than the hypothesis of a supposed return to some benign natural relationship of human to landscape, as postulated by Dean and Gray, or even than Selby's interest in competing cultural constructions of the land, is the fact that the lyric depicts a human being in a latently ecophobic stance that partly defines the species – that of being the would-be manager of fire and combustion. *'All humans manipulate fire, and only humans do so'* (Stephen J. Pyne).[30] So 'Mid-August at Sourdough Mountain Lookout' depicts the human in archetypal mode, as the exclusive overlord of fire, high on the tower above the forest. 'No human society has lacked fire, and none has failed to alter the fire regimes of the lands it has encountered' (Pyne, 27).

Pyne sums up:

> We are truly a species touched by fire. Fire opened the night by providing light and heat. It protected caves and shelters. It rendered foods more edible, leached away toxins from cassava and tannic acid from acorns, and killed bacteria that caused salmonella, parasites that led to trichinosis, and waterborne microbes. It interacted with every conceivable technology. . . . Fire was power. . . . (24)

Fire is an instance of a human tool that has physically altered the very physiology of the species as well as its behaviour. Cooking made new diets accessible, giving humans relatively small teeth for their body size and, decisively, perhaps enabling the development of the brain, the body's most energy-hungry organ. 'Certainly fire altered social relationships. Groups defined themselves by their shared fire . . .' (24).

Fire is both an object of fear and means of exploiting natural resources, including cooking and innumerable forms of useful industry, as well as the destructive effects of fossil fuel combustion.

In even so simple an act as lighting a space against the dark and the dangers of night-time, fire is already mildly ecophobic.

The topic of fire, both in its fearfulness and its indispensability, may highlight the intellectual and moral challenge of the Anthropocene, as against overly simple or moralistic diagnoses of the environmental crisis. Not only does combustion seem implicated in technological and medical triumphs that no-one would wish to see reversed, but the Anthropocene also forms an indeterminate but insidious threshold at which many actions previously normal or insignificant have become, often in all innocence, themselves destructive, simply by virtue of human numbers and power. The kind of major forest fire being risked by ill-informed fire-watching policies in the 1950s would probably become even more damaging in the changed planetary atmosphere of 2014, the time of writing and one of unprecedented firestorms in California.[31]

The question of fire-use and of the destructiveness of the human species seems a huge one to foist on a tiny lyric, a breach of decorum and scale of a kind endemic to the Anthropocene. Nevertheless, one reasonable, if narrow, thematic reading of 'Mid-August at Sourdough Mountain Lookout' would find in it one definitive image for the Anthropocene as the ape of fire playing with fire.

Emergence and anachrony

Literary criticism has often been the institution of a continuous revisionism, a site in which newly significant issues or previously overlooked forms of social wrong begin to be discussed through new readings of texts in the tradition. Contemporary readers come to read the texts and issues of the past in new ways and, in so doing, affirm a sense of their own difference from that which they have inherited. In this way, criticism as an institution also became a conduit for a specific post-enlightenment understanding of the historical process and of modernity, as one in which the human is engaged progressively in ever more illumined forms of self-understanding and self-liberation from the ignorance, limitations or prejudices of the past.

Eco-historicist readings are one symptom of this retrospective gain in perspective. Gillen D'Arcy Wood writes that 'The eco-historicist method historicizes our current crisis moment by making ecological languages of the past speak to the present'.[32]

A good example is Ken Hiltner's previously mentioned analysis of the controversy over the burning of highly sulphurous coal in seventeenth-century London.[33] Yet this renewed interest in kinds of thought previously overlooked must also avoid the danger of positing the Anthropocene in terms that make it continuous with a long and varied tradition of thought on the relations between weather, climate and human cultures, instead of also being a drastic break with these. Ecocritical reading cannot just be some act of supposed retrieval, but now becomes also a measure of the irreversible break in consciousness and understanding, an emergent unreadability. For instance, pollution in London would not have been of concern to people in seventeenth-century Massachusetts. In the twenty-first century this is no longer so clear.

So it would be a simplification to claim that an awareness of the Anthropocene highlights simply the parochialism or intellectual limits of older ways of thinking. For the deficiencies and evasions coming to light are to a significant degree also themselves new, not simply 'faults' that have at last been uncovered. For we are talking about emergent effects not known before human impacts crossed a certain fuzzy threshold to interact in unaccounted and newly significant ways with the finitude of the Earth, and about the kinds of retrospective re-evaluation of past cultures and assumptions they entail.

A corollary of emergence is that previous norms become uncertainly anachronistic. Two recent critical essays take up the issue of how texts are constituted in a kind of *anachrony*, always readable, that is, in times and ways that are not those of their own day, just as, say, *Hamlet* can be the object of numerous psychoanalytic readings of interest and force despite the fact that psychoanalysis did not exist as a mode of thought until the twentieth century. Kate Rigby reads a poem by the Australian poet Judith Wright, 'Dust', written during a drought-ridden summer of 1942–3, as a form of what Rigby calls 'prophetic witness'. Images of desiccation, recalling prophetic books in the Old Testament, cannot but suggest forms of human wrong-doing and responsibility, obscure retributions, the protest of the Earth, yet now in ways little envisaged in the 1940s:

This sick dust, spiralling with the wind,
is harsh as grief's taste in our mouths
and has eclipsed the small sun,
The remnant earth turns evil.[34]

For Rigby the text becomes a kind of 'biting and stinging eco-prophetic witness', calling us to a sense of environmental responsibility.

J. Hillis Miller's paper 'Anachronistic Reading' is similar in argument.[35] Miller's concern is the fact that Wallace Stevens's poem 'The Man on the Dump', published in 1942, cannot now but be read as a text that prefigures climate change and a planet drifting towards the condition of a vast garbage dump. Stevens's original concern was in part the need of modern poets to purge new work of 'images', ideological relics of a cultural past that stand in the way of seeing things without illusion. While Stevens's concern with the poet as cultural legislator, the maker of supreme fictions (to replace, for example, those of religion), may now seem merely anachronistic, Miller's concern is a *creative* anachrony inherent in literary language itself. That is, since writers will, necessarily, not be able much to predict the affect and the effects of reference that a text may produce in a future reader, it is always possible that new, unforeseen contexts will alter the text retrospectively, giving it changed and perhaps prophetic force.

Nevertheless, the kind of Anthropocene criticism proposed and practised by Miller and Rigby is arguably still only a kind of interpretative dead-end. The kinds of reading demanded by the Anthropocene surely need to be rather more sophisticated than finding its image in any past text that deploys waste land or desert motifs. Its emergent unreadability cannot be so easily decoded. After all, it may be that texts with no apparent 'environmental' focus can be shown to be most implicated in environmental damage (such a text is considered in Chapter Five).

The concerns opened by Snyder's lyric offer one particular example of the kind of altered perspective that may be set to overtake numerous rereadings of inherited texts. For instance, backcasting from the unfolding scenarios of the Anthropocene, does William Wordsworth's poetry appear now primarily as a voice of proto-ecological protest in the context of the first industrializing society, or does his celebration of a supposedly providential 'nature' as a spiritualizing force in his own life read mainly as another version of the kind of arrogant anthropocentrism which many ecocritics read as a primary cause of our current predicaments? Is the work of Oscar Wilde, with its transgressive hedonism, more a claim for individual freedom or a celebration of an insidious culture of consumerist 'self-making' as a 'lifestyle' choice? Does the book of Genesis, granting humanity dominion over the beasts, implicate itself in the mass extinction now under way? The number of texts open to such revisionist questions would be unlimited. Can one now truly decide which primary texts are 'environmental' in their issues or not? They all are in some sense, and those least explicitly 'environmental' may actually be the ones most in need of reconsideration. For a critic to evaluate competing versions of the significance of a text increasingly involves something as near to impossible as anticipating the hindsight of a future that must now be conceived in terms beyond simple enlightenment conceptions of progressive human self-liberation and self-understanding. The work of thought may now expand to include questions of climate, of nonhuman lives and of probable futures.

One answer to these questions about alternative readings of Wordsworth and Wilde is to refuse in advance the demand to see either writer as meaning merely the one thing. In effect, the meaning of a past text is a site of emergent effects. The retrospect of the Anthropocene makes it even more impossible to accept that any context to be reconstructed is going to be unitary rather, than, in Martin Jay's words 'a dynamic force field of contending contexts, both synchronous and diachronous, that never fully resolves itself into a single meaningful whole with a clear order of influence'.[36]

A further partial reading here of Snyder's lyric would find its impetus in the fact that the text is 'paratactic' in its mode of construction. That is, it presents a series of images much in the way of a mere list – smoke, fir cones, rocks and meadows, flies, not remembering, drinking water, looking down

(Down valley a smoke haze
Three days heat, after five days rain
Pitch glows on the fir-cones
Across rocks and meadows
Swarms of new flies.)

with only minimal connectives between them or any syntax ascribing causality or purpose between one thing and other. So rather than rushing to hypothesize all these things as the expression of some unifying underlying psychic state, a reader might stay with this disjunctiveness. The poem would not then be taken as expressing some true human essence realizing itself in some act of contemplative retrieval or a self-possessed move on the game board of national landscape politics. This fourth possible reading would read the poem in terms of a condition even of uncertainty, hiatus, disconnection etc. There is the isolation in empty space, to the point of loss of identity, as if Snyder's 'I cannot remember' inhered between each line and the next and between the two very different stanzas.

In his book, *Inventions*, Gerald Bruns offers some seemingly straightforward observations about the interpretation of past texts. He aims to illustrate the difference between mere knowledge, simply factual knowledge for instance, and a supposedly deeper, more genuine 'understanding'. It is, striking, however, how far Bruns's points can no longer apply in the kinds of cases we are now considering:

> To understand a sentence is to understand the situation in which it occurs, which time provided, and also takes away; and, when time has done its work, scholarship or imagination must be brought into play, often to no effect. To understand anything is to understand a situation, but the understanding of any situation requires that you enter into it in order to become part of what you would understand. This is the basic hermeneutic principle, whose corollary is that only outsiders know things, but insiders understand them. A situation cannot be understood except by one who is already contained in it.[37]

The cognitive and ethical claims of the Anthropocene underline just how deeply a text is *not* completely 'understood' by being resituated solely in the cultural context of its time of production. It jumps out, lingers and may have unexpected consequences (recalling Ulrich's Beck's aphorism: 'We live in the age of unintended consequences').[38] To turn again to Snyder's poem, its emergent sense exceeds that of the situation in which it occurred, or, more strictly speaking, that situation is being reconceptualized as a context that must now also include the present and an uncertain future. Furthermore, a reader's being part of the situation of the past text at issue is not the guarantor of a more secure understanding, as it was for Bruns.

Conclusion

The relatively clear-cut case of rereading Snyder's 'Mid-August at Sourdough Mountain Lookout' instantiates a sense of anachronism set to become a general malaise of the Anthropocene, as people come to realize how deeply inherited modes of thought and practice are contaminated by unintended side-effects, producing a general retrospective derangement of meaning. This is not a matter of conceptions and assumptions from our own time supposedly interfering with the scholarly enterprise of recreating the significance of a text in its 'original context'. It is rather that this 'original context' is now being understood on far broader spatial and temporal scales and these make earlier notions of that 'original context' look like kinds of containment. The disruptions of the Anthropocene ('the death of nature') are set to be so massive as to pose anew major questions of what criticism and literary interpretation are for, and in relation to what emergent or unknown norms. The more degraded and dangerous the once-natural environment becomes, the more the future or possible futures will insist on themselves as part of any context to be considered or critical method to be used. Later chapters will try at least to sketch some possible moves on this difficult game board.

Notes

1   Simon Prosser, 'Emergent Causation', *Philosophical Studies* (2012) 159, 21–39, 21.

2   Such a description is apt but would still not quite match the difficulties of thinking the Anthropocene. For the initial state of the Earth system has never been known, and perhaps never can be known, well enough to enable hard and fast predictions about its future behaviour in the first place.

3   'The Deconstruction of Actuality', 536.

4   Derrida's *On Hospitality* (2000) argues how the supposedly inviolable interiority of the home is already de-constituted, turned inside-out, by its multiple embeddings in public space, the state, the telephone line, monitored emails, etc., yet there is residual idealism in Derrida's exclusive attention to systems of law and communication (61). His focus on the moment of decision in

individual consciousness and its pathos (its ordeal of undecidablity, etc.) seems inadequate in a context in which things have now become overwhelmingly more political than people. Nothing in Derrida's work seems to allow for a situation in which it is not irrational to connect a patio heater in London immediately with the slow inundation of Tuvalu in the Pacific. Thus *On Hospitality* mentions TV, email and internet, but not the central heating system, cooking appliances, washing machine or car, all of which have physical effects beyond their immediate local horizon (*On Hospitality: Anne Dufourmantelle Invites Jacques Derrida to Respond*, trans. Rachel Bowlby. Stanford, CA: Stanford University Press, 2000).

5 *The End of Nature* (New York: Random House, 1989), 96.

6 *The Gary Snyder Reader: Prose, Poetry, and Translations* (Washington, DC: Counterpoint, 1999), 399.

7 Timothy Gray, *Gary Snyder and the Pacific Rim. Creating Countercultural Community* (Iowa City: University of Iowa Press, 2006), 107.

8 Tim Dean, *Gary Snyder and the American Unconscious: Inhabiting the Ground* (New York: St Martin's Press, 1991), 21.

9 Nick Selby, '"Coming Back to Oneself / Coming Back to the Land". Gary Snyder's Poetics', in John Tallmadge and Henry Harrington (eds), *Reading under the Sign of Nature: New Essays in Ecocriticism* (Salt Lake City, UT: University of Utah Press, 2000), 179–97.

10 See www.youtube.com/watch?v=Y2UbkRI6vXg.

11 *Overtime: Selected Poems* (London: Penguin, 1999), 5–20.

12 Quoted in Selby, '"Coming Back to Oneself"', 187.

13 Herman Rapaport, *The Literary Theory Toolkit: A Compendium of Concepts and Methods* (Oxford: Wiley-Blackwell, 2011), 34.

14 'Eco-Historicism', in Gillen D'Arcy Wood (ed.), special issue of *The Journal for Early Modern Cultural Studies* 8.2 (Fall/Winter 2008).

15 'Renaissance Literature and Our Contemporary Attitude to Global Warming', *ISLE* 13.3 (Summer 2009), 429–42.

16 Ted Steinberg, *Down to Earth: Nature's Role in American History* (New York: Oxford University Press, 2009), 141.

17 *Back on the Fire: Essays* (Emeryville, CA: Avalon, 2007), 83.

18 Williams, *Paterson* (New York: New Directions, 1963).

19 Atwood, *Oryx and Crake* (Toronto: McClelland and Stewart, 2003).

20 'The Posthuman Comedy', *Critical Inquiry* 38 (Spring 2012), 533–53, 534. Wai Chee Dimock writes: 'An Americanist hardly needs any knowledge of English literature, let alone Persian literature, Hindu literature, Chinese literature. It is as if the borders of knowledge were simply the replicas of national borders. And yet, what does it mean to set aside a body of writing as "American"? What assumptions enable us to take an adjective derived from a territorial jurisdiction and turn it into a mode of literary causality' (*Through Other Continents: American Literature Across Deep Time* (Princeton, NJ: Princeton University Press, 2006), 3).

21 Bruce Braun and Sarah J. Whatmore (eds), *Political Matter: Technoscience, Democracy, and Public Life* (Minneapolis, MN: University of Minnesota Press, 2010), xxii–xxiii.

22 For a discussion of this, see my *The Cambridge Introduction to Literature and the Environment* (Cambridge: Cambridge University Press, 2011), 161.

23 See *The Ecological Thought*, 38–40.

24 *Bodily Natures: Science, Environment, and the Material Self* (Bloomington, IN: Indiana University Press, 2010), 15–17.

25 Kate Daniel (ed.), *The Book of the Dead*, in *Out of Silence: Selected Poems* (Evanston. IL: Northwestern University Press, 2000), 37–40.

26 Bear, *Darwin's Radio* (New York: Ballantine, 1999) and *Darwin's Children* (New York: Ballantine, 2003).

27 Alaimo criticizes Shira Wolosky's reading of Rukeyser in terms of the power of modes of discourse, in order to, in Wolosky's words, '"expose [. . .] not only the complicity of medical, industrial and legal institutions but also the ways in which this complicity takes place through specific modes of language"' (47). Such a constructivist reading 'risks losing sight of the materiality of human bodies and environments' (Alaimo, 48).

28 Alaimo allies her argument with Heise's recognition that environmental arguments need to inculcate 'not so much a sense of place as a sense of planet' (15), yet she still determines 'trans-corporeality as the transit between body and environment [as] *exceedingly local*' (emphasis added). If her mode of concern with the toxicity can involve vaster scales that is only because, as Alaimo writes, to trace 'a toxic substance from production to consumption often reveals global networks of social injustice, lax regulations, and environmental degradation'. So oddly, while trans-corporeality entails a direct concern with connections between bodies, to trace it on the more than local scale is still a matter of discourse and

law, the very approach Alaimo criticizes in those thinkers who risk 'losing sight of the materiality of human bodies and environments' (48).

29 Alaimo only cursorily mentions global warming, not following up the ramifications (20).

30 Stephen J. Pyne, *Fire: A Brief History* (Seattle, WA: University of Washington Press, 2001), 24, Pyne's emphasis.

31 See Anna Williams, 'California Burning', *New Scientist*, 16 August 2014.

32 Gillen D'Arcy Wood, 'Introduction: Eco-historicism', *Journal for Early Modern Cultural Studies* 8.2 (Fall/Winter 2008), 1–6.

33 Hiltner, 'Renaissance Literature and Our Contemporary Attitude to Global Warming'.

34 Quoted by Rigby, 'Writing in the Anthropocene: Idle Chatter or Ecoprophetic Witness?' *Australian Humanities Review*, Issue 47, November 2009, www.australianhumanitiesreview.org/archive/ Issue-November-2009/rigby.html

35 'Anachronistic Reading', *Derrida Today* 3 (2010), 75–91.

36 Martin Jay, 'Historical Explanation and the Event: Reflections on the Limits of Contextualization', *NLH* 42 (2011), 557–71, 561.

37 Bruns, *Inventions: Writing, Textuality and Understanding in Literary History* (New Haven, CT: Yale University Press, 1982), 180.

38 Beck, *World Risk Society* (London: Polity, 1999), 119.

CHAPTER FOUR

Scale framing

*What could be more private than a couple deciding
to have a baby or not?
What could be more public than a couple deciding
to have a baby or not?*

A scale (from the Latin *scala* for ladder, step or stairs) usually enables a calibrated and useful extrapolation between dimensions of space or time. Thus a 'cartographic scale' describes the ratio of distance on a map to real distances on the Earth's surface. To move from a large to small-scale or vice versa implies a calculable shift of resolution on the same area or features, a smooth zooming out or in. With climate change, however, we have a map whose scale includes the whole Earth but, when it comes to relating the threat to daily questions of politics, ethics or specific interpretations of history, culture, literature or other areas, the map is often almost mockingly useless. Even the climatology works on a less than helpful scale. For, paradoxically, it is simpler to predict futures for the planet as a whole, a closed system, than to make forecasts for specific areas.

Policies and concepts relating to climate change invariably seem undermined or even derided by consideration of scale effects: a campaign for environmental reform in one country may already seem effectively negated by the lack of such measures on the other side of the world. A long fought-for nature reserve, designed to protect a rare ecosystem, becomes, on zooming out, a different place.

Scale effects

The Anthropocene is itself an emergent 'scale effect'. That is, at a certain, indeterminate threshold, numerous human actions, insignificant in themselves (heating a house, clearing trees, flying between the continents, forest management) come together to form a new, imponderable physical event, altering the basic ecological cycles of the planet.

The force of the notion of a 'carbon footprint' relates to scale effects. If it were just a matter of my own emissions there would be no controversy and no need for the idea of a personal 'footprint'. The size of my carbon footprint is of no interest or significance in itself except in relation to the incalculable effect of there being so many millions of other footprints having an impact over an uncertain timescale. This is something beyond my individual horizon entirely. The concept of a 'carbon footprint' is one in which the finitude of the planet is inherent – crudely speaking, if the planet were larger, my personal footprint would be smaller. The phrase 'carbon footprint' becomes a very peculiar catachresis, collapsing huge and tiny scales upon each other and instantiating a problem that Hans Jonas highlighted about 'all traditional ethics' – that it 'reckoned only with noncumulative behavior'.[1] The emergent force of scale effects is confusing because they take the easy, daily equations of moral and political accounting and multiply them both by zero and by infinity: for example the greater the number of people engaged in modern forms of consumption then the less the relative influence or responsibility of each, but the worse the cumulative impact of their insignificance.

Thinkers like Sarewitz and Allenby are essentially talking about emergent scale effects. Deborah MacKenzie hypothesizes that 'once a society develops beyond a certain level of complexity it becomes increasingly fragile. Eventually it reaches a point at which even a relatively minor disturbance can bring everything crashing down'.[2] Scale effects underlie the way material and non-cultural elements inhabit and distort what may be presented as purely cultural political issues – not in the welcome sense, advocated by green thinkers, of reminding us of how deeply 'culture' is embedded in and part of 'nature', but as emergent, interference phenomena. As a result of scale effects, what is self-evident or rational at one scale may well be destructive or unjust at another. Hence, progressive arguments designed to affirm individual rights and help disseminate Western levels of prosperity may even resemble, on another scale, an insane plan to destroy the biosphere. Yet, for, say, any individual household or motorist a scale effect in their actions is invisible. It is not present in any phenomenon in itself,[3] but only in the contingency of how many other such phenomena there are, have been and will be, at even large distances in space or time.

Can the Leviathan of humanity en masse, as a geological force, be represented? No, at least not in the realist mode still dominant in the novel. Its effects are global and non-localizable. Its modes of appearance as a totality are only in graphs, statistics and computer projections and modelling – of CO_2 emissions, population figures, waste generation, proportion of the Earth's land surface used and so on. It cannot be pictured adequately in some sensuous image in the way that, for example, poverty can be depicted in the form of an ill-fed family huddled together in one shabby room, greed by the image of a luxury car next to a swimming pool, or nuclear war by the image of a mushroom cloud. Nevertheless, any literary representation of environmental issues – and which issues now are not in the end? – over the past century at least, must be a representation in part of this emergent human or planetary reality.

Scale framing

A constitutive, unavoidable element of any representation, evaluation or literary reading is to presuppose or project a certain scale in space and time for its issues. A certain scale must make up the fundamental structure of any imaginable experience, or of any model of the world. Broadly speaking, it would be difficult to describe the development of a geological feature on a time scale of hours, or even of a decade, while it is conversely difficult to imagine what a novel's interior monologue would look like if one tried to present it over a geological time scale. In fact, the nonsensical impossibility of such an idea already underlines how the topic of this chapter, scale, forms a pervasive, decisive but almost universally overlooked structural feature of any sort of reading.

'Scale framing' is recognized in discussions of environmental and other politics as a strategy for representing complex issues in ways that make them more amenable to thought or overview, while at the same time running grave risks of being a simplification and even evasion. Hence essays on scale framing are often also exercises on cognitive bias, whether intentional or accidental. One small but significant example appears in controversies in the United States over possible action to protect the endangered Steller Sea Lion, whose habitat stretches across the northern Pacific. The US National Marine Fisheries Service had investigated the plight of the sea-lion, but in ways that were soon challenged in the courts by environmental groups. At issue was a spatial scale framing. The Fisheries Service investigated threats to the animals by deciding to focus primarily on critical habitat and on how the sea-lions there interact with local influences, an approach that seems rational but which excluded consideration of fishery-wide practices that would affect the animals in other parts of their range, as well as excluding questions about national fisheries management more broadly.[4]

As the Earth turns into a novel, partly incalculable hybrid entity where human effects interact in emergent ways with partially understood ecological systems, with counter-intuitive interactions that cross the continents, many habitual modes of thought, understanding and action now emerge as constituted by a kind of increasingly anachronistic 'scale framing', that is discursive practices that construct the scale at which a problem is experienced as a mode of predetermining the way in which it is conceived. Crucially here, to frame the scale at which one considers a problem is also sometimes a way of evading it – for example thinking of private vehicle use solely in terms of individual right, or environmental issues as solely a matter of green consumer choice (Allenby and Sarewitz's Level I). As Emma Hughes writes of the example of scale framing in relation to GM crops in Britain, 'by giving people a boundary you are installing a sense of agency or control'.[5]

A good example of unacknowledged scale framing in environmental thinking is the emerging but uncertain subdiscipline of 'ecopyscology', the study of the relation of human psychic health to environments. Ecopsychological theorists trace destructive and ultimately self-destructive attitudes to the natural world back to some broad, psychological diagnosis: that individual human beings, compared to their hunter-gatherer ancestors, are in a condition of arrested development, are autistic, or are suffering from a condition of trauma first induced by the turn to agriculture (in which nature becomes conceived as something to control and manipulate, not to live with), or from a form of dissociative disorder, the inability to make true connections between phenomena.[6]

I do not believe the arguments of ecopsychology are ultimately convincing. Instead, the 'madness' at issue is less a matter of individual psychology than of scale effects. Ecopsychologists almost always diagnose a kind of dysfunction normally applied to an individual only – autism, trauma, insanity, dissociation and so on – but then apply it to whole societies.[7] In effect, in ecopsychology, the social body is understood as the individual writ large. What is wrong with this is that it makes little allowance for how scale effects render collective effects different in kind as well as impact from individual ones. Small amounts of deforestation are different in quality as well as quantity from large-scale logging on every continent. In relation to human behaviour 'ecopsychology' becomes an instance of the fallacy called 'methodological individualism', the postulate or assumption the 'the behavior of any social group must ultimately be explained in terms of properties of the individual members, who collectively constitute that group' (James H. Fetzer).[8]

A lot of the moralism that reflects badly on green politics comes from this. The terms that ecopsychologists apply to whole societies, such as 'autistic', 'dissociation disorder', 'trauma' etc., are really tropes or catachreses, that is, figures of speech applied to a collective condition for which there is no literal name, only the trope taken from individuals. So when specific people are accused of these there is a certain failure of proportion, a scapegoating. This may be why environmental moralism, targeted at any individual, always seems over the top as it tries to implicate that person in damaging the Earth.

Scale framing as miniaturization: Two cases

Other forms of scale framing may lurk in seemingly innocent or neutral procedures of reading and criticism. Take, for example, a recent 'postcolonial' ecocritical reading, Christa Grewe-Volpp's essay 'No Environmental Justice without Social Justice: A Green Postcolonialist Reading of Paule Marshall's *The Chosen Place, the Timeless People*'.[9] Grewe-Volpp's article exemplifies an extremely common way of proceeding in the literary criticism of novels: the critic homes in some chosen text and highlights how specific cultural or environmental issues play out within it, usually suggesting this particular text as offering some sort of explanatory model or norm of use in the real world. However, the plural and contradictory contexts of the Anthropocene now highlight some limits in this way of valuing novels.

Marshall's novel of 1968 concerns the imaginary Bourne island on the edge of the Caribbean. As background to Marshall's novel of 1968, Grewe-Volpp gives a full account of the writer's bestowal of the island with a representative Caribbean history – British colonialism, the African slave trade, sugar plantations, the deep shadow of the nearby United States, economic dependency and a strong and growing division between a Westernized, privileged minority and the deprived majority. The island is divided between a developed West, with the various tourist industries of the Caribbean, and a neglected and impoverished East, its town of Bournehills devastated by the environmental effects of sugar-cane production, with the international sugar-cane industry effectively continuing the violations of the monoculture plantocracy that preceded it. The novel follows a small group of US scholars researching a long-range development project and coming to terms with the implications of what they actually find on Bourne Island. The crucial character is Merle Kinbona, the owner of the guest house where the researchers initially stay, descendant of an English plantation owner and black slaves, with her hybrid identity expressed in her clothing and interests.

Marshall's method is rendered as the exploring of real environmental, political and social situations through imaginary encounters, and Grewe-Volpp's reading initially traces the various cultural and political problems that the novel dramatizes (the racism deep in one of the American characters, the way the impoverished people of Bournehills have resisted the neo-colonialism of earlier Western development projects). Grewe-Volpp's critical work is like that of most critical and ecocritical readings of novels, that is to recast the text's specific events into a more transparently legible kind of general cultural politics. Kinbona's story in particular is read symbolically as that of a possible future for the island. The latent symbolism may seem obvious enough here: a person of the mixed ethnic and cultural descent characteristic of the Caribbean begins, as the novel ends, planning a trip to Africa to be reconciled with a daughter by a long-estranged African husband. She also vehemently rejects an offer of money from Harriet Amron, wife of the leader of the development project who tries to bribe Kimbona to leave the island after discovering an affair with her husband. This attempted bribe and its vehement rejection is seen by Grewe-Volpp as a symbolic refusal of all outside development projects for the island, though in fact the scheme at issue had been shown as sensitive and having a great deal of genuine local support.[10] Grewe-Volpp's essay concludes by also giving heavily symbolic significance to a possibility that Kimbona mentions before leaving for Africa, that is that she might get involved in local politics on her return. Grewe-Volpp puts great weight on this to argue that: 'the narrative loci lead us to conclude. . . . That once responsibility is restored to the people who live in close symbiosis with the land, they will take care of its needs as well, if only for their own benefit' (236).[11]

Grewe-Volpp's final wrapping up of the novel is not untypical of how many critics read realist novels such as this: a critic's job is taken to mean highlighting the book as enacting in fictional miniature a cultural politics that could be held usefully to apply, scaled-up again, to innumerable people and situations in actual life. Such miniaturization, however, is in danger of turning Marshall's portrayal of the social, psychic and emotional complexities and nuances of a predicament into a kind of bioregional parable.[12] Grewe-Volpp's final argument about restoring 'autonomy' to the local people is easy to agree with – but so easy in fact that, intellectually, one finds one has got almost nowhere by doing so. It is a classic instance of the fallacy of scale framing to offer Kimbona's story of self-assertion at the individual level as projecting the supposed viability of some general transformation at the level of a population as a whole. Grewe-Volpp's positing that direct ownership of land by its inhabitants should lead to its ecological health is also a claim refuted by the counter-examples of many politically autonomous communities across the world, where the temptations of trading for short-term profits still override broader considerations. The critical slogan 'No Environmental Justice without Social Justice' may in fact be variably fragile or convincing, depending on the scale of consideration and inclusion at issue.

Scale framing may be particularly clear in the case of a reading of a fictional island. Nevertheless, too many ecocritical readings make their arguments through a comparable process of intellectual miniaturization. Bearing in mind the intractable challenges of the Anthropocene, it will surely become harder in the future to be satisfied with an ecocritical method whose contribution to knowledge remains only to take up a work of fiction and affirm in it values and environmental truisms most readers of the criticism would hold in any case.

Scale framing, or rather how to confront both its inevitability in some form and its potential evasiveness, is also the underlying issue in Adam Trexler's overview of climate change novels over the past 40 years, *Anthropocene Fictions* (2015).[13] With admirable thoroughness, Trexler takes up more than 150 novels that involve climate change in some way. With a topic of such global scope, involving so many factors, the question of its categorization in some sort of coherent literary representation becomes especially acute. No finite piece of writing can encompass a topic that seems to entail thinking of almost everything at once – climate, culture, politics, population dynamics, transport infrastructure, religious attitudes: 'How can a global process, spanning millennia, be made comprehensible to human imagination, with its limited sense of place and time?' (5). This is effectively a study of various modes of scale framing, assessing their relative scope and weaknesses.

Nevertheless, Trexler sees in the novel form itself a potential to avoid many dangers of simplifying the Anthropocene. It is a literary form that can be comprehensive, capable of taking up an issue such as environmental degradation, and treating the social, personal, political, cultural and aesthetic aspects of it non-reductively, all between the same covers, as opposed to what is seen as the pre-emptive framing of it in non-fictional accounts, in purely scientific, purely political or purely economic terms.

Some kind of scale framing is inevitable to any representation and Trexler notes, as many have done, the resort in innumerable so-called Cli Fi novels to cultural stereotypes, to dystopian or apocalyptic scenarios, with a focus on future environmental disasters such as devastating flooding or desertification or on future eco-fascist regimes, corporate tyrannies or collapsed societies. Such approaches evade most of the present-day moral, political dilemmas by simply jumping ahead to some far more straightforward depiction of future disaster.

Even what is recognized as one of the most successful narratives of climate change in the mode of future realism, Kim Stanley Robinson's 'Science in the Capital' trilogy (2004–7),[14] emerges on scrutiny as an exercise in scale framing to a degree that fatally undermines its plausibility as making a useful contribution to the debate. Robinson skilfully imagines the kinds of crises and metamorphoses undergone by political and social institutions in the American capital in response to the crisis of sudden climate change (with Washington suffering severe flooding). A reductive framing, however, lies in the way Washington politics is simplified, overlooking the plurality of US domestic factors that would stymie the vast programmes of emergency measures and economic reforms pushed through by Robinson's fictional president. It also lies in the narrowness of so US-centric a focus on a global issue, resting on the unlikeliness of what Trexler describes as 'a simplistic, last-minute emissions deal with China' (126). The most significant scale framing at work is Robinson's presentation of all the significant action in terms of social mobilization and 'a de-emphasis of the real, material agency of things' (166), as innumerable physical processes in the Earth's systems become less and less reliably predictable.

So even Robinson's ambitious project is a form of intellectual miniaturization, its scale framing still simplifying the Anthropocene in terms largely dictated by the aesthetic, dramatic, and narrative constraints of presenting things in some easily apprehensible empirical scenario, sensuous images or plot of human actions, characters and motive. This is not to make the facile point that any literary text can always be shown to have excluded some issue or implication in order to achieve the relative coherence or understanding which it does possess. Rather, the omissions, simplifications and contortions of plot and probability that Trexler is describing read more provocatively. They trace the disruptions to given categories of thought inherent in trying to think the Anthropocene. Tobias Menely and Margaret Ronda, in an essay on waste, repeat a point of some power: They write: 'The paradigmatic instance of this displaced agency, *unavailable to narrative representation*, is the tipping point, where positive feedback loops related to forest dieback, permafrost methane release, and the ice-albedo effect generate – in some scenarios – "runaway" climate change, independent of human action' (emphasis added).[15] As the contingent emergent sum of innumerable and probably incalculable processes happening across the Earth at divergent time scales, a 'tipping point' per se is neither unitary nor representable in any one, sufficient image.[16] Scale effects in particular defy sensuous representation or any plot confined, say, to human-to-human dramas and intentions, demanding new, innovative modes of writing that have yet convincingly to emerge.[17] This issue is considered further in Chapter Nine.

Overpopulation

Another issue of scale concerns the fact of human overpopulation. Overpopulation is meant here in the strict sense as the situation in which the population of a species exceeds the long-term carrying capacity of its ecological context, in this case humanity and the context of the Earth as a whole. An ever-growing population produces threshold or scale effects that erode the possibility of acceptable, practicable or moral choices for the human future. A UN report of 2012 reads:

> [a]s the world's population looks set to grow to nearly 9 billion by 2040 from 7 billion now, and the number of middle-class consumers increases by 3 billion over the next 20 years, the demand for resources will rise exponentially. Even by 2030, the world will need at least 50 per cent more food, 45 per cent more energy and 30 per cent more water . . . at a time when a changing environment is creating new limits to supply.[18]

The latest report of the Intergovernmental Panel on Climate Change (IPCC) affirms:

> Globally, economic and population growth continue to be the most important drivers of increases in CO2 emissions from fossil fuel combustion. The contribution of population growth between 2000 and 2010 remained roughly identical to that of the previous three decades, while the contribution of economic

growth has risen sharply. (IPCC Fifth Assessment Synthesis Report, November 2014)[19]

Both economic and population growth have outstripped the effects of any emission reduction measures since the turn of the century. Nevertheless, addressing population growth is not part of any proposed mitigation strategy in the IPCC, even though other lifestyle and behavioural changes are discussed. It is not clear whether this is because it is seen as not amenable to policy intervention, or that the topic is simply too politically and culturally toxic to touch – it simply disappears from the report.

The cultural and political toxicity of the issue soon becomes clear. For instance, there have been widespread arguments that raising people across the globe to more Western-like levels of prosperity and consumption must address the phenomenon of couples feeling the need to have children as a kind of insurance for their old age. Yet, merely making Western modes of life more widespread would form an evasive and anthropocentric agenda whose implementation would actually see accelerated levels of habitat loss across the world to support levels of human consumption set to exceed capacity after the short term.[20] The seemingly obvious and just policy of calling for a massive redistribution of wealth from North to South would be a political impossibility while, in Stephen Gardiner's words, 'the development necessary for the less developed nations to reach a stable or even declining population would, on present technologies, involve a catastrophic increase in energy consumption, and so in environmental impact per person'.[21] On top of this, increased longevity almost everywhere and the reduction of infant mortality – indisputable human goods – are also factors in overpopulation, facts which must complicate any would-be simplistic diagnosis of the issue.

Answers to overpopulation that appeal to economic 'development' on the current model also discount the moral claim to life of other species and assume a total human entitlement to the planet. The question should not be how many human beings can the 'resources' of the planet sustainably support, but, in Eileen Crist's words: 'How many people, and at what level of consumption, can live on Earth without turning Earth into a human colony founded on the genocide of its nonhuman indigenes?'[22]

Overpopulation was a controversial but widely discussed issue in the 1970s, after ground-breaking work by Paul Ehrlich and by the 'Club of Rome'.[23] However, by the time that ecocriticism emerged as widely recognized school in the early 1990s, the topic had become muted and politically suspect, almost taboo. The almost total absence of the issue of population from environmental debate until very recently can be traced to the same factors that led to the dominance of social-ecological types of argument in environmental criticism more generally – that is, the attempt to frame most issues in terms of an extremely understandable but often more narrowly conceived social justice agenda. A decisive moment in this changed perspective on population was the International Conference on Population and Development (ICPD) held in Cairo in 1994. Here, environmental and social goals such as addressing poverty through alleviating population growth and defence of the nonhuman environment were 'supplanted almost entirely by individual goals defined in terms of sexual and reproductive health and rights'.[24] The long internationally drafted document from Cairo made no mention of the strong interrelationship between population growth and the environmental degradation and poverty linked to population pressures.[25] Attention to the geomorphic, large-scale effects of overpopulation gave way to the closely related yet crucially distinct issue of improving the autonomy of women, understood to be the most decisive issue affecting the frequency of pregnancies. A priority becomes helping all girls to have access to education, and women to family planning, with contraception being made easily available.

Who would take issue with such obvious goods? There should not be much real conflict in practice between populationists and social justice advocates, as giving more power to women, including the questioning of both social/patriarchal and religious pressures to have children, tends to have the effect of encouraging life-choices that involve fewer pregnancies. However:

> While the agendas of the human rights and environmental groups should not be seen as fundamentally at odds with each other, they are nonetheless not the same. The human rights agenda is about protecting freedoms and rights of individuals here and now. The environmental agenda . . . has been about protecting the natural and human environments, now and in perpetuity.[26]

In effect, with the rights agenda, the longer time-scale effects (with their massive scenarios of human and nonhuman misery) are overlooked or assumed to take care of themselves. For several decades demographic concerns came increasingly to be tinted as latently racist, anti-woman, anti-immigrant and anti-poor. There were even caricatures of campaigners on population as advocates of oppressive forms of 'population control' that violate the rights of women. 'Thus, representatives from the feminist and social justice movement became strange bedfellows of the Vatican and other conservative religious advocates'.[27]

From a strictly populationist point of view, the advocacy of individual rights would be described starkly as a means to an end, namely reduced population rates (although these themselves would also be understood as a matter of enabling the future material conditions making any sort of rights agenda meaningful), while for thinkers influenced by the Cairo consensus, such improved rights are an end in themselves.

The difficulty, again, is scale effects – the way a growing population harbours emergent properties such that the more people there already are, the greater becomes the latent rift between the two dominant stances on the issue, that is to say, the more, on the one side, an exclusive focus on individual rights risks becoming an evasive lower-level answer to a Level III issue, and the more, on the other side, a narrowly populationist agenda risks endorsing present or immediate injustice.

Bryan G. Norton describes a situation that will be familiar to that increasing proportion of people who live in a large city. Stressing how 'environmental values are inherently and unavoidably scalar, contextual and emergent',[28] Norton highlights how increased consumption and population are correlated at the individual scale with diminishing freedom of choice, as the loading capacity of an environment is approached (40). Overpopulation also erodes the significance of each individual voice in any supposed democracy by the mere fact of the law of large numbers and the increasing complexity of infrastructure and regulation required to make society function. Albert A. Bartlett writes:

> when the population of the region around the town grows to become a gigantic urban metroplex with, say, ten times the population of the town, the voice of one citizen in the town

in solving the regional problem is diluted by another factor of ten. With regional population growth, all manner of problems from pollution to transportation become regional problems, and this expansion of the problems greatly diminishes the voice of individual citizens in finding solutions to the problems.[29]

Overpopulation in the sense at issue in the Anthropocene means extrapolating this kind of regional problem (which may be only local, answerable by making more space available elsewhere) to a global one (where there is no space elsewhere). Protection of the environment is easy to defend as maintaining the scope of human options in future societies,[30] yet this fact is very unlikely to quieten the demands of the present, as the immediate pressures of overpopulation and of poverty come to reinforce each other. Leon Kolankiewicz writes of the destruction of rain forest in Honduras, where the logging trucks are followed by 'land-hungry *campesinos*, applying traditional slash-and-burn agriculture: *sustainable when population density is low, but destructive when it is too high.* These desperate settlers were claiming and clearing any patch of standing forest' (emphasis added).[31] Tragically, at a certain threshold, it comes increasingly to matter that the rightful claims of subsistence agriculture can erode the rainforest as well as the large-scale logging companies that do so far more culpably.

GAME-THEORETIC DYNAMICS

Scale effects are also implicated in a culture's entrapment in the kinds of impersonal dynamic highlighted by 'game theory' – the mathematical modelling of situations of conflict or cooperation between agents pursuing their own interests in relation to a shared resource or problem. Garrett Hardin's controversial game-theoretical parable, the 'tragedy of the commons',[32] has become a frequent reference in discussions of climate change and the near impossibility of reaching or keeping agreements on adequate measures to mitigate it. Darkly, it has even been influential in informing the policies of bodies at the centre of international capitalism, such as those of the IMF and the World Bank.[33]

Hardin's notorious parable depicts the destruction of a piece of common grazing land by herdsmen variously competing for its use.

Each individual herdsman, knowing the others will be facing the same pressures and perhaps thinking in the same way, feels he has no alternative but to try to graze a few more cattle on the land if he can. Inevitably it would seem, the land is destroyed by overgrazing simply through each herdsman acting in their rational self-interest – something that becomes inevitable if there are *already* too many herdsmen. Seemingly rational behaviour at one, individual scale becomes irrational and destructive on a larger one. Hardin intended this parable to debunk the very notion of a commons, depicting it as a resource that must inevitably destroy itself through misuse, as opposed to systems of private property – each herdsman responsible for his own plot of land, which Hardin then supposed safe from over-exploitation.

Hardin's parable has been discredited in several significant respects. Critics observe that he overlooks the long history of real commons, which have often been very successful, based as they are on longstanding agreement and shared responsibilities and penalties.[34] However, the tragedy of the commons is more compelling as 'a problem of *scale* [rather] than a problem of *lack of private* property ownership'.[35] Rebuttals of Hardin's 'tragedy of the commons' often envisage alternative scenarios at what is implicitly a local or regional scale, one at which effective communication and agreement between the parties concerned can easily be envisaged. But this is not at all easy to conceive for human populations spread across the various continents – why would one group in Bolivia feel much compulsion to restrain themselves to reciprocate the actions of another group in Poland, say, or vice versa? The list of conditions for any effective agreement on the climate would be: that resource use can be monitored, verified and shared, that the parties know and trust each other; that outsiders and freebooters can be easily excluded; and that the rules are easily enforced. Yet on the planetary scale, these conditions will become strained to breaking point. The situation becomes all the murkier in that we are addressing dangers that emerge at thresholds which are still uncertain and multiple, arising with the cumulative effect of many marginal and dispersed decisions. All in all, the situation in relation to the planetary commons forms a game space in which one cannot even be sure what move one is making.[36]

Recently, Stephen Gardiner has taken up varieties of game-theoretical argument more subtle than Hardin's to argue that climate change represents the 'perfect moral storm', that is, a global environmental tragedy arising from 'the unusual interaction of a number of serious and mutually reinforcing problems, which creates an unusual and perhaps unprecedented challenge'.[37] The new move Gardiner makes is a characteristic expansion in the scale of the object of consideration, to include competition across the dimension of time as well as space. Just as in the old 'tragedy of the commons' model, each user of the commons would be tempted to appropriate just a little more space, so in Gardiner's extension each human generation, living with the immediately surrounding effects of a cumulative environmental degradation, will very probably find itself doing only the minimum or less to reduce its own ecological impact, tacitly leaving more adequate action to the next generation. He hypothesizes that even were current governments across the world to achieve some sort of binding and enforceable agreement on carbon emissions, there would still be very good reason to suspect its adequacy. This is 'the tyranny of the contemporary' (154). The frightening element in Gardiner's argument about generational buck-passing is that, for a later generation living in the probably more intractable conditions produced by the neglect of its predecessors, inadequate short-term measures inevitably become even more attractive, further degrading the life of people in the future, a domino effect of intensifying environmental degradation.

The 'developed' countries squander resources in often trivial ways on a massive scale, even as they promulgate systems of economics that portray such vandalism as a benefit ('increased GDP'). Yet thinkers who try to represent the ecological violence of overpopulation as entirely a matter of excessive consumption in the 'developed' world look increasingly like people attempting to keep the arguments on more ethically comfortable and intellectually convenient terrain. If we are deploying the 'Anthropocene' to name a blurred and messy threshold then one of its most insidious effects becomes an increasing clash between the human rights agenda and the pressures of environmental integrity and safety. Expanding population not only consolidates individual poverty, as more people must share a finite world, but it also plays a large role in increased water scarcity, erosion of topsoil and biodiversity loss. As more people are forced to live in vulnerable areas, such as floodplains, more will be the victim of 'natural' disasters.

The 'Anthropocene' may also name this threshold or scale effect constricting the scope of plausible human action at the planetary level, increasingly transforming situations of Level II complexity into ones of a Level III perplexity and the scene of simultaneous pressures from incompatible demands. A scale effect is never visible in itself. Of carbon emissions, all one will ever see is a person driving a car, a house being heated, melting snow or whatever, and not the innumerable other sources of pollution, now and in the future across the planet, that make each particular triviality transmute into something significant. Overpopulation is clearly a hyperobject in Morton's sense, although absent from his book, *Hyperobjects*, bar a brief mention (140), and it exemplifies one elusive feature of such objects – non-locality. Global overpopulation cannot be seen as such in any one place. It is measured statistically and entails the combined effects of there being people elsewhere, even in sparsely inhabited areas across the planet. Morton writes 'When you feel raindrops, you are experiencing climate change, in some sense. In particular you are experiencing the climate change known as global warming. But you are never directly experiencing global warming as such' (*Hyperobjects*, 48). Might one not rewrite this as follows: 'Whenever you meet any other people you are now experiencing overpopulation in some sense, but you never directly experience overpopulation as such'?

Literary representations of overpopulation

Just as the scale effects of pollution cannot adequately be represented in the image of, say, a smoke stack or even many smoke stacks, so any literary effort to represent global overpopulation in sensuous or perceptual terms is immediately vulnerable to the criticism that this representation is 'really' of something else. Overpopulation in relation to the Earth as a whole is a scale effect that, again, cannot be seen: 'most people don't yet know how to process it [overpopulation] as a problem at the personal level' (Ronnie Hawkins),[38] and this disjunction between immediate perception and broader understanding challenges literary representations of the issue. Just as climate change fiction and cinema has inevitably drifted towards sensationalist and often unhelpful images of implausibly instant and very cinematic disasters, what literature there is on overpopulation has tended to present often xenophobic images of claustrophobia-inducing urban crowds. This tends to be the way of various dystopian and other narratives of the 1960s and 1970s, when the so-called Population Bomb was a widespread public issue.[39]

In the best currently available survey of literary representations of overpopulation, Heise discusses this generation of fictions in an analogous way. Without herself dismissing the serious ecological pressures from expanding human populations, she argues that the various scenarios in these narratives from 40 and 50 years ago actually reflect situations that are not necessarily cases of global overpopulation at all. Rather they depict fear of loss of individuality in a crowded urban space, a sense of claustrophobia perhaps reinforced by class or racial prejudice and anxieties, or they reflect the fact of increased human visibility when poverty forces people onto the streets, or they continue older modes of depicting totalitarian societies with their restrictive regulations, including forms of coercive birth control.

As a scale effect, overpopulation in relation to the present and future carrying capacity of the planet does not – in fact it cannot – appear as such in an indisputable way, only certain, local symptomatic effects. The point is not that such things as overcrowding are not obvious and credible images of regional population pressures, but that, since overpopulation as a distributed and truly *global* issue is not visible in itself, the 'over' in 'overpopulation' is a judgement relating to scale effects over space and time. Consequently, any particular, local representation of it by a writer will always be susceptible to being read by a critic as 'really' responding to some other concern. As Andreu Domingo writes of certain novels concerned with overpopulation, 'the main characters are frightened of being absorbed into the masses, of being confused with them. The taboo, the unmentionable, is contamination by poverty'.[40]

It is the potentially insidious nature of global overpopulation as a scale effect that it can never be seen directly, but must be modelled in statistics and in specific side-effects that can always be argued as being 'really' something else, such as capitalist greed or urban overcrowding. Correspondingly, even some supposed curb or reduction in the human population will have no easily visible symbol or image comparable, say, to say the aesthetically attractive picture of some rainforest newly 'saved' from logging companies. Other arguments trying to dismiss overpopulation as a false problem, a screen of other concerns, instantiate a similar logic of misrecognition. For instance, Andil Gosine's 'Non-White Reproduction and Same-Sex Eroticism: Queer Acts against Nature' dismisses 'overpopulation' as an issue, defining it as an attempt to 'pit blame for global ecological disaster on the reproducing proclivities of the world's poor',[41] and highlighting instead 'industrialization, overconsumption, and capitalist territorialisation' (153). Gosine's argument is plausible as a critique of elements of some dystopian fictions of the 1960s and 1970s but how convincing would it be to ascribe to population activists such as Al Gore, Paul Ehrlich, David Attenborough, Eileen Crist and others such crass motivation for their activism as fear of 'Sex between Third World Men and Women' (163)? To trace elements of racism in arguments such as Garrett Hardin's making of 'overpopulation' *the* root of the environmental problem is one thing, but to give the impression that such racism explains most of the debate is merely absurd.[42] The UN itself is a main voice of concern about population and it was the Chinese themselves who introduced the notorious one-child policy for their own reasons. Intellectually at least, arguments as extreme as Gosine's are reassuring even in their evasiveness, for they force the terms of discussion back into such familiar and well-practised fields of debate as prejudice about race and sexuality.

Critical of narratives of overpopulation in images of urban overcrowding, Heise also builds an interesting argument about other depictions of it which may seem less questionable. Here, however, the same point can be made in reverse – the depictions of increasing population which she endorses are really being approved for representing something else quite separate from it. John Cage's experimental poem 'Overpopulation and Art' (1992) and the novels *Earth* by John Brin (1990) and *Stand on Zanzibar* (1968) by John Brunner are praised as depictions of overpopulation whose focus on global communication media can be seen to contribute to the urgent project of humanity achieving a truly cosmopolitan, planetary sense of identity. In Brin's science fiction parable, the energies inducing global collapse help create a peculiar symbiosis between the planet as a physical, geological entity and the human in the modified form of a sentient, 'super-intelligent' internet. More plausibly, in Cage and Brunner a crowded planet becomes the occasion for rethinking the relation of the individual to the local and to the global, 'an opportunity to rethink individual and collective relationships to local places and global systems' and thus to develop 'an eco-cosmopolitan awareness and presence' (90). Heise continues:

> earlier class-coded paranoias about the consequences of omnipresent crowds of humans for the individual transmute into a celebration of physical crowds that merge with or metamorphose into virtual ones, thereby gaining access to a different category of space that is not envisioned as a scarce and unevenly distributed resource. (90)

Thus the local individual comes to re-envisage his or her identity on a more global scale. The significant question, however, about this partial migration into virtual reality is this: what does it really have to do with the issue of planetary overpopulation? Is this a depiction of overpopulation at all? Would not the points about increased communication and virtual crowds, and the emergence of a new, more global sense of identity, also hold true if the human population were, say, half, a tenth or even a hundredth (i.e. 70 million) of its current total of 7 billion and growing? Given the finite nature of the number of contacts any one person can have, a network of a million people (a minute fraction of the world's population) may feel subjectively no less vast than one of a billion or more. So, Heise's point that dystopian portrayals of overpopulation were really about something else also applies in its way to the more utopian accounts which she endorses. These projects are not representations of overpopulation either: they are more truthfully seen as idealizations of the social effects of communications technology.[43] In sum, the tragic dynamics of the Anthropocene and its scale effects remain as elusive as they are inescapable.

Finally, work like Domingo's or Heise's, on cultural representations of overpopulation, does not consider how the scale effects of the Anthropocene might also affect ecocriticism's own mission of influencing the social imaginary. For the greater the scale of an environmental issue, in time or in space, and the larger the human populations involved and the keener the competition between them for space and resource, the less plausible it becomes to assign credible influence to affecting the cultural 'imaginary' or identification with some sort of species-being, or to making new

FIGURE 4 *The nonlocality of scale effects: Two images, both of overpopulation.*

cultural bonds. In effect, environmental deterioration itself seems set to render increasingly unreal the current strategies of environmental cultural politics. The utopian dream of overpopulation as a sort of extended internet and basis for an ecocosmopolitan identity may look like the inverse image of this more plausible, darker prospect, and both prospects need to be considered.

Notes

1   Hans Jonas, *The Imperative of Responsibility: In Search of an Ethics for the Technological Age* (Chicago, IL: University of Chicago Press, 1984), 7.

2   MacKenzie, 'Are We Doomed?', *New Scientist*, 5 April 2008, 33–5, 33.

3   For readers familiar with phenomenological terms, one can say that no 'eidetic reduction' will flush it out.

4   Becky Mansfield and Johanna Haas, 'Scale Framing of Scientific Uncertainty in Controversy over the Endangered Steller Sea Lion', *Environmental Politics* 15 (2006), 78–94.

5   Hughes, 'Dissolving the Nation: Self-deception and Symbolic Inversion in the GM Debate', *Environmental Politics* 16 (2007), 318–36, 324.

6   This is a summary of the various diagnoses for environmental ills offered by the contributors of essays to Theodore Roszak, Mary E. Gomes and Allen D. Kanner (eds), *Ecopsychology: Restoring the Earth, Healing the Mind* (San Francisco, CA: Sierra Club Books, 1995).

7   In some overviews of human society offered by ecopsychologists
    terms such as 'sanity' and 'madness' become shifted drastically,
    even arbitrarily. Conventional psychotherapy is asserted to serve a
    conception of human normality that is actually deeply destructive:
    'the deepest of our repressions, the form of psychic mutilation that
    is most crucial to the advance of industrial civilization, namely, the
    assumption that the land is a dead and servile thing that has no
    feeling, no memory, no intention of its own' (Theodore Roszak, in
    Ecopyschology, 7).

8   James H. Fetzer, 'Methodological Individualism: Singular Causal
    Systems and their Population Manifestations', *Synthese* 68.1 (1996),
    99–128, 99.

9   In Timo Müller and Michael Sauter (eds), *Literature, Ecology,
    Ethics: Recent Trends in Ecocriticism* (Heidelberg: Winter, 2012),
    227–37.

10 One should also add, to be scrupulous, that the withdrawal of the
    project leader, Saul Amron from leading the scheme was a result of
    his wife's pulling strings with powerful connections in the United
    States (forced to confess this, she commits suicide).

11 In fact the novel's last page returns to the theme of the endurance of
    the local impoverished population and seems to dramatize the island
    as having come full circle since its opening scene. A main road
    depicted then as having been washed away because of inadequate
    upkeep is now about to be destroyed once more with the return of
    the rainy season.

12 Grewe-Volpp transforms the novel's tentative final trajectory into
    a definite, individualistic tale of self-realization (a liberal parable
    in effect): 'Merle liberates herself from authoritarian systems from
    patriarchal abuse when she goes to reclaim her daughter, from
    poetical and economic abuse when she decides to go into politics
    and work for the improvement of her people and work for the
    improvement of her people . . .' (236).
        It is worth remembering here that Edouard Glissant, the
    celebrated novelist and environmental and independence activist
    for the French Caribbean colony of Martinique, rejects as too
    impracticable the notion of an autonomously self-sufficient
    Martinique, seeing a viable future for that island after French
    colonization instead in the growing of expensive, organic food
    for an international niche market. See Eric Prieto, 'The Use of
    Landscape: Ecocriticism and Martinican Cultural Theory', in
    Elizabeth M. DeLoughrey, Renée K. Gosson and George B.
    Handley (eds), *Caribbean Literature and the Environment:*

between Nature and Culture (Charlottesville, VA: University of Virginia Press, 2005), 236–46, 244–5.

13 *Anthropocene Fictions: The Novel in a Time of Climate Change* (Charlottesville, VA: University of Virginia Press, 2015).

14 *Forty Signs of Rain* (New York: HarperCollins, 2004); *Fifty Degrees Below* (New York: HarperCollins, 2005); *Sixty Days and Counting* (New York: HarperCollins, 2007).

15 Tobias Menely and Margaret Ronda, 'Red', in *Prismatic Ecology*, 22–41, 38.

16 Erle C. Ellis argues against the widespread image of a single tipping point for the future of the planet: 'the concept of a global tipping point has major policy implications. It suggests that below some threshold nothing serious will happen, but after that all will be lost. Holding such a view risks breeding complacency on one side and hopelessness on the other' ('Time to forget global tipping points', in *New Scientist*, 9 March 2013, 30–1, 31). There is no empirically perceptible 'point', only innumerable possible such thresholds, often not perceived as such until crossed, which in turn influence other and larger and smaller scale natural systems. Secondly, the 'tipping point' image simplifies by its easy visualizablity, and thus misrepresents the elusive and even insidious nature of global environmental issues.

17 Trexler argues for a re-evaluation of so-called genre fiction, such as action thrillers and other popular as opposed to 'literary' novels. Genre fiction, such as thrillers involving new technology or material inventions, is 'frequently preoccupied with humans interacting with things, and their innovations more often than not emerge from new assemblies of characters and nonhumans. This means that the agency of things is often clearer in such genres than in character-driven fiction' ('Novel Climes: Anthropocene Histories, Hans-Jörg Rheinberger's Trace and Clive Cussler's Arctic Drift', *Oxford Literary Review* 34.2 (2012), 295–314, 302). These observations lead, however, to what some may see as a slightly unfair account of 'canonical criticism' as preoccupied 'with authentic character, author-geniuses, and master texts' (*Anthropocene Fictions*, 27).

18 'A New UN Report on Uur Impending Overpopulation' (February 2012), awww.mercatornet.com/demography/view/10244#sthash.8G3Mv3ml.dpuf
    For a useful overview of varying official framings of the population issue since the alarmist arguments of the 1960s and 70s, see Diana Coole, 'Too many bodies? The return and disavowal of the population question', *Environmental Politics* 22 (2013), 195–215.

19 IPCC Fifth Assessment Synthesis Report, www.ipcc.ch/pdf/ assessment-report/ar5/syr/SYR_AR5_LONGERREPORT.pdf

20 To appeal to the obvious desire to eradicate poverty and its degradations should not disguise the ways in which this argument might also be rather convenient for the agenda of an ever-expanding capitalism, whose deeper interests lie in ever more numerous markets.

21 Gardiner, 'The Real Tragedy of the Commons', *Philosophy and Public Affairs* 30 (2005), 387–416, 401.

22 'Abundant Earth and the Population Question', in Philip Cafaro and Eileen Crist (eds), *Life on the Brink: Environmentalists Confront Overpopulation* (Athens, GA: University of Georgia Press, 2012), 141–53, 145.

23 Ehrlich, *The Population Bomb* (New York: Ballantine Books, 1968); Donella H. Meadows, Dennis L. Meadows, Jorgen Randers and William W. Behrens III, *Limits to Growth* (New York: New American Library, 1972).

24 Don Weeden and Charmayne Palomba, 'A Post-Cairo Paradigm: Both Numbers and Women Matter', in *Life on the Brink*, 255–73, 255.
     Howard Beck and Leon J. Kolankiewicz describe the metamorphosing agenda of the US group 'Zero Population Growth', founded in 1968 in the wake of the impact of Paul Ehrlich's *The Population Bomb*. They trace how a social justice agenda came to eclipse the initial environmental focus: 'New staff were hired less on the basis of their environmental expertise and commitment and more because of their commitment to women's issues' ('The Environmental Movement's Retreat from Advocating U.S. Population Stabilization (1970–1998): A First Draft of History', *Journal of Policy History* 12.1 (2000), 123–56, 135)

25 Ibid., 134.

26 Ibid., 144–5.

27 Weeden and Palomba, 257.

28 Byran G. Norton, 'Population and Consumption: Environmental Problems as Problems of Scale', *Ethics and the Environment* 5 (2000), 23–45.

29 Albert A. Bartlett, 'Democracy Cannot Survive Overpopulation', *Population and Environment* 22.1 (September 2000), 63–71, 66–7.

30 Norton, 'Population and Consumption', 43, nt 13.

31 'Overpopulation versus Biodiversity: How a Plethora of People Produces a Paucity of Wildlife', in *Life on the Brink*, 75–90, 76.

32 Garrett Hardin, 'The Tragedy of the Commons', *Science* 162 (1968), 1243–8.

33 Rob Nixon, 'Neoliberalism, Genre, and "The Tragedy of the Commons"', in *PMLA* 127 (2012), 593–9. It is striking how often accounts of Hardin's parable overlook the fact that it was the issue of overpopulation that concerned him, not the kind of more abstract prisoners' dilemma-type situations they focus on. Ironically too, as he himself came partly to recognize (see Nixon, 597), the 'tragedy' that Hardin projects as an attack on the very idea of common ownership actually applies more clearly to the institutions of private property in a capitalist profit-driven market. Alan Carter writes: 'Private property in land has meant that farmers have to sell their products on the market, and they can only remain profitable by undermining the long-term fertility of their soil, which they will be driven to do' (*A Radical Green Political Theory* (London: Routledge, 1999), 33). The situation Carter describes has played itself out in Australia, where pressured private farms find themselves overstocking or overcultivating their properties, the practice of 'flogging the land' (Jared Diamond, *Collapse: How Societies Choose to Fail or Survive* (London: Penguin, 2006), 393).

34 He also ignores other possible solutions to the tragedy, such as the situation in which there is common ownership of the cattle as well as the land, making strong shared interests in safeguarding both (see Carter, 33–4). Futhermore, in applying the parable to the issue of overpopulation, Hardin makes the bizarre assumption that people will be inclined to have as many children as they can unless externally restrained. Above all, he overlooks the crucial point about the environmental effects of human population, that this is not just a matter of numbers of people but of environmental impact *per head,* with each new person born in North America having 40 or 50 times the environmental impact of one born in a far poorer region (see Norton, 23). This fact answers the deplorable tendency in Hardin's argument to see overpopulation as an issue primarily in the developing world, rather than a matter of resource use per head.

35 Norton, 36, Norton's emphasis.

36 One need not rely on the controversial Hardin in this context. The economist Petros Sekeris has recently deployed a game-theoretical model of competing resource use to show that, whenever there is some possibility of future violent conflict over a depleted resource, the effect is merely to accelerate resource grabbing on all sides. See his 'The Tragedy of the Commons in a Violent World', *RAND Journal of Economics* 45 (2014), 521–32.

37   Gardiner, *The Perfect Moral Storm: The Ethical Tragedy of Climate Change* (Oxford: Oxford University Press, 2011), 7.

38   Ronnie Hawkins, 'Perceiving Overpopulation: Can't We See What We're Doing?', in *Life on the Brink*, 202–13, 207.

39   Examples of texts at issue would be Anthony Burgess, *The Wanting Seed* (London: Heinemann, 1962); Harry Harrison, *Make Room! Make Room!* (New York: Doubleday, 1966); Kurt Vonnegut, 'Welcome to the Monkey House' (New York: Delacorte Press, 1968); and Robert Silverberg, *The World Inside* (New York: Doubleday, 1971).

40   Domingo, '"Demodystopias": Prospects of Demographic Hell', in *Population and Development Review* 34 (2008), 725–45, 731.

41   In Catriona Mortimer Sandilands and Bruse Erickson (eds), *Queer Ecologies: Sex, Nature, Politics, Desire* (Bloomington, IN: Indiana Press, 2012), 149–72, 149.

42   For the more convincing arguments against claims that human population growth is the root environmental problem rather than a dire element of it, see Norton, 'Population and Consumption'.

43   Heise's argument also overlooks the issues of information overload. See neuroscientist Daniel Levitin's *The Organized Mind: Thinking Straight in the Age of Information Overload* (New York: Dutton, 2014). Levitin observes that 'in 2011, Americans took in five time as much information every day as they did in 1986. . . . At some point we are going to exceed our capacity to deal with everything. Maybe we already have' ('It's All Too Much', *New Scientist,* 16 August 2014, 26–7).

CHAPTER FIVE

Scale framing: A reading

How would it be to read and reread the same literary text through a series of increasingly broad spatial and temporal scales, one after the other, paying particular attention to the strain that this puts on given critical assumptions and currently dominant modes of reading? The issues can be tested through a practical reading experiment.

Raymond Carver's late short story, 'Elephant' (originally published in 1988),[1] is a comic monologue consisting of the complaints and then gradual acceptance of his situation by a male blue-collar worker who is continually being pestered for money by hard-pressed relatives in other parts of the United States. Most of 'Elephant' happens between domestic interiors linked by telephone. The narrator's recently unemployed brother, a thousand miles away in California, requires immediate help to pay the mortgage on his house, seems later to be able to forgo more borrowing because his wife might sell some land in her family, but finally comes asking for money once more. He has already had to sell their second car and pawn the TV. The narrator's daughter has two children and is married to:

> A swine who wouldn't even *look* for work, a guy who couldn't hold a job if they handed him one. The time or two he did find something, he overslept, or his car broke down on the way in to work, or he'd just be let go, no explanation and that was that. (390)

The narrator's aged mother, 'poor and greedy' (387) relies on the support of both her sons to maintain her independent lifestyle amid signs of failing health. The narrator's son demands money to enable him to emigrate. A divorced wife has to be paid alimony. Struggling with his resentment as he writes all the cheques, the narrator reaches a turning point with two dreams. The one alluded to in the story's title is of how his father used to carry him on his shoulders when he was a child, and he would feel safe, stretch out his arms and fantasize that he was riding an elephant. The next morning, giving a kind of private blessing to all his relatives despite their demands, he decides to walk rather than drive to work, leaving his house unlocked. Walking along the road, he is stretching out his arms as in his dream of childhood when a workmate called George stops to pick him up. George has a cigar and has just borrowed money to improve his car. Together they test it for speed:

> 'Go', I said. 'What are you waiting for, George?' And that's when we really flew. Wind howled outside the windows. He had it floored, and we were going flat out. We streaked down that road in his big unpaid-for car. (401)

The comic drama is that of an increasingly exasperated monologue interspersed with accounts of phone calls with their awkward but manipulative requests for money. Financial support of distant family members turns almost into its own mini-business as 'the first of the month [. . .] I had to sit down and make out the checks' (392). The crescendo is intensified by new turns of event, the bill collectors hammering with their fists on the door of the brother's house, the theft of all the furniture from his daughter's trailer, the son's discovery of his allergy to cocaine (so ending a possible 'career' as a drug dealer). The comedy is in the repetition, the rising tempo, like the moves in a theatrical farce.

Turning now to the new questions posed by climate change, what kind of readings emerge of such a text? First, perhaps, that if 'Capitalism must be regarded as an economy of unpaid costs', then 'Elephant' could easily read as a kind of environmental allegory, as a narrative of a chain of unpaid debt and unearned support extending itself into the final image of the large unpaid-for car. This relatively obvious first reading, however, can be deepened by considerations of scale.

Any broadly mimetic interpretation of a text (i.e. one reading it not as self-contained artefact but as a reproduction of the real in some sense) always assumes a physical and temporal scale of some sort for its act of representation. It is a precondition of any such mapping, though almost never explicit in the interpretation. The scale at which one reads a text, and the scale effects implicated, drastically alter the kinds of significance attached to elements of it; but, as we will see, that scale cannot itself give criteria for judgement.

Three scales can be used. First, we could read the text on a (critically naïve) personal scale that takes into account only the narrator's immediate circle of family and acquaintances over a time frame of several years. At this scale there is a certain humanist cosiness about the text, as if the Carver story were already a cynically commercial screenplay. Family loyalty wins out against misfortune; love and forgiveness prevail in a tale of minor but genuine domestic heroism. The reading could refer to Carver's own defence of short stories as throwing 'some light on what it is that makes and keeps us, often against great odds, recognizably human'. In this respect 'Elephant' would even come close to being a kind of Carver schmaltz.[2]

One can also imagine a close reading of 'Elephant' at this scale that hypothesizes a deeper psychology at work in the speaker, that he is in unacknowledged need of the dependency of others and lets himself be manipulated by them. Here, the critic would become like an amateur psychoanalyst reconstructing the dynamics of an internal self-image, with perhaps a special focus on the memory of being carried on the shoulders of his own father, whose position, of course, he is taking in supporting the rest of the family. For all his complaining, his monologue would thus become a story of implicit Oedipal triumph, of taking the place of the father.

To imagine any of the fraught characters in this text taking into consideration their environmental impact (not entirely implausible for a text of 1988) seems fanciful. In this respect the naïve first scale is the one that represents the experience of environmental questions for most people across the globe – it is an non-issue, almost something to laugh at or to dismiss in anger in the struggle for economic safety. This kind of scalar entrapment in the immediate is the human norm, albeit often involving cycles of poverty far more severe than those suffered by these American characters.

Immediate monetary benefit at the individual scale feeds a process of entrapment that forecloses the thinkability of other modes of life. For instance, if I buy cheap bananas from Jamaica I may feel I am helping to support people in a relatively impoverished part of the world, yet, on a longer scale, I may also be helping to perpetuate environmentally destructive kinds of agriculture, trapping workers there in the trading nets of international capitalism. There are analogies here with the menial jobs at issue in 'Elephant' (the unspecified blue-collar work of the narrator, the monotonous work canning fish considered by his daughter).

A second scale at which to read the text is that almost always assumed in literary criticism. Spatially, it is that of a national culture and its inhabitants, with a time frame of perhaps a few decades, a 'historical period' of some kind. This scale framing characterizes almost all criticism on Carver, placing his work in the cultural context of the late-twentieth-century United States. Kirk Nesset, writing in 1995, is representative: 'Carver's figures dramatize and indirectly comment upon the problems besetting American culture, particularly lower middle-class culture, today'.[3] Other topics prominent in discussions of Carver are broadly located at this scale, such as unemployment and consumer culture as they affect personal relationships, the ideals and realities of American domesticity, and this society's materialism and its concepts of gender, especially masculinity, and coupledom. Such scale framing enables an interpretation of the final scene of 'Elephant' as a temporary moment of escape from the denigrations and frustrations of American consumer capitalism, focused on the private car as an image of individual freedom and mobility.

A third, larger, hypothetical scale is, of course, the difficult one, and the one at which scale effects and a certain impersonal ecological dynamic start to become visible and shade out more conventional considerations. This scale could be, spatially, that of the whole Earth and its inhabitants, and placing 'Elephant' in the middle of a, let us say, 600-year time frame, from 300 years before 1988 to 2288, 300 after, while bearing in mind authoritative plausible scenarios for the habitability of the planet at that time.

An initial impulse about the idea of reading at the third scale expresses a sense of disproportion, that trying to read 'Elephant' at this scale simply does not 'make sense'. Yet once again this does not adequately respond to our new knowledge that *not* to read at this scale is now become an evasion.

What, then, is being held off? Viewed on very long time scales, human history and culture can take on unfamiliar shapes, as work in environmental history repeatedly demonstrates, altering conceptions of what makes something 'important' and what does not. It is easy to argue that, globally, the two major events of the past three centuries have been the industrial exploitation of fossil fuels and a worldwide supplanting of local biota in favour of an imported portmanteau of profitable species: cattle, wheat, sheep, maize, sugar, coffee, eucalyptus, palm oil etc.[4] Environmental history situates the vicissitudes of human societies in terms of many under-conceptualized material events and contingencies, many of them all the more decisive for not falling within history in terms of a realm of human representations and decisions – the insights of systems ecology, population studies, the contingencies of diseases and disease resistance, of the domestication of plants and animals. Environmental history has none of metaphysical features of the concepts of history famously criticized by Derrida in *Of Grammatology* (1967),[5] being neither linear, nor teleological, nor a matter of tradition as the development or accumulation of knowledge or culture. As the issue of climate change now reminds us, environmental history is often a matter of unforeseen and unintended consequences. The list of genuinely significant historical agents thus soon extends itself beyond the human in a rather bewildering way: cotton grass competes with us for water, wheat replaces a native flora over large portions of the Earth, agriculture in general enables storage of food, facilitating the growth of sedentary lifestyles, villages, towns, cities, but also encouraging disease, parasites etc. Environmental history underlines how deeply the agency of the human is far more circumscribed and saturated with illusion than one might suppose.[6] Thus it is that most of the world's wheat, a crop originally from the Middle East, now comes from other areas – Canada, the United States, Argentina, Australia – just as people of originally European descent now dominate a large proportion of the Earth's surface. This huge shift in human populations, including slaves as well as domesticated animals and plants, has largely determined the modern world, with its close connections between destructive monocultures in food production, exploitative systems of international trade and exchange and the institution of the modern state, in effect a huge bubble of population and consumption expanding at a rate that drives innumerable other species into oblivion and which cannot be supported by the planet's resources for long. It is the transitory world of this bizarre, destructive and temporary energy imbalance that developed world populations currently inhabit and take for a stable and familiar reality, even as the interference of scale effects increasingly come to fracture it.

Reading at the third scale also renders both obvious and incongruous the 'methodological nationalism' that characterizes almost all middle-scale readings of Carver. Even so seemingly uncontroversial a phrase as Carver's own 'the dark side of Reagan's America'[7] may instantiate methodological nationalism in proportion to the degree in which the national sphere and its cultural agenda serve exclusively to enframe, contain and shape an analysis.

To read Carver in exclusive relation to American culture would still seem innocent enough were it not that, at the expanded scale, certain familiar critical assumptions about ethics and cultural politics in most readings of this writer now come to look parochial and damaging. The rhetoric of social marginalization and impoverishment common in readings of Carver becomes at the very least complicated by the fact that, on a global scale, while their distress is undeniable, none of the characters in 'Elephant' is actually poor in a material sense. The narrator has a house to himself and also a car, and liked to eat out at restaurants. The supposedly impoverished brother had two cars and was forced to sell one of them to help keep his house. The supposedly poverty-stricken daughter, with her husband and children, lives in a trailer but has at least one car. The brother's wife is a land-owner and the son requires money to do something most living people will never do, that is, to travel in an aeroplane to another country. The mother does not live with any of her children but is maintained in a household of her own. It is not the number of people but the number of separate households demanding support that is the real economic issue in 'Elephant', the keeping the property each represents. The culture of independence affirmed in the narrator's indignant work-ethic also effectively serves an economic infrastructure that sets up a continuous dependency on high levels of consumption and the car, and, as a result, produces a pervasive and intensifying sense of entrapment. 'If nothing succeeds like success, nothing also entraps like success' (Hans Jonas).[8]

In sum, as Robert Savino Oventile remarks, in an exclusively US context a politicized criticism at this social-cultural scale remains tied to narratives of inclusion and 'recognition of the other' that also functions as the soft face of an expanding US capitalism, for it is based on norms of prosperous, national inclusion structurally in denial of its parasitism on the rest of the world: 'Tied to narratives of progress, these critical programs rely on visions of a future that, on inspection, project versions of the present, only cleansed of the contradictions and impasses making the present possible'.[9]

In his 'On Hospitality' (2000) Jacques Derrida argued how the supposedly self-contained 'inner' realm of the at-home, the house, the personal household, is constitutively breached by its embeddedness in the outside, public space, increasingly so with such technologies as email, the telephone, television and so on.[10] At the third scale, however, which Derrida does not pick up, everything and everyone is always 'outside': a person registers there less in terms of familiar social co-ordinates (race, class, gender and so on) than as a physical entity, representing so much consumption of resources and expenditure of waste (not the personality or the attitude, but the 'footprint'). The effect of embedding 'Elephant' within the third scale is to turn the text into a peculiar kind of gothic, a doppelganger narrative. Characters as 'persons' and responsible agents are now doubled by themselves as mere physical entities. The larger the scale the more thing-like becomes the significance of the person registered on it (even as scale effects have given humans en masse the status of a geological force). The issue is not the way some modes of critical reading exclude consideration of nonhuman agency, but the more uncomfortable business of reading the human, so to speak, on the same level as nonhuman agency, that is, reading people as things.

The emergent scale effects of the Anthropocene intervene in our reading in an even mocking way. Events or actions that might have seemed straightforward in the past – the narrator's helping his family – emerge as following an invisible, environmental dynamic bound up with the contingency of how many other people are also actively engaged in practices that produce pollution or waste, or take up land etc., along with the often unpredictable effects of natural entities caught up in these processes, such as the heat-absorbing properties of the ocean, of the declining tundra. The significance of the speaker's actions takes on new meaning at a level of consideration never of relevance before.

Because one cannot get an assured overview upon it, the third scale is not so easy to describe as a mode of 'framing' – it is easier to characterize as an *unframing* of both the first and second scales as they now seem to become incoherent. An experimental reading at this scale also seems to imply a more 'anthropological' kind of criticism. The third-scale reading is indifferent to whether or not there is an Oedipal dynamic to the speaker's actions. It does not build up any image of psychological depth. It does not deepen so much as flatten. A kind of environmental 'unconscious' of unthought side-effects emerges that has nothing to do with personal complexes or psychic dynamics, but which is situational, contextual, the unregarded realm of what can't be helped simply by going to buy food or get to work, the unattended-to physicality of what passes without thought.

Plots, characters, setting and trivia that seemed normal and harmless on the personal or national scale reappear as destructive doubles of themselves on the third scale, part of a disturbing and encroaching parallel universe, whose malign reality it is becoming impossible to deny. We can no longer sustain the fiction that significant historical agency is the preserve of intentional human action alone. The material infrastructure that surrounds and largely dictates the lives of the people, the houses, the cars, the roads, may partially displace more familiar issues of identity and cultural representation as a focus of significance. Technology and infrastructures emerge not only as inherently political but as doubly and unpredictably politicized in scale effects that deride the intentions of their users or builders. 'Elephant' could be described in terms of what William Ophuls calls 'energy slavery',[11] the oppressive, all-pervading and destructive effects of being born into a fossil-fuel-based infrastructure as aggressive as an occupying army.

'Petro-minimalist realism'

Described this way, highlighting nonhuman agency, the famous 'minimalist realism' of Carver's writing even begins to sound like a kind of so-called magic realism, a term more usually applied to non-Western texts that blend the conventions of as-if-real representation with mythic or spiritual elements that, to some Western readers at least, may seem magical in their use of characters and agencies other than the human. A suggestive text to compare with 'Elephant' in this respect would be another that is deeply engaged with the effects of fossil fuels and questions of literary representation, the Nigerian writer Ben Okri's 'What the Tapster Saw' (1999, first published 1987), almost exactly contemporary with 'Elephant'.[12]

The term 'petro-magic realism', invented by Fernando Coronil with particular reference to Venezuela and oil wealth,[13] has also been applied to the profound and often disruptive effects of oil extraction in Nigeria, where the building of roads, bridges and hospitals served as a simulacrum of public 'development' helping disguise the dubious legitimacy of the central state amid promises of quasi-magical transformation and modernization.[14]

The context of Okri's short story of 1987 is the Nigerian boom in oil extraction that has devastated large areas of that country, and which was later to lead to the execution, on trumped-up charges, of the writer and activist Ken Saro-Wiwa. The supplanting of an economy based on palm oil by one based on petroleum extraction is a trauma that finds expression in the peculiarly hybrid and unsettled form of 'What the Tapster Saw'. The protagonist of Okri's story, whose job as a tapster entails the tapping of palm oil, falls from a tree while trespassing on Delta Oil Company territory. In a subsequent coma he imagines himself surrounded by various bizarre, magical creatures. Okri depicts Delta Oil Company territory in the terms of a Yoruba magical forest of strange transformations (though Okri is not Yoruba himself). The reader can trace there 'the oil company employees trying to level the forests' to drill for oil (187, 188–9), using witch-doctors to 'drive away the spirits', or to influence the weather, even exploding the forest with dynamite, with a 'weird spewing up of oil and animal limbs from the ground' (189). The effect on the tapster, however, is an inability to integrate these events into any narrative he can recognize. Sarah L. Lincoln argues that the 'magical-realist style deployed in "What the Tapster Saw" serves to thematize, as well as to express formally, the subjective, social, and semiotic disjunctures of Nigerian life under pressure from an oil-based economy' (161). She writes:

> After his fall, he notices features of the landscape that recall the ecological effects of oil drilling – a 'viscous', stagnant, iridescent river (185); wounded trees; foul-smelling smoke that irritates his eyes and skin; and 'thick slimes of oil' that coat everything (189). Though the wandering tapster is unable to identify the source or reason for these sensations, which appear to him as semiautonomous actors in their own right, the reader's eyes, free of cobwebs, recognize the landscape of degradation described most memorably by Ken Saro-Wiwa, and understands the tapster's travels through what [Amos] Tutuola called the 'deads' town' as a prophetic vision of the fate of the forest.[15]

It may seem far-fetched to suggest a similarity between the seemingly mundane reality of Carver's suburban world and the tapster's obscure dream of unknown agents and weird creatures of strange intimacy and bizarre motivation.[16] Considered on the third scale, however, the differences become matters of degree and of conventions of recognition as to what is normal. Carver's so-called minimalism in short story technique also projects a realm of disjunctive surfaces and personal isolation in which the lack of a completely reliable sense of relation between cause and effect, intention and result, effort and reward, is accompanied by a pervading sense of insecurity and redundancy. The late-capitalist alienation projected in Carver's style is more homologous with the nightmare forest of the tapster's psychic disintegration than might first appear.[17]

The reading of Carver at the third scale underlines the fragility and contingency of effective boundaries between public and private, objects and persons, the 'innocent' and 'guilty', human history and natural history, the traumatic and the banal, and (with technology) the convenient and the disempowering. A futural reading of 'Elephant' would thus be more object-centred, aware of the capricious nature of nonhuman agency and suspicious of the way contemporary criticism, even ecocriticism, tends to interiorize all environmental issues as ultimately questions of subjective attitudes or belief, of humanity acting reflexively upon itself (even 'humanity destroying itself'). In sum, at the third scale a kind of non-anthropic irony deranges the short story as an easily assimilable object of any given kind of moral or political reading.

The very notion of 'magic realism' has proved vulnerable to criticism.[18] Associated with so-called third-world literature, it tends to posit its 'realism' side as an implicit, supposed Western norm against which the beliefs or customs of local or indigenous cultures define their difference through the 'magic' element. However, the juxtaposition of Carver and Okri suggests here a slightly different reading. This is to read Carver's kind of US realism as a privative form of 'magic realism'. That is to say, the affective, psychological and material effects and conditions of a high-energy infrastructure – thing-agency, so to speak – pervade the whole physical and psychic space of Carver's text, but are simply taken for granted there as some sort of inertly given norm, at work in generally assumed expectations of prosperity, opportunity, support and personal mobility in the characters, as well as in the narrator's indignant work-ethic. For instance, there is nothing really 'private' about a car.[19] Along with the households demanding to be sustained, the politics of energy slavery reappear even in such seeming daily trivia as how the daughter's partner allegedly loses the chance of a job because his car broke down, or the way the narrator's brother promises, 'I've got this job lined up. It's definite. I'll have to drive fifty miles round trip every day, but that's no problem – hell, no. I'd drive a hundred and fifty if I had too' (83). Cars also proliferate themselves through their parasitism on ideologies of individual 'freedom' – 'Elephant' ends with the narrator in the passenger seat, on a high-of-speed urging on George, complete with cigar, to drive as fast as he possibly can.

Some implications

Simon Levin writes, in a scientific context: 'That there is no single correct scale or level at which to describe a system does not mean that all scales serve equally well or that there are not scaling laws'.[20] However there are crucial differences between reading a literary text at multiple scales and the function of scales in scientific modelling and explanation. In such modelling, suppression of detail is seen as a strength of work at large scales, where broad results emerge as patterns overriding individual variations. A literary reading clearly works in no such way. Assumptions of scale are always at work in any reading, but, as we shall see, reading at different scales can suggest different judgements of value but cannot easily be used finally to decide between them.

The three different scales produce readings of 'Elephant' that conflict with each other, yet can the third scale act as some final frame of reference or court of last appeal, deciding for us how to read the text? An ecological overview is in danger of feeding a reductive green moralism, keen to turn ecological facts into moral imperatives on how to live, blind to the sense of helplessness dominant in 'Elephant' at the first scale. While it highlights the hidden costs of lower-scale thinking, the third scale's tendency to register a person primarily as a physical thing is evidently problematic, almost brutally removed from the daily relationships, moral questions, hopes and struggles that it ironizes. For instance, although this essay chose the less controversial example of cars, the most environmentally significant aspect of the situation projected by the text would be the reproduction of people themselves. The fact that the narrator has fathered two children would be more crucial – in the brutal terms of physical emissions – than either his lifestyle or property. ('With climate change and other global ecological threats looming, the last thing the world needs is more Americans' (Eileen Crist and Philip Cafaro).[21])

A mode of critical reading focused solely on the immediate physical sources of carbon emissions could soon drift towards the eco-fascistic. Under eco-managerialist schemes, people come increasingly to be conceived less and less as citizens of a polity than consumers of a resource in need of administration. So reading at several scales at once cannot be just concerned with the abolition of one scale in the greater claim of another but a way of enriching, singularizing and yet also creatively deranging the text by embedding it in multiple and even contradictory frames at the same time (so that even the most enlightened-seeming progressive-seeming argument may have one in agreement at one scale and in vehement disagreement on another). The overall interpretation of 'Elephant' offered here can only be a multiple, self-conflicting one. The acts of the narrator remain of great personal generosity even if, at the same time, scale effects ironically implicate them, however minimally, in incalculable evil. The text emerges – simultaneously, depending on the scale at issue – as (1) a wry anecdote of personal heroism, (2) a protest against social exclusion, and (3) a confrontation with the entrapment of human actions and decisions within a disastrous impersonal dynamic they do not comprehend, as well as the various containments of inherited modes of thinking.

So the challenge must be to continue and deepen the critique of individualistic conceptions of identity, right, etc., enmeshed as they are in the slow-motion catastrophes of international capitalism, without letting such a critique become an implicit endorsement of alternative, latently eco-fascistic forms of social control. In terms of Carver's story, it would mean not letting the impersonal dynamics of the third scale obliterate the immediate sense of things at the first scale. A renewed intellectual and ethical onus falls on those middle-scale modes of criticism that confine themselves to national, cultural horizons, and in the process implicitly endorse social and political norms without consideration of the wider cost of their scale framing. The implications of the experimental reading of Carver seem to point, as do Stephen Gardiner's game-theoretical analyses, to the question of civil disobedience – that is, if it seems hard realistically to envisage some better mode of life supplanting the current systems of destruction, one can at least refuse them support.[22] Gardiner writes that politicians have power delegated by citizens and 'if the attempt to delegate effectively has failed, then the responsibility falls back on the citizens again, either to solve the problems themselves, or else, if this is not possible, to create new institutions to do the job'.[23]

Ecophobia?

Awareness of the Anthropocene turns 'Elephant' into drastically different, even contradictory text(s), depending on the scale at which it is read. This contradictoriness may highlight and questions a little-theorized but widespread working hypothesis in ecocriticism: this is that given forms of human 'oppression' make up a unitary monolith, of which ecophobia, racism, sexism and unjust hierarchy are all co-conspiring and mutually supporting parts, such that to question or call on one must be at once to implicate the others.[24]

A good example of such lumping together is the critical term 'ecophobia' as originally coined by Simon C. Estok by analogy with homophobia, xenophobia or other forms of human prejudice or bigotry. Deployed in an ecocritical reading of Shakespeare, ecophobia names for Estok 'an irrational and groundless fear or hatred of the natural world, [something] as present and subtle in our daily lives and literature as homophobia and racism and sexism'.[25] It would then follow that a politicized criticism alert to the Anthropocene would be one that developed skills in reading ecophobia in the most unexpected places, even in, say, ostensibly green texts or the policies of some environmental thinkers.

However, so straightforward a definition of ecophobia exemplifies the temptation in ecocriticism for kinds of intellectual and moral simplification. Estok, reading Shakespeare's plays, draws on the intellectual resources of ecofeminism, social ecology and related forms of ecocritique to argue that destructive attitudes towards the natural world in these texts are always inherently associated with forms of human-to-human injustice. This exemplifies here a pervasive, intellectually convenient and increasingly brittle assumption among most Western ecocritics – that arguments in defence of the nonhuman environment will always somehow support and be supported by the latest developments of a left-liberal humanist programme of ever-expanding social inclusiveness, so that to support the one cause, say fighting prejudice about gender, is necessarily to aid the others, such as ecological health. Rebecca Bach argues:

> Attempting to ally all of these liberatory theories and practices leads Estok to some suspect claims.. . . In general, the evidence the book presents for Shakespeare's ecophobia is not entirely persuasive. Estok shows us that Shakespeare's plays often extol nature's virtues. But he often takes evidence of natural dangers as signs that a play is essentially ecophobic. It is more accurate to say that the plays present the natural world as sometimes nurturing and beautiful and sometimes dangerous. This vision of nature is certainly anthropocentric, but it can be as ecophilic as it is ecophobic.[26]

Whatever the merits of Estok's proposal, the Anthropocene represents in any case a threshold across which things become more complicated. Estok's topic is environmental destruction in the seventeenth century, using early modern texts as the basis for describing a more general condition, ecophobia. Yet, however similar some seventeenth-century and twenty-first-century issues may be, this does not allow for those threshold effects at issue in the 'Anthropocene', and the very different agency of technologies and other material entities in the twenty-first century. A difficulty is that cultural and political action in one place or by one group is now more caught up in an impersonal game space whose dynamics become remorseless in proportion to the number of other 'players' involved and the scale effects of their dispersal in space and in time, for many of the significant players are in the future. '[T]he key point is that the structure of people's values, even when those values are in some sense shared, can undermine the collective pursuit of those values' (Gardiner).[27]

Estok's slightly moralistic version of ecophobia does not fit well the tragic dynamic of the Anthropocene as a threshold at which, even after one has acknowledged the depredations of international capitalism and forms of environmental colonialism, it may now still be simply things like the desire for improved health and living conditions (and subsequent population increases), better travel facilities and the need for food production that drive destructive behaviours such as overfishing, the destruction of the habitats of other species or rising carbon emissions. Estok's monochrome version of 'ecophobia' does not fit, for example, the huge programme of road building that is about to roll across the continent of Africa, with many surely welcome effects such as connecting numerous remote areas, enabling farmers to market their crops in newly reachable towns, combating poverty and enabling access to medical support, but also enabling large mining operations, legal and illegal, and cutting across irreplaceable wild habitat, opening up once remote areas to poachers and loggers, and even threatening the great wildlife migrations in the Serengeti.[28] This scenario is not all plausibly ascribable to some irrational hatred of the natural world, but to the side-effects of hideously complex and often morally contradictory pressures.

The various scalar readings of 'Elephant' suggests that if one had the job of saying what 'ecophobia' could mean in the threshold environmental conditions now at issue, as opposed to the seventeenth-century contexts of Estok's readings of Shakespeare, it would be redefined in more tragic terms as: *an antipathy, dismissive stance or sheer indifference towards the natural environment, including attitudes which, however understandable in the past, tend now in the emergent contexts of the Anthropocene to become directly or indirectly destructive, even in ways that may not have been the case before.*

Notes

1　'Elephant', in Raymond Carver, *Where I'm Calling From: The Selected Stories* (London: Harvill Press, 1993), 386–401.

2　Quoted in Kirk Nessset, *The Stories of Raymond Carver: A Critical Study* (Athens, OH: Ohio University Press, 1995), 104.

3　*The Stories of Raymond Carver*, 7.

4　'Environmental history' is a still relatively recent and ill-fitting newcomer in the academy. Prominent examples are John R. McNeill's *Something New under the Sun: An Environmental History of the Twentieth Century* (New York: Norton, 2000); Robert Marks, *The Origins of the Modern World: A Global and Ecological History* (Lanham, MS: Rowman and Littlefield, 2002); Alfred W. Crosby's *Ecological Imperialism: The Biological Expansion of Europe 900–1900* (Cambridge: Cambridge University Press, 1986); Clive Ponting, *A Green History of the World* (New York: St Martin's Press, 1991); Sing C. Chew, *World Ecological Degradation: Accumulation, Urbanization, and Deforestation 3000 BC-AD 2000* (Walnut Creek, CA: Altamira Press, 2001); Jared Diamond, *Guns, Germs and Steel: A Short History of Everybody for the Last 13,000 Years* (1997; London: Vintage Books, 2005), and his *Collapse: How Societies Choose to Fail or Survive* (London: Penguin, 2005).

5　*Of Grammatology* [1967], trans. Gayatri Chakravorty Spivak (Baltimore: Johns Hopkins University Press, 1976).

6　Crosby's *Ecological Imperialism* has been criticized for using a rather simple dichotomy of European and non-European people. For other reservations about Crosby's study, see Tom Griffiths, 'Introduction' to Tom Griffiths and Libby Robin (eds), *Ecology and Empire: Environmental History of Settler Societies* (Edinburgh: Keele University Press, 1997), 1–16, 1–8.

7　Marshall Bruce Gentry and William L. Stull (eds), *Conversations with Raymond Carver* (Jackson, MI: University Press of Mississippi, 1990), 201.

8　Jonas, *The Imperative of Responsibility*, 9.

9　'Paul de Man Now, or, Nihilisms in the Right Company', *Symplokē* 21 (2013), 325–39, 328.

10 *On Hospitality: Anne Dufourmantelle Invites Jacques Derrida to Respond*, trans. Rachel Bowlby (Stanford, CA: Stanford University Press, 2000), 61.

11 Ophuls, *Requiem for Modern Politics*, 169–74.

12 In Okri, *Stars of the New Curfew* (London: Vintage, 1999), 183–94.

13 Coronil, *The Magical State: Nature, Money, and Modernity in Venezuela* (Chicago, IL: University of Chicago Press, 1997).

14 See Jennifer Wenzel, 'Petro-Magic-Realism: Toward a Political Ecology of Nigerian Literature', *Postcolonial Studies* 9 (2006), 449–64.

15 *Expensive Shit: Aesthetic Economies of Waste in Postcolonial Africa*, Ph.D. thesis, Duke University 2008, 155.

16 For detailed analysis of the decisive interrelationships in the United States between urban sprawl, the interests of oil companies, urban planning, the culture of induced automobile use, and capitalist imperialism, see George A. Gonzalez *Urban Sprawl, Global Warming, and the Empire of Capital* (Albany, NY: SUNY Press, 2009).

17 Compare Lincoln on an aspect of Okri's style:
the short, declarative sentences that define Okri's style here, frequently beginning 'He saw' or 'He heard', or featuring inanimate objects in subject positions ('Thick slimes of oil seeped down the walls'; 'Noises were heard below'), create an environment in which the senses are assailed by one new thing after another, with few transitional modifiers to help us make connections between or among these experiences. (pp. 160–1)
Readers of Carver will recognize here analogues of his so-called minimalist style, if slightly less prominent in the monologue 'Elephant' than elsewhere. If Okri uses short, disjunctive sentences that tend to animate the inanimate, Carver's often do the reverse, rendering people as inanimate things. Examples would be 'The blind man let go of his suitcase and up came his hand' ('Cathedral' in *The Selected Stories*, 292–307, 296); 'I slap him before I realize. I raise my hand, wait a fraction of a second, and then slap his cheek hard. This is crazy, I think as I slap him' ('So Much Water so Close to Home', *The Selected Stories*, 173–93, 180).

18 Okri himself dislikes the term. See Robert Fraser, *Ben Okri* (Tavistock: Northcote House, 2002), 10.

19 Michael S. Northcott writes: 'The ascription "private" is increasingly problematic when applied to automobiles. Their use requires the public maintenance of an extensive concrete, steel and

tarmac infrastructure, representing one half of the built space of European and American cities' (*A Moral Climate: The Ethics of Global Warming* (London: Dartman, Longman and Todd, 2007), 215).

20 Levin, 'The Problem of Pattern and Scale in Ecology', *Ecology* 73 (1992), 1943–67, 1953.

21 'Human Population Growth as If the Rest of Life Mattered', in *Life on the Brink*, 3–15, 10.

22 *The Perfect Moral Storm*, 433.

23 Ibid., 403.

24 For example, Ynestra King writes that the 'ecofeminist movement and culture *must* show the connection between all forms of domination, including the domination of nonhuman nature' (emphasis added) ('The Ecophobia Hypothesis: Re-membering the Feminist Body of Ecocriticism', in Greta Gaard, Simon C. Estok and Serpil Oppermann (eds), *International Perspectives in Feminist Ecocriticism* (London: Routledge, 2013), 70–84, 78).

25 *Ecocriticism and Shakespeare: Reading Ecophobia* (Basingstoke: Palgrave, 2011), 4.

26 Rebecca Ann Bach, Review of *Ecocriticism and Shakespeare: Reading Ecophobia,* by Simon C. Estok, and of Dan Brayton and Lynne Bruckner (eds), *Ecocritical Shakespeare*, in *Shakespeare Quarterly* 64.1, Spring 2013, 110–13. Richard Kerridge also criticizes the notion of 'ecophobia' in Estok's book on Shakespeare as too 'undifferentiated' and 'resistant to historicization' ('Ecocriticism' in *The Year's Work in Critical and Cultural Theory* 21 (English Association, 2013), chapter 18, 1–30, 28).

27 *The Perfect Moral Storm*, 57.

28 Andy Coghan, 'Africa's Road to Riches', *New Scientist,* 11 January 2014, 8–9.

CHAPTER SIX

Postcolonial ecocriticism and de-humanizing reading: An Australian test case

One of the functions of culture has been to provide the human image with a basic, but specific form – so that when someone looks in the mirror in the morning, what looks back is an individual with personality, with beliefs, duties, someone who may be looking well today, or in a bad mood, or who is late for work perhaps . . . and rarely, what is at least equally truly, a member of a ruthless species of ape wearing clothes, superficially intelligent but caught up in natural and ecological processes that it can barely see, let alone comprehend.

Anat Pick suggests:

> Do not literature, the arts, and the 'humanities' at large reflect the incomplete becoming – the struggle of the human to assume and inhabit a definite form? To come to terms with and give shape to an entirely incidental embodiment? It is only after this initial humanizing that other animals can be brought into the field of human semblance [in notions of the 'anthropomorphic']¹

This chapter continues the project of trying to gauge the break in consciousness and understanding emergent with the concept of the Anthropocene. The particular focus is on Australian literary history and on one text of 1901 by the (once) iconic nationalist writer, Henry Lawson (1867–1922), an author still associated with the cultural foundations of modern Australia. How deeply do retrospective insights now alter it? What is proposed is a 'de-humanizing' reading, meant here in the largely positive sense, that is, critiquing the way a text or cultural practice reinforces by its limited scale framing delusory conceptions of human action and identity.

Why Australia in particular? Even in 1901, Australia stands out as a particularly stark exemplar of the challenges of the Anthropocene. For instance Australia, then as now, is comprised of heavily urbanized areas built on the very edge of the continent, cities heavily dependent on the export of material resources such as coal and agricultural produce from a vast and sparsely inhabited interior. This gulf between the city and 'the Bush' entails a psychic disjunction between human settlements and the ecosystems in which they are embedded, often in a disavowed dependence. This instantiates the general point made by the late Australian philosopher Val Plumwood in 2008 about illusions of localism across the modern world, the 'split between a singular, elevated, conscious "dwelling" place, and the multiple disregarded places of economic and ecological support, a split between our idealized homeplace and the places delineated by our ecological footprint'.[2] Another significant parallel with the Earth of the twenty-first century would be the fact that, even in 1901, if then less regarded, the damage to Australia's ecosystems was already permanent and irreversible.

An Australian test case recommends itself because that country's modern history is, more legibly than elsewhere, not just a history of human beings. Many of its victims, and some of its winners, are nonhuman. The European settlement was a matter of the partial but often extensively destructive supplanting of one biota by another, partly by human intent, as with wheat crops and cattle, but often without it, as with accidental infestations of introduced rabbits and cane toads. This constituted a massive environmental experiment, resulting in widespread soil degradation and other damage, something whose analogy with the wider Earth of the twenty-first century is obvious enough. Not in any country, but perhaps least of all Australia, should one continue to write criticism and history as if it were a matter of human agency alone. It would like trying to understand the cuckoo without making reference to other birds.

Yet this is precisely the method of a recent authoritative survey of Australian Literature from a postcolonial perspective. Graham Huggan's *Australian Literature: Postcolonialism, Racism, Transnationalism* forms a model of postcolonial literary criticism as it stood in 2007,[3] with its attention to how competing human groups in colonial and postcolonial contexts define themselves through strategies of uneven social inclusion and exclusion. It stands out for its attention to critical method, yet it is striking how anachronistically such an anthropocentric focus now reads.

Setting up a reading experiment

This chapter's reading experiment, which does not presuppose prior familiarity with its object text, falls into two parts. The first approaches a short story of 1901 by Lawson with the tools of a kind of postcolonial approach that is now becoming anachronistic, that is, one which assumes the autonomy of human culture, seeing human beings and groups as defining themselves exclusively by relation to each other, in forms of social inclusion and exclusion. A second, 'de-humanizing' reading evaluates the drastic reconfigurations of context that emerge with the concept of the Anthropocene.

Lawson's 'Telling Mrs Baker' was first published in *Blackwood's Magazine* for October 1901, during Lawson's brief stay in England.[4] This also happens to be the year of 'federation', that is, the year in which the separate British colonies came together to form the country still today called 'The Commonwealth of Australia'.

Lawson was working at a crucial moment in Australian literary and cultural history, that of the so-called Australian Legend of the 1890s. This term, coined by Russell Ward in the 1960s, describes prominent features of the cultural nationalism of the Australian colonies in the 1890s, the decade before Australia emerged as a new, federated nation.[5] The idea of the Legend focused on the particular Bush ethos that grew up among pastoral workers in the sheep and cattle stations, and the value of this ethos as the expression of an emerging nationalism. Some basic elements of the Legend still persist in popular images of Australia that focus on the Bush and pioneer experience, valorizing a blokeish egalitarianism and a stoical ethos of patriotic loyalty and pride. Recently, however, critics have highlighted with unease the Legend's positing of archetypally Australian figures in terms of a masculinist idealization of Bush life (though, then as now, Australia was one of the world's most urbanized countries). The form that such cultural nationalism took may also be marked by the context of the 1890s, a time of both drought and economic depression in Australia.[6]

However, another revisionist point now suggests itself. In the changed light of the Anthropocene, Lawson emerges no longer as an icon of Australian nationalism but as a fascinating writer of environmental conflict and degradation, and, to a degree unknown to himself, of the effects of these in terms of cultural and personal self-conceptions.

For instance, an environmental hatred marks 'Telling Mrs Baker' and many of Lawson's other stories. The Bush and the Outback seem to deride any given European cultural associations of 'nature':

> Somebody told me that the country was very dry on the other side of Nevertire. It is. I wouldn't like to sit down on it anywhere. The least horrible spot in the Bush, in a dry season, is where the Bush isn't – where it has been cleared away and green crop is trying to grow.[7]

In Lawson's undoubtedly ecophobic misreading the outback is essentially anti-cultural, anti-human and anti-humanist, mostly similar to landscapes that have been ruined by waste or abuse. Australian nature does not seem 'natural' in any acceptable sense but is a kind of dump: 'We crossed the Macquarrie – a narrow, muddy gutter with a dog swimming across, and three goats interested.'[8] 'The country looks as though a great ash-heap had been spread out there, and mulga scrub and firewood planted – and neglected.'[9] One story indulges the geological fiction that the very rock is rotting.

Such a land seems good only for changing into something more recognizably European, pastoral, pretty and profitable. In the version of Lawson prominent in the Australian Legend, the denigration of the continent's native environment and exaggerations of its 'weirdness' became part of an idealization of those engaged in its culturalization, the workers and settlers that faced such realities, the new supposedly Australian (masculine) types, stoical, loyal, egalitarian (at least with fellow Europeans), taciturn even sardonic and resourceful. However, it is tragically ironic that the forms of agriculture and pastoralism being idealized and still generally practiced in Australia are now widely understood to be destructively at odds with the Australian climate and soil, a lack of understanding that underlies, although unacknowledged, significant issues in 'Telling Mrs Baker'.

With early twenty-first century Australia suffering a particularly intense instance of the climatic syndrome of long drought followed by extensive flooding, the calls become louder for modes of agriculture less at odds with its natural context. Two decades ago, Ian Anderson wrote,

> Agriculture is one of the mainstays of Australia's economy. But ironically, the country is not well suited to the European styles of farming that are practised. . . . The country's soils are thin – most are less than 10 centimetres deep – and contain little organic matter. The weather is not dependable either, often fluctuating between prolonged drought and severe flooding. Added to this, Australia's native mammals have padded feet that do minimal damage to soil. By comparison, the hooves of imported animals are far more destructive.[10]

First reading

'Telling Mrs Baker' is the story of two drovers who return to lie to one Mrs Baker about the supposedly brave and noble death by fever of her husband, Bob Baker, nicknamed 'the Boss', droving cattle across the Australian Bush – when he actually died from alcohol poisoning. Baker's death is grotesque and sordid. At one point he strips naked in despair to try to hang himself in the scrub, and his posthumous effects expose him as a sexual predator on the wives of friends. Nevertheless, his two friends, Andy M'Culloch and the narrator, believe that 'it isn't Bush religion to desert a mate in a hole' (198). Having stuck with Baker in life, they now contrive to tell an exonerating lie about his death to Mrs Baker when they return to the small town of Solong, towards Sydney. This comic confrontation of the sexes makes up most of the narrative.

FIGURE 5 *Drought.*

Bob Baker is introduced at the opening of the story as a former 'squatter', or landowner, in the business of keeping sheep and breeding racehorses. However, he fell into ruin by spending too much time in Sydney in 'swell hotels' (196), following up his horse-racing interests. 'So after a pretty severe drought, when the sheep died by the thousands on his runs, Bob Baker went under, and the bank took over his station and put a manager in charge' (196). He seems to take to excessive drinking when he becomes a drover (197), and maybe even 'hadn't been quite right in his head before he started drinking – he had acted queer sometimes . . . maybe he'd got a touch of sunstroke or got brooding over his troubles' (198) (Figure 5).

Huggan tries to rescue Lawson from his now dubious status as a white nationalist Australian icon. His method of reading (which Huggan even formalizes into the working of four 'discursive categories') is primarily to underline the unjust, socially constructed nature of some category of identity (whiteness, maleness, etc.) by a counter-stress on what its excludes, denigrates or evades in order to constitute itself. In Lawson's case, this means counter-readings that 'focus on racial exclusionism, spurious appeals to solidarity, and a sexual division of labour that highlights the vanities and insufficiencies of men' (*Australian Literature*, 56). All three points immediately suggest a reading of 'Telling Mrs Baker' in which Lawson's work would be endorsed in a strained, very qualified way, by being retrospectively gauged against contemporary norms of equity and personhood:

> While it would be optimistic, to say the least, to convert Lawson into a surreptitious champion for Aborigines, stories like 'The Bush Undertaker' suggest that he was certainly aware, like most of his contemporaries, of the racialized anxieties underlying white-settler claims upon the land they selected for their own. (*Australian Literature*, 58)

Within this critical framework, 'Telling Mrs Baker' would be most explicitly about the 'constructions' of gender that the colonial situation sets up. The domestic Mrs Baker, 'with nothing particular about her in the way of brains' (202–3), is lied to in ways that help her sustain a self-image as the loving wife of a brave man who heroically succumbed to the perils of the frontier. She also consents to her husband's invented 'last wish' (201) that she return to Sydney. That city appears here as the place of domestic security and illusion, of a willing ignorance about the real hardships of the land on which it depends. An earlier passage in the story has the narrator mock his presumed urban readership –'Sounds queer to you city people, doesn't it?' (199).[11]

The lie to Mrs Baker can be said to cast her in a protected and patronized feminine role, while her being kept in that role also helps sustain the lie of her husband's heroism and self-sacrifice. The moral situation is complicated, however, by a kind of doubling. Bob Baker has a brother, Ned, and Mrs Baker a sister, Miss Standish from Sydney (no first names are given for the women). Both siblings are counterparts. Ned Baker is like his brother in pitting himself against a hostile, heavily damaged environment. He is 'fighting the drought, the rabbit-pest, and the banks, on a small [sheep] station back on the [New South Wales/Queensland] border' (198), set in hopeless 'God-forsaken scrubs' (199). But Ned Baker is also unlike his alcoholic brother, being reliable, honourable and hard-working. He helps clear up the mess of his brother's death. He avenges himself on a publican who exploited Bob's infatuation with a girl employed as a lure in the pub.

Miss Standish is likewise a counterpart to Mrs Baker. Whereas Mrs Baker seems happy to be stupid, Miss Standish is pictured as an intelligent, attractive young woman, dressed in a metropolitan style. She also writes short stories for *The Sydney Bulletin*. Miss Standish soon sees through the lie being told to her sister and has to be silenced by a carefully aimed wink. Later she follows the men as they leave, thanks them and kisses them warmly on the mouth. Australian readers of 'Telling Mrs Baker' in 1901 would have recognized in the reference to the *Bulletin* an acknowledgement of a leading organ of the Australian cultural nationalism of the 1890s, one that helped consolidate a (masculinist) image of the 'Australian' as defined and distinguished by a relationship to the Bush, with many of the selectively egalitarian values associated with Lawson and the Australian Legend.

All in all, Lawson affirms values of loyalty and endurance in the bushmen, never doubting the value of the colonial enterprise, while mocking images of pompous heroism. The two mates who contrive to lie to Mrs Baker in Lawson's story are depicted in a slightly sentimental way, as comically gauche, very awkward with women, but determinedly loyal in an act of deception never doubted for a kindness. The story falls into two parts: the account of Baker's decline and death and the scene in Mrs Baker's parlour as the lie is told. The domestic scene is one of diffidence and a kind of comic sentimentality, with the men's clumsy fumbling with hats, in what is represented as a feminine space. They decline the offer of tea: 'we didn't feel we could handle cups and saucers and pieces of cake successfully just then' (203) and there is the awkward pathos of little Bobby Baker asking if his father has 'gone up among the stars' then immediately asking for a penny; the slightly theatrical nature of Mrs Baker's grief, and the final kiss on the lips from Miss Standish as they leave (the story ends, 'I don't think it did either of us any harm' (209)). In effect, the second part of 'Telling Mrs Baker' displaces attention from the stakes of the lie about Baker to the comedy of its telling. Its mild sentimentality 'humanizes' the characters and the situation. Miss Standish, as a writer who idealizes bushmen, seems likely to produce more copy for *The Sydney Bulletin* along similar lines ('I like the Bushmen! They are grand men – they are noble!' (208)).

Second reading

No real precedents exist for reading at the scale required by the Anthropocene. As with the readings of Carver and Snyder, one first clear step is the rejection of methodological nationalism, something which has been especially strong in Lawson's case, almost defining his image. The larger context must place Lawson's work in relation to European imperialism and the colonization of much of the world between 1600 and 1900. In addition, Lawson's drovers and bushmen are engaged in an industry of livestock and meat production that remains an increasing source of habitat destruction and atmospheric pollution across the world. Today, animal agriculture has been argued to be a greater source of greenhouse gases, directly and indirectly, than all the world's transportation systems.[12] Again, shifting the scalar context produces new ironies of retrospect in the way in which present-day or future readers may consider a past literary text.

What becomes especially visible in this Australian context is the need to read colonization as an interspecies affair, not just a matter of human to human interactions. An alternative reading of 'Telling Mrs Baker' might test the implications of the fact that human beings have always existed as part of a community of animals. Human beings could not exist and cannot be understood without other species, whatever the tendency of modern societies to keep livestock hidden away in factory-like enclosures while people live as if red meat were on tap, like water from a reservoir.

A further reading of Lawson's story might then pivot upon the following passage, which it is perhaps easy to skim over if read with an exclusively human interest in tracing the decline of the Boss and the reaction of his mates:

> We had two other men with us, but had the devil's own bother on account of the cattle. It was a mixed-up job all-round. You see it was all big runs round there, and we had to keep the bullocks moving along the route all the time, or else get into trouble for trespass. The agent wasn't going to go to the expense of putting the cattle in a paddock until the Boss sobered up; there was very little grass on the route or the travelling-stock reserves or camps, so we had to keep travelling for grass. (197)

What Lawson does not write is that, in passing across and obliterating the numerous boundaries of the traditional inhabitants, such high-pressure pastoralism also drove out many native animals as it also displaced or destroyed Aboriginal societies. The repeated denigration of the outback as unnatural wasteland is evidently in the service of Eurocentric notions of humanity and food production, and implicitly, the eradication of native flora, fauna and other people.

The Bush that Lawson's characters struggle with did not constitute 'wilderness' but a depopulated landscape that is now understood to have been altered by generations of Aboriginal fire management. The hybrid quality of the Bush, shaped by human and nonhuman influences alike, is further underlined by the accident of its catastrophic infestation by the introduced European rabbit. This demonstrates just how far the role of Europeans in colonizing these spaces 'was less a matter of judgement and choice than of being downstream of a bursting dam' (Alfred Crosby).[13]

Ecological devastation became a chief agent of rapid colonization and conquest. Even the native grasses were lost. Eric Rolls writes of the first years of the British colony:

> The only things not thriving in the Colony were Australian grasses. Their roots had run in a spongy soil full of humus. They were accustomed to fire, to drought, and flood, to deficiency of nitrogen and phosphorus, to the gentle feeding of sharp-toothed kangaroos at the clumped butts, and the picking of their seeds by parrots and pigeons and rats. They had never had their whole seed heads snatched in one mouthful; they had never been trampled by cloven hooves; their surface roots had never had to run in hard ground.[14]

The very weeds were introductions, like dandelions, or like 'plantain, the Englishman's foot'. Former settler colonies like Australia were founded largely on the basis of the eradication of indigenous biota for the benefit of the narrow, fragile ecosystem of an originally European agriculture and husbandry.

No indigenous animals appear at all in the wide Australian landscapes of 'Telling Mrs Baker': it is almost as if they never existed. All the animals named are introductions: sheep, rabbits, horses, cattle, dogs. No Aboriginal people appear either. This unremarked absence takes on a sinister quality if one remembers Adrian Franklin's statement that 'The colonization of Australia involved the meeting of one culture that defined itself as absolutely different from animals with another that defined itself as indistinguishable from animals.'[15] The invisibility of indigenous life in Lawson's text is also grimly appropriate in another way. The defeat of the Aborigines was to a significant degree owing to the least visible members of the European biota, viruses and bacteria, including some ultimately derived from domesticated animals. Europeans arrived on the shore of Australia, as they did for North America, in ships stacked with livestock, after centuries of living with domestic animals and birds, sharing both their diseases and immunities. In effect settlers and their animals formed a kind of social unit, one whose members were to a degree mutually intelligible through each other's signals. Wherever the cattle ran, even over wide areas, they brought with them the jurisdiction of their human owners. In a striking expansion of significant scale, Deborah Bird Rose suggests 'the conquest of Australia did not begin in 1788. It began about 10,000 years ago when our ancestors domesticated cattle.'[16] British settlers and transported convicts arrived on the shore of a continent inhabited by hunter-gathers with little or no resistance even to chickenpox or other 'minor' ailments. So the highlighted stoicism and toughness of some of Lawson's bushmen is undercut by the way in which the European conquest of much of the world was to a large degree an accident of microlife. This is also the time that Africa suffered the epizootic or animal epidemic of rinderpest (perhaps accidentally carried by invading Italian troops),[17] devastating cattle and pastoral ways of life, making that continent more vulnerable to a ruthless scramble for territory between European powers.

So the broader, planetary context for 'Telling Mrs Baker' effects another derangement of scale, it is both vaster than the normal focus (Australian society c. 1900) and yet also concerns the very small and unperceived, microorganisms, diseased resistance, unregarded seeds. It involves ecological ignorance and sheer accident as much as it does planned and executed schemes of colonization.

'Telling Mrs Baker' pivots around a dichotomy between those who know the truth about the pressures of moral degradation in the Bush but require others who need to be lied to and those who need to be lied to, such as Mrs Baker, or indeed city people on the whole. While in *Heart of Darkness* (1899) Joseph Conrad's anti-hero Kurtz seems to succumb to what is controversially depicted as the barbarism of indigenous Africans, Baker's initial antagonist was his own fecklessness, then the Australian environment – the drought in which 'the sheep died by thousands on his runs' (196) – and his inability to resist pubs in settlements along the droving trails. The Bush was not 'wilderness' as a space of benign self-discovery or assertion, but one in which received Western categories of the human (Giorgio Agamben's 'anthropological machine')[18] may break down.

The bigger picture of Australia's invasion and conquest demonstrates how far people need to be seen as part of large social, technical and biological groupings and structures, including vital nonhuman elements (meteorology, geology, bacteria), just as, for comparison, the attitudes, frustrations and manipulativeness dramatized in Carver's 'Elephant' arose in the mixed spaces of possibility and entrapment created by certain forms of 'advanced' infrastructure. It would be less accurate to say that the Australian colonists brought with them kinds of pastoral and arable agriculture that at least in the very short term appeared superior to the practices of the Aborigines than that those practices were an essential if unacknowledged part of what made them who they were.

As John Miller writes, '[W]e need to rethink. . . . What we mean by "human" and "animal" because climate change, among other interlinked factors, has made it impossible for these terms to mean what we thought they meant.'[19] One resource for such recontextualization, and especially suggestive for reading a text about someone collapsing from alcoholism in the Bush, is the anthropologist Tim Ingold's notion of 'inversion', devised to critique idealistic notions of human agency that portray it in overly unitary and self-contained terms. Ingold describes the 'logic of inversion' as misrepresenting human agency as a central, sovereign determinant of events, ascribing what are really the effects of multiple, contextual factors to the supposed act or nature of a unitary, human agent whose actions are then understood as the outer expression of an inner intention or character.[20] To try to undo the logic of inversion at work in a text or the understanding of its contexts is necessarily to unwind, as plural and dispersed, effects of agency that have been misleadingly condensed into a few human decisions, actions or characteristics. Ingold defines 'inversion' in more detail as follows:

> Thus the organism, moving and growing along lines that bind it into the web of life, is reconfigured as the outward expression of an inner design. Likewise the person, acting and perceiving within a nexus of intertwined relationships, is presumed to behave according to the directions of cultural models or cognitive schemata installed in his or her head. (68)

By 'cultural models', Ingold could well be referring to a powerful and all-pervasive mode of human self-idolatry: the tendency to explain in terms of internal personal, social or national characteristics perceived advantages or disadvantages that more truly pertain to external multiplicitous human and nonhuman agents, matters of geographical accident or of deep history. Examples would be such cultural directives as the supposedly civilizing missions of Australian pastoralism or, in the United States, of the 'manifest destiny' of expanding European settlement.[21] To work to undo the strategy of 'inversion' is to transform what seems the work of few interacting points or agents into the work of a far more multiplicitous and plural web, such as a whole ecological/geographical and biological context traced over larger spatial and temporal scales, even back to the Neolithic in the case of colonial Australia. One can hypothesize that the larger the scale of consideration in this respect the weaker the perceived illusions of 'inversion' appear, and the more 'de-humanized' may become the significance of the person registered at that scale.

Baker's alcoholism presents an ambiguous case for 'inverted' or humanist ideas of agency. It is a condition in which external circumstances and personal intent seem uncomfortably contaminated. 'Identity' is not here something asserted in relation to some 'excluded other': it becomes the site of a crisis of volition and responsibility. Alcoholism lies in a grey area between categorization as a disease (more so now than in Lawson's time) and as a moral failing. In 'Telling Mrs Baker', drinking is seen to represent moral weakness, an easy escapism compared to the kind of dutiful behaviour enacted by Ned Baker. This is why it must be covered up. Even Bob Baker's obvious despair, when he attempts to hang himself in the Bush, is not seen to challenge the condemnation of alcohol as an indulgence. It is preferable for the others to maintain the fiction of a noble and unchanged personhood beaten by ill luck than to puzzle at a derangement of that personhood itself. The whole humanist edifice maintained by the final lie is thus, paradoxical as it may seem at first, better maintained by presenting Baker as the victim of entirely external forces for which he had no responsibility (fever, illness). What the bushmen defend in their lie about Baker are certain, supposedly supremely 'human' attributes (devotion to a patriotic enterprise, love for dependents, monogamy and an executive dignity of self, even in defeat), as opposed to the story of squalid physical vulnerability in which these things evaporate:

> while our eyes went off him for a few minutes he slipped away into the scrub, stripped himself naked, and started to hang himself to a leaning tree with a piece of clothes-line rope. We got to him just in time . . .

> Sometimes, towards the end, he'd be sensible for few minutes and talk about his 'poor wife and children'; and immediately afterwards he'd fall a-cursing me, and Andy, and Ned, and calling us devils. He cursed everything; he cursed his wife and children, and yelled that they were dragging him down to hell. He died raving mad. It was the worst case of death in the horrors of drink that I ever saw or heard of in the Bush. (198–9)

The Bush is heavily damaged space in which the fauna is either exterminated, driven out or being homogenized according to its compatibility with European occupation, yet also one in which lines of demarcation and control are fragile and can break down into the dubious category of the feral, as with the plagues of feral rabbits and feral cats in modern Australia. 'Feral' is also a word that could sum up Baker's transformation. Alcoholism in the Bush is presented as a terrifying collapse of the distinction of human and nonhuman, with loss of such human-defining features as clothes and any family and social bonds. The human as would-be overlord of animal life – droving cattle from the back of a horse – is reduced to a toxic, naked insanity in a rabbit-infested ruin of an ecosystem. The scene of drunken collapse in the Bush would also link Baker with one degrading image of Aboriginal people at a time when native communities, then as now, were often ravaged by alcohol abuse.[22] In Lawson's then shifting the focus from Baker's death to the comically gauche domestic drama of the lying scene (the largest portion of 'Telling Mrs Baker'), any concern with the implications of Baker's collapse seems answered only by an indulgent theatre of humanizing sentimentality. This mismatch of feeling and reality works as a feint of narrative closure, though with a slight element of cultural mockery in its reference to *The Sydney Bulletin.*

The lie to Mrs Baker sustains a strategy of 'inversion' by forcing a strict divide between the realm of chance – of the supposed misfortune of a 'fever' (199) – and that of human character and action. Bob Baker is to be presented as a hero unfairly struck down by elements beyond his control, and the line between human dignity and chance is to be strictly asserted, if only as a needed fiction. Saving Baker's dignity by a lie is the way in which Lawson's narrative asserts the dignity of the other bushmen, with their loyalty and self-sacrifice for a friend. Yet the retrospective ironies of the Anthropocene highlight another level of delusion and of unrecognized chance. To reread the European invasion and conquest of Australia in more 'dehumanizing' terms, as the often misrecognized action of a kind of cross-species entity – that of 'human + cattle + innumerable forms of microorganism – is to see the whole colonial context and its values as a matter of ecological, geographical and deep-historical contingency.[23]

Conclusion

Let us review this reading experiment. The kind of anthropocentric postcolonial theory exemplified in our first reading moved to explain all the issues in the text in terms of human-to-human relationships, especially their iniquities. It works within the frame of received arguments on equity, gender and power relations and it makes Lawson's text symptomatic or exemplary of them. The second reading does not overlook such inequities but sees in the desire to enclose all the issues raised by the text within the frame of human-to-human relationships a kind of denial comparable even to the staged lie about how Baker died, as against the place of biological accident – including effects beyond normal time scales of consideration – and climate. The first reading of Mrs Baker had an 'explanatory' tone. The second, de-humanizing reading has no, or at least no adequate, answers to the situation it describes, even while it highlights further issues of human injustice (to Aboriginal people especially, but also kinds of sexism).

A 'de-humanizing' reading of 'Telling Mrs Baker' makes it impossible to see this text of 1901 Australia solely in terms of the notion of formative 'social discourse' used in Huggan's *Australian Literature*, that is, 'the sum of "available ways of speaking [and] writing in which social power operates to produce certain objects and effects" (Susan Sheridan)'.[24] Such once-dominant critical conceptions now appear themselves as a form of 'inversion', a reading forcibly subsuming what were really the effects of diverse elements of geography, psychology, politics, environment and chance into the working of a disciplinary formula operating in self-enclosed cultural terms.[25]

As in the case of the reading of Carver's 'Elephant', the additional consideration of a far broader temporal and spatial scale has the effect of rendering the more familiar, manifest drama of character, plot and so on mildly epiphenomenal. The readings of both Carver and Lawson also reinforce a counter-sense of the human as a creature of broader impersonal dynamics (geographical, biological, technologic and demographic) playing themselves out in the narratives of individual lives but invisible to the way those see themselves and their goals. It has traced, in issues of disease resistance, the absence or presence of other animals, soil erosion, matters further removed from the awareness of Lawson or his readers than critical readings normally do.

In both cases, the broader scale ironizes the text in novel ways. As with Carver's protagonist, action which seems generous or noble on the surface (more problematically so in Lawson's case) also feeds into a more destructive dynamic on the broader scale, unsustainable resource use and 'energy slavery' on the one hand, the evasive idealization of the degradation of Australian ecosystems on the other.

Critical reading in relation to the Anthropocene becomes a measure of an irreversible break in consciousness and understanding between the past and present. Increasingly violent droughts and floods in contemporary Australia change the significance of a plot set in Lawson's 'federation drought'. The lie being told to Mrs Baker becomes seen as bigger and as more compromised than either its fictional tellers or their author could have known. The break in understanding between past and present produces both a sense of intellectual liberation, as older certainties re-emerge as anachronisms, but also the irony of tracing in the past modes of thought and practices that are to be condemned from out of a world in which many of their effects have already become irreversible. Analogously, the greatest challenge for critics engaged with climate change may be how to acknowledge that climate change is inevitable, already under way, without paralyzing our ability still to imagine a future worth struggling for.

Finally, as before, the expanded, ecological scale cannot simply be taken as revealing a 'truth' that completely negates the drama at the normal scales of human-to-human interactions. To return to the example of Carver's 'Elephant', it is not difficult to imagine many other texts, whether by Carver or by others, whose reading would open upon the same global ecological contexts when taken on the broadest scale. Almost any twentieth-century Western text with some focus on urban life, making the usual normative assumptions about lifestyle made possible by a fossil fuel-based infrastructure, must lead to the same large-scale context. Likewise, with Lawson, many other texts concerning droving and settler colonization (other texts from the time of the 'Legend' or, in North America, writers such as Willa Cather) would have opened a path leading back to the vast geographical and biological contexts at issue. It is only by keeping alive simultaneously questions at smaller, more 'human', scales that the readings of 'Elephant' or 'Telling Mrs Baker' also retain some specificity, even as their events are rendered more disconcertingly epiphenomenal. The broadest scale intervenes to deepen, ironize and 'de-humanize' the others, but not fully to supplant them as some general and repetitive last word about depressing or tragic ecological realities.

Knowledge of the broader context deepens our own sense of the destructive ignorance at work in the lie to Mrs Baker. Nevertheless, and in unresolved tension with it, it would still be reductive to set aside Lawson's comedy, even his dubious sentimentality, in order to reread the events of the text solely at the broader scale in which human beings are just the playthings of long-term ecological, material and social contingencies. In its way, the lie about Bob Baker remains a defence of certain norms of personhood against just such a reduction, an assertion of human dignity even as a loyally sustained fiction, even if caught up in social and ecological complexities beyond the comprehension of Lawson's time.

Notes

1 *Creaturely Ethics: Animality and Vulnerability in Literature and Film* (New York: Columbia University Press, 2011), 83.

2 'Shadow Places and the Politics of Dwelling', *Australian Humanities Review*, 44 (March 2008), http://www.australianhumanitiesreview. org/archive/Issue-March-2008/plumwood.html

3 *Australian Literature: Postcolonialism, Racism, Transnationalism* (Oxford: Oxford University Press, 2007). The methodological anthropocentrism of this book seems all the more surprising in that it coincides with its author's turn to postcolonial ecocriticism, as seen in a special issue of the journal *Interventions*, 'Green Postcolonialism', 9.1 (2007) coedited with Helen Tiffin.

4 In John Barnes (ed.), *The Penguin Henry Lawson Short Stories* (London: Penguin, 1986).

5 Russell Ward, *The Australian Legend*, 2nd edn (Melbourne: Oxford University Press, 1966).

6 Huggan's *Australian Literature* highlights the kinds of omissions that had given the 'Legend' its false sense of comprehensiveness: The Legend, although still periodically reinvented, now stands at something of a crossroads; it is increasingly seen as the limited product of an equally limited number of middle-class writers and intellectuals during the period roughly from the 1930s to the 1960s, who shared a somewhat inflationary sense of the justice of the national cause. The Legend's alleged radicalism has been exposed, as have its pretentions to egalitarianism. The modern consensus view is that it overprivileges white-settler experience by excluding Aborigines; male experience by marginalizing women; rural experience by ignoring the city (*Australian Literature*, 55).

7 'In a Dry Season', *Penguin Henry Lawson*, 37–9, 38.

8 Ibid.

9 Ibid.

10 'Australia's Growing Disaster', *New Scientist* 29 July 1995, 12–3.

11 The lying in 'Telling Mrs. Baker' could also be compared to the more famous lie that ends Joseph Conrad's contemporary novella, *Heart of Darkness* (1899). The narrator Marlow returns from a traumatic trip to the colonial heart of Africa, where he has witnessed one Mr Kurtz die in horror after succumbing to indigenous practices of savagery. He visits Kurtz's former fiancée

in Belgium. As if maintaining the fictions of more commonplace adventure stories, Marlow lies to her as she asks:
'"His last word – to live with", she insisted. "Don't you understand I loved him – I loved him – I loved him!"
I pulled myself together and spoke slowly.
"The last word he pronounced was – your name."' . . . (*Heart of Darkness* (London: Penguin, 1988), 121)

12 See, for instance, the facts highlighted by the activist film/ documentary, 'Cowspiracy', http://cowspiracy.com/fact-check/

13 Crosby, *Ecological Imperialism*, 192.

14 *A Million Wild Acres* (Ringwood, VA: Penguin Australia, 1981), 28.

15 Adrian Franklin, *Animal Nation: The True Story of Animals and Australia* (Sydney: University of New South Wales Press, 2004), 48.

16 *Reports from a Wild Country: Ethics for Decolonization* (Sydney: University of New South Wales Press, 2004), 74.

17 See Phoofolo, Pule, 'Epidemics and Revolutions: The Rinderpest Epidemic in Late Nineteenth-Century Southern Africa', *Past & Present* 138 (1993), 112–43; Clive A. Spinage, *Cattle Plague: A History* (New York: Springer Science & Business Media, 2003).

18 *The Open: Man and Animal*, trans. Kevin Attel (Stanford, CA: Stanford University Press, 2004).

19 John Miller, 'Biodiversity and the Abyssal Limits of the Human', 209.

20 *Being Alive: Essays on Movement, Knowledge and Description* (London: Routledge, 2011), 63.

21 One of Walt Whitman's best-known rhetorical devices is a good example of 'inversion' being deployed in process as kind of a literary device. In Sections 15 and 16 of his nationalistic *Song of Myself* (1892 version), the American persona of the poem is dramatized as encompassing in the one form vast spaces and vast varieties of people. The 'I' of the poem's speaker, and by identification the reader too, encompasses

> A Southerner soon as a Northerner, a planter nonchalant and hospitable down by the Oconee I live,
> A Yankee bound my own way ready for trade, my joints the limberest joints on earth and the sternest joints on earth,
> A Kentuckian walking the vale of the Elkhorn in my deer-skin leggings, a Louisianian or Georgian,
> A boatman over lakes or bays or along coasts, a Hoosier, Badger, Buckeye;
> At home on Kanadian snow-shoes or up in the bush, or with fishermen off Newfoundland,

At home in the fleet of ice-boats, sailing with the rest and tacking,
At home on the hills of Vermont or in the woods of Maine, or the
Texan ranch,
Comrade of Californians, comrade of free North-Westerners,
(loving their big proportions,)
Comrade of craftsmen and coalmen, comrade of all who shake
hands and welcome to drink and meat, ...

http://www.poetryfoundation.org/poem/174745

This is to cite only a few lines from over a hundred in a structure
of parallel sentences, with powerful cumulative effect. Such a list
stages Ingold's process of inversion in action. The contingency of
a wide geographical extent, as well as cultural variety, is being
interiorized by the poem's speaker and his readers, and appropriated
into an identificatory fantasy of unitary self-aggrandizement.
Certain recurrent American nationalist values emerge here as partly
to be read as an effect of geographical contingency – the historically
sudden appropriation of a whole continent and its resources (in part
made possible by the accident of competing immune systems and
disease), enabling an expansive conception of national personhood,
of a culture of opportunity or enterprise, an ideology of self-making
in large open spaces, etc.).

22   See the Australian government report, 'Alcohol and Health in
Australia', c. 2009, www.nhmrc.gov.au/your-health/alcohol-
guidelines/alcohol-and-health-australia

23   Ingold's critique of atomistic notions of identity as personal
property can be related to attempts to extend the scope of notions
of personhood beyond the individual. In *The Community of Rights:
The Rights of Community* (Montreal: Black Rose Publishing,
2012) Daniel Fischlin and Martha Nandorfy argue that, especially
in the global south, environmental questions must be interpreted as
pushing notions of rights and citizenships beyond a limited human
reference. They see a new and difficult cosmopolitics emerging from
the less compartmentalized context of southern environmental
concerns, with people living in the direct consequences of
deforestation, poisoning and drought, for whom making
distinctions between their own 'rights' and those of the nonhuman
ecosphere around them would make little sense. The notion of a
'community of rights' embracing the nonhuman also corresponds
to now widely recognized views of what the 'human' is in the first
place, understandings that reject the individualistic focus of now
dominant liberal and (worse) neoliberal conceptions in favour of
definitions of personhood that include a whole field of constitutive

relations to the nonhuman environment. To refer back to Lawson's context, sheep farming and mass cattle-droving across ancestral Aboriginal lands constituted a violation of native personhood.

24 *Australian Literature*, 23.

25 Huggan's *Australian Literature* (2007), for all its merits, also becomes interesting as an instance of how once dominant modes of reading in postcolonial criticism may now appear as more sophisticated versions of Ingold's 'inversion'. By 2007, this book's still representative anthropocentric methodology is becoming visibly formulaic.

Huggan's summarizes the four discursive strategies claimed to make up the internal dynamics of cultural representation:

Literature is one instrument among others for the deployment of . . . often complex discursive strategies. Four strategies can be picked out briefly here for closer consideration: the representations of otherness and the racial/sexual other; the production of racial stereotypes; the use of race as a signifier of exclusion; and the appropriation of race as a self-affirming marker, in which the previously marginalized racial other re-emerges as a self-validating writing subject. (24)

Attention to these discursive strategies enables the modern critic to reread literary tradition in Australia as the arena for contested forms of identity politics, primarily those based on appeals to supposed national, racial or sexual difference. Huggan also shows just how far later and supposedly more enlightened principles of explanation, such as notions of 'culture' or 'ethnicity', could also form an anti-progressive cultural politics whose dynamics an awareness of these discursive strategies can help make visible. Nevertheless, these strategies are entirely constituted within the framework of an anthropocentric model of the cultural, treated as an effectively autonomous sphere determined exclusively by competing human identity claims.

Huggan's first and second strategies can be considered together. These are 'the representation of otherness and the racial/sexual other; the production of racial stereotypes' (24). He endorses the argument from Homi Bhabha that 'stereotypes are products of the desire for fixity in ideological constructions of otherness', providing a would-be secure general image of the other whose function of dependability is necessarily 'fraught with anxiety and ambivalence', or at times an image of idealization as well as of fear (the murderous savage but also the innocent 'child') (25).

This self-other dialectic produces a seemingly neat formula for sketching the workings of structures of domination and prejudice in a colonial context: the supposedly secure identity, say, of a masculinist self-image as hero, sustains its fantasy of justified authority by 'othering' people as 'the native', different and inferior. At the same time, the 'marginalized' other retains, in this set-up, a pivotal position that is immediately ready to be celebrated as its 'subversive' potential, one seen as revealing the socially 'fabricated' nature of the terms in which the oppressor conceives it, or as offering a person branded as 'other' a fertile artistic site for their own social critique. These last points correspond to Huggan's third and fourth 'strategies' ('the use of race as a signifier of exclusion; and the appropriation of race as a self-affirming marker, in which the previously marginalized racial other re-emerges as a self-validating writing subject', i.e. an author in his/her own right).

Once one has grasped the basic formal structure of this argument, and its dependence on a simple self-other dialectic (sometimes abbreviated as 'othering'), Huggan's literary history of Australia risks acquiring a rote quality. The job of the critic becomes effectively to trace the working of these cultural strategies. Thus, whereas a writer or critic may represent certain ethnic and other differences as natural or given, the critic will highlight instead their 'constructed' nature, and hence their complicity in form of social hierarchy and exclusion. Reading Australian literature in terms of these 'discursive strategies, which frequently collide and intersect with one another' (25), the undoubted insights of Huggan's survey become undermined by a sense of the formulaic. For instance, in relation to 'othering' as the definition of the self's identity through the exclusion or demonization of the other, Huggan draws the logically inevitable point that a 'tactical exclusion [of this kind] can end up drawing attention to itself, reinstalling the excluded other as an unsettling absent presence' (25). This point is then ripe to be modulated, in turn, into two logical consequences as to methods for reading specific texts. Either (a) an interpreter can offer a reading of the text at issue that brings to light and is critical of such strategies of exclusion or omission, showing them to be constitutive of the text's seeming coherence, as in the texts held to exemplify the Australian Legend, now re-evaluated as 'excluding Aborigines; . . . marginalizing women; . . . ignoring the city' (55); or (b) the critic can offer a reading of the primary text as itself knowingly dramatizing and making visible such 'exclusion' or 'othering', through its own strategies of irony or polyvocality. So while some texts associated the 'Legend' become the object of the first option, Huggan's more appreciative account of Miles Franklin's novel *My Brilliant Career* (1901) exemplifies the second. That is, the sometimes hackneyed discourse of the narrator-protagonist in that book is seen as being presented by Franklin in latently ironizing terms, as theatricalizing a colonial discourse that others in that society might have wished to present as merely given or natural. Huggan is referring to passages such as a piece of callow patriotic ranting in which the young female speaker seems to take up the masculine bombast of the Legend, or echoes bad nineteenth-century Australian poetry. Thus, *My Brilliant Career*, offering a 'pastiche of seemingly incompatible literary styles', can be claimed as being 'foundational in its capacity both to locate itself within an "indigenous" Australian tradition and to provide the grounds for that tradition's effective critique' (60). Huggan's own reading of Lawson also follows this second method. Lawson is seen as different from 'the Legend's standard masculinist account' because of the way his text highlights the fragility of cultural norms of the masculine (58). In Huggan's words: 'Lawson's focus . . . is often on male failure and inadequacy' (58).

Alternating between these two critical strategies, which are both anthropocentric kinds of middle-order scale framing, it is no wonder that Australian literary history can be said so often to show a tense interplay between 'oppositional' and 'complicit' modes of 'postcolonialism' (30).

CHAPTER SEVEN

Anthropocene disorder

It is too early to know if it is too late
(Bronislaw Szerszynski).[1]

Awareness of scale effects, in however partial a form, produces some distinctive psychological and emotional phenomena. One is the unstable tone of numerous environmental slogans, clichés and arguments, at once both portentous and trivializing. Thus a sentence about the possible collapse of civilization can end, no less solemnly, with the injunction not to leave electronic equipment on standby. Greenpeace's guide *How to Save the Climate* urges its reader to take showers instead of a bath and to measure time spent in the shower by singing a brief song.[2] The latent crisis of scale and agency underlies a derangement of linguistic and intellectual proportion, a breakdown of 'decorum' in the strict sense.

For others, the environment is now increasingly experienced not just as an object of physical perception but in new kinds of affect: an unusual flood can lead to rage against the crass advertising of a cheap airline; the violence and noise of a newly built local road may induce a sense of nausea at the hypocrisies of systems of politics dominated by the short-term demands of international capitalism. The very glare of the sun takes on fearful qualities: the sight of the sea and the sky is no longer of entities totally untouched by the human. This is also the realm of feeling sick at the sight of a mountain gouged out by mining. It means finding TV programmes that celebrate the natural world increasingly unbearable, for they already feel like re-animations of the dead.

Yet the Anthropocene itself, and its alarming future scenarios, is never visible in any immediate sense. This can often mean not being able to know if such feelings in response to any individual place under threat or environmental issue form an overreading or an underreading of the broader state of things. It is becoming increasingly plausible to connect freak weather events happening across the planet (certain extreme heat events in various countries, flooding in Northern India, drought in the North Island of New Zealand)[3] such that they make, together, a new level of overall meaning; call it the Anthropocene for short. At the same time, for the majority of people unaware of the complexities of scientific modelling, the availability of such an overarching schema for interpreting anomalous phenomena can render it a self-fulfilling mode of perception. We ask, what is the 'cause' of the mysterious diseases affecting amphibians, of the rise in the cost of coffee, the loss of a local road bridge to flooding? The answer is 'global warming' of course. Outside of the authoritative but still controversial precisions of climate modelling, the Anthropocene as an explanatory reference still hovers uncertainly in the space between empirical observation and self-fulfilling prophecy.

David Wood's scalar gap between 'what I can see and what may really be happening' increasingly feeds into a psychic syndrome that can be nicknamed 'Anthropocene disorder', a state of mind likely to become more widespread as the biosphere continues to degrade. The phrase is coined to name a new kind of psychic disorder, inherent in the mismatch between familiar day-to-day perception and the sneering voice of even a minimal ecological understanding or awareness of scale effects; and in the gap between the human sense of time and slow-motion catastrophe and, finally, in a sense of disjunction between the destructive processes at issue and the adequacy of the arguments and measures being urged to address them. In response, the mind is suspended, uncertainly, between a sense of rage and even despair on one side, and a consciousness of the majority perception of such reactions as disproportionate and imbalanced on the other.

Anthropocene disorder is also the emotional correlate of trying to think the implication of trivial actions in scale effects that make everyday life part of a mocking and incalculable enormity. The situation presents itself as both a generalization and yet a trivialization of Derrida's notion of genuine decision[4] as a negotiation with the undecidable (to turn a light on, to buy a particular kind of pineapple, to fly to a conference). The awkwardness is that, even as its stakes become higher, the term 'decision' becomes diluted almost out of recognition in relation to the kinds of daily banality implicated in climate change. Even the most ordinary actions become 'decisions' of acquiescence. At the same time, the very element that renders such actions potentially disastrous in the longer term, the effects of scale, also includes, necessarily, the almost complete irrelevance of my own 'decision' at the present time. Yet the less my share of the blame, the greater the overall responsibility.

How does one respond to or even perceive a scale effect – something that is totally invisible in any individual action or object but which forms a powerful and even disastrous 'entity' when considered in a global context? The emotional instability at issue relates to the way in which, with the spectrality of scale effects, there is no clearly proportionate response.[5]

Take, for example, that icon of environmentalist loathing, the urban four-wheel drive or SUV (Sports Utility Vehicle), needlessly driven for its supposed status, a notorious source of pointless pollution, symbol of the destructive nature of car culture more generally. To condemn an SUV is on the surface the stance of a simple or even simplistic green moralism, familiar and perhaps a little self-righteous.

This gut reaction of repugnance is in fact heavily mediated. It involves some knowledge about the climate, conveyed by technologies of communication; it is informed by a sense of the power and destructiveness of the oil industry, of the environmental vandalism caused by road building, as well as of the political and economic institutions that sustain and defend all this. It also involves a sense of the insidious dangers of scale effects – and on top of these, like the worst possible bad joke, comes the thought of leading climate scientist James Hansen's argument that to burn all of the planet's fossil fuels would lead ultimately to the total destruction of all life on Earth. Hansen surmises:

> After the ice is gone, would Earth proceed to the Venus syndrome, a runaway greenhouse effect that would destroy all life on the planet, perhaps permanently? While that is difficult to say based on present information, I've come to conclude that

if we burn all reserves of oil, gas, and coal, there is a substantial chance we will initiate the runaway greenhouse. If we also burn the tar sands and tar shale, I believe the Venus syndrome is a dead certainty.[6]

Such a scenario is impossible either to forget or to think dispassionately. Is Hansen's scenario all too plausible or is it a sort of frustrated hyperbole? The question merely intensifies the condition that this chapter nicknames 'Anthropocene disorder' (Figure 6).

Scale effects inhabit, contaminate and destabilize the meaning of an individual action or object such as an SUV, precisely in that its significance as an individual object is in a kind of

FIGURE 6 *The dead Earth.*

suspense, depending on just how many other sources of pollution there are or may be. So the particular SUV is a simulacrum of indeterminate others, its occupier is a kind of doppelganger, the one thoughtless or irresponsible driver is also all the other imaginable thoughtless or irresponsible drivers. This may be another reason why an environmentalist's repugnance at the one car, like much green morality, always seems disproportionate in each individual case.

In effect, a contingency, the finitude of the Earth and its incalculable ramifications, acts so as to divide, spectralize and alter the nature of each particular act or thing in an imponderable way. My act of condemnation is likewise spectralized, that is, it will remain an ineffective gesture of empty anger unless somehow also generalized, duplicated by innumerable others in innumerable times and places, and carried over into action.

So the affective force of the icon of the SUV is to be a bad-dream-like condensation of causal links over large stretches of both space and time, to other such machines and sources of pollution. This more truly imagined SUV is paradoxically also a *spectral* one, not in the sense of a diminished reality but in the sense of never being truly localizable, never just in one place but acting as a power at a distance, and also in its refusal to disappear, for the image and its force persists even if the particular SUV in front of me is taken out of service and crushed.

In sum, the more 'truly' the SUV is depicted in its connections and their implications, the more it may also seem to become a phantasmagoria of fears and the bizarre. The further 'out' into the real one thinks, then the more 'internal' the image of the one SUV must become. It is another insidious effect of the Anthropocene that psychically it induces, undecidably, a condition akin to paranoia.[7] How far is what is happening, including the thought of the complete destruction of the biosphere, out there or 'in the mind'?

Anthropocene disorder and ecocriticism

Anthropocene disorder is often in evidence beneath ecocritical writing. It is the emotional correlate of the kinds of cognitive overload described by Allenby and Sarewitz. It also inheres in the dilemma that workers in the humanities already feel when confronted with the scientific evidence for the dangers of climate change. As Richard Kerridge puts it in an interview:

> A threat like that, identifiable only by specialist scientists, demands of non-experts a special scrupulous exactness about the limits of our own knowledge. We have to confess our own reliance on debates in which we cannot intervene, yet not allow our uncertainty to become vacillation or passivity. [. . .] We are called upon to act with unprecedented collective decisiveness on the basis of a probability that we cannot assess for ourselves, is not yet tangible, yet is catastrophic in its implications.[8]

In the writing of ecocriticism, the overwhelming sense of the global stakes at issue accompanies, in individual work of specific texts, the sense that the readings may well be perceived to get things out of proportion in each case – can one *really* link up a comic monologue by Raymond Carver to implications of what might be the end of the world? This discordancy, this lack of balance, is what makes consideration of even a seemingly simple lyric like Snyder's 'Late August at Sourdough Lookout Mountain' representative of numerous other seemingly trivial actions and modes of thought in the Anthropocene, a general 'getting-things-out-of-proportion' that yet can't be dismissed. In effect, massive questions, often seeming too big for any one individual not to evade them, now inhabit, disturb or distort thinking about even the most ordinary-seeming daily actions. For instance, someone's commuting to work not only raises issues of the environmental impact of transport systems, such as the destructiveness of private car use, but also, and more profoundly, the question also raised in Snyder's lyric: what *is* human 'work'?

In her review of Morton's *Hyperobjects*, one might say that Heise is diagnosing a case of Anthropocene disorder in that critic's sometimes hyperbolic style:

> he [. . .] moves far ahead of science in relating everything from heat and droughts to species extinction, Hurricane Katrina, and the 2011 Tōhoku earthquake and tsunami to global warming: claims that most climate scientists would feel uncomfortable with, given the difficulty of establishing causal relations between

individual weather events (let alone earthquakes or extinctions) and long-term climate patterns.[9]

Objections like this exemplify how far literary and cultural criticism is now being driven to discuss issues and forms of expertise well beyond its usual scope. The difficulty is that modes of recognized intellectual procedure and a cogency of argument have depended on clear disciplinary demarcations, on each discipline of knowledge having its own hard-proven modes of evidence and argument, yet these have been breaking down.

Anthropocene disorder names a feeling of a break-down in the senses of proportion and of propriety when making judgements. Anthropocene disorder in this sense does not spare the latest intellectual trend in ecocriticism, the so-called material turn associated with Alaimo's 'transcorporeality' and with a 'material ecocriticism'. 'Material ecocriticism', with its stress on human embodiment amidst plural material and nonhuman agencies, has become a heading under which more and more critics have been working, affirming how familiar lines of demarcation no longer hold between areas of life and between intellectual or disciplinary categories '[M]aterial ecocriticism, focuses [. . .] on how "the linguistic, social, political and biological are inseparable" (Serpil Oppermann)'.[10]

This breakdown of normal disciplinary frames is exciting but also vertiginous. For Levi R. Bryant, since 'ecology' cannot now be confined to the disqualified notion of a realm of nature separate from the human then it must now mean simply a 'discourse on *relations and interrelations*'.[11] Thus it must be also a 'social ecology' which could look at how institutions effect gender identities (296), or 'the effects of smartphones on human relationships' (301), or the effects of material geography or other nonhuman influences on human social formation . . . – in effect, an 'ecology' of everything and anything.

This is another of the contrary tensions of the Anthropocene. On the one hand, a critic must now be suspicious of kinds of environmental, ethical and political containment that have operated in past forms of scale framing. On the other, how can the increasingly felt need to read a text or issue in relation to – effectively – almost everything else retain some kind of coherence and discipline? The deepest methodological challenge for 'material ecocriticism' is the relation of its theory to its practice. How to move from general tenets (for instance that 'the linguistic, social, political and biological are inseparable') to specific, disciplined interpretations of a text, even while demonstrating that 'All things connect and cannot escape into separation' (Steve Mentz)?[12] In practice, this breakdown of the barriers between intellectual disciplines can become too easily a breakdown of intellectual standards. In recent critical anthologies of such readings, such as *Prismatic Ecologies* and *Material Ecocriticism* (2013),[13] the manifesto aim of acknowledging matter as a form of emergent agency, and of 'regarding material configurations as texts' (Serenella Iovino),[14] can result in readings that follow a long, even torturous path through the specifics of very disparate texts or events, linked by rather loose threads or even just by association, all in order finally to conclude on a noncontroversial point that might just have been argued more directly at the start, with less expenditure of the reader's time. For instance, Ben Woodard's essay 'Ultraviolet' performs the idea of a kind of 'ultraviolet ecology', one, that is, which would acknowledge natural entities and forces as extending well beyond the limits of the human sense system. Yet readers find themselves asking, once they have finished the essay, if they actually needed to work through exegeses of such disjunctive things – Johann Wilhelm Ritter's discovery of ultraviolent radiation (fatal in Ritter's case), elements of F. W. J. Schelling's *Naturphilosophie*, the horror tales of H. Lovecraft (abruptly introduced as having an analogous sense of nature as ultimately inscrutable and alien) and finally some episode of *Star Trek* – all in order, in the final paragraph, to make a general point most readers would always have endorsed in any case, that is the need to reject preconceptions of 'nature' as limited to the pleasantly green and visible.[15]

The ethical thrust of the new materialism is that of most ecocriticism more widely, to influence the cultural imaginary,[16] and to do so by inspiring 'a greater sense of the extent to which all bodies are kin', 'inextricably enmeshed in a dense network of relationships'.[17] This is to instil a newly chastened 'welcoming humanism', meaning one that fully acknowledges human imbrication in material processes and that promulgates a vague ethic of care: 'the effort to listen to the world in the entirety of its voices is essential to the very project of being humans' (Serenella Iovino).[18] It is an aim that seems incontrovertible but also extremely vague. After all, a reader of 'material ecocriticism' can only be reminded so many times that ecology is all about interdependence (or that 'The ontological vision of the material turn is the picture of a world of inter-connected dynamics' (Iovino))[19] and that this should reinforce an ethic of respect for 'the other'. Yet material ecocriticism's attention to the agential effect of matter, as these emerge in new configurations, does not consider directly the most salient of such phenomena, the emergence of the human *en masse* as a new kind of thing, a Leviathan more like a geological force than a reflective being, along with kinds of threshold and scale effects that mock or erode old categories of ethics and politics, even though these are all we have.

Anthropocene disorder is coined to name a lack of proportionality, not out of a sense of old norms of consideration and demarcation calling to be restored, but of a loss of proportion *tout court*, vertiginously and as yet without any clear alternative. A self-proclaimed 'material ecocriticism' will only exacerbate this sense of disorientation if it does not move beyond the reaffirmation of easy ethical/'ecological' truisms.

Anthropocene disorder and nihilistic anti-humanism

Anthropocene disorder also effects a deep sense of bemusement and wonder at the nature of humanity itself, as well as disgust. Awareness of the Anthropocene has the dual effect of both highlighting assumptions deriving from 'humanism' – the view that human beings are a unique and, for some thinkers, the exclusive source of moral worth in the known universe – and questioning its now not so hidden costs. In environmental contexts, humanism becomes another version of anthropocentrism, the evaluation of all other beings solely as they relate to human use or aims. The knowledge of the collapse of whole ecosystems in the wake of human demands for resources undermines at a stroke the credibility of any claim that moral value resides solely in humanity.

Besides humanism in this broad sense, the widespread use of the word 'human' in ordinary language is now coming to seem an increasingly evasive and empty term of approval or tolerance.

To be afflicted with Anthropocene disorder is to find the very word 'human' more opaque the more it appears. Take a sentence such as 'the thought was only human', or the description of certain actions or attitudes as being 'human', or 'fully human', 'human and understandable', or phrases such as 'an intensely human story', or 'this film reminds us what it means to be a human being'. The platitudinous pseudo-profundity of such language forms a spurious gesture of intellectual closure, often tinged with an element of species narcissism.

This is not just a feature of colloquial language. It permeates intellectual discussion. For instance, the editor's introduction to *Passions of the Earth in Human Existence, Creativity and Literature* (2001) repeats the word 'human' like a mantra. The essays being introduced are seen as affirming 'processes through which the living being . . . distils a specifically human significance of life that makes it fully human . . . [with the] corresponding human "elemental passions of the soul"';[20] or, 'we will investigate our specifically human situation, the situation of the human condition within the unity-of-everything-there-is-alive'[21] and so on. If one counts it, in this not unrepresentative text, the word 'human' in a vaguely approbative sense appears in more sentences of this editor's introduction than not, almost like an incantation supposed, magically, to conjure up its own authority. The empty phrase 'fully human' even appears in this sense in Patrick Curry's attempt to dissociate the term 'humanism' from kinds of human self-aggrandizement, signifying instead 'the need to be humane, including but extending beyond humanity, in order to be fully human'.[22] Like the word 'natural', 'human' seems to operate in countless texts almost with the deliberate aim of benumbing thought. Yet now the clear emergence of the species as a capricious planetary agent reinforces how we barely know what the human is, even as we cannot but keep acting as if we did. The empty and even rather stupid word recurs ubiquitously, as a kind of blind spot immediately hidden by some simplified projection. Its meaning, otherwise hollow or tautologous, is really just this anaesthetic effect.

Alf Hornborg's question remains:

The natural scientists need to understand the specificity of the human species. Why do humans, of all species, pose such a threat to biodiversity? Biologists are not equipped to understand the driving forces of environmental degradation, for instance, in culture, politics, and economy. Conversely, social scientists trained to think in terms of 'social constructions of nature' are ill equipped to visualize a biophysical environment objectively endangered by human activity.[23]

In the humanities, most readings of the sources of human destructiveness will trace it to some social or cultural dysfunction – say to modes of exploitative hierarchy – often with the implication that some more ecologically benign form of human nature exists to be restored. On the other hand, anti-humanist thinkers such as Tom Cohen and Claire Colebrook read the categories of the human and the cultural per se as inherently out of kilter with the physical environment, as always potentially if not actually destructive.[24] One emergent effect of the current threshold in world affairs may be a realization of the degree to which human activity is caught up in and emerges from an impersonal dynamic it cannot command.

Baird Callicott hypothesizes not only that the realm of human work and practices is caught up in such a dynamic, but also that a certain latent destructiveness has been inherent in it from the first. He asks why our species has become such a catalyst and accelerator of capricious geological and meteorological forces. The question must dwarf any one answer, but a basic factor may be a kind of scalar disjunction inherent to the humanity per se. In this regard, Callicott makes a trenchant redefinition of the distinction between the natural and non-natural or cultural:

> What renders strip mines, clear-cuts and beach developments unnatural is not that they are anthropogenic – for, biologically speaking, *Homo sapiens* is as natural a species as any other – but that they occur at temporal and spatial scales that were unprecedented in nature until nature itself evolved another mode (the Lamarckian mode) of evolution: cultural evolution.[25]

By 'Lamarckian', Callicott is referring to a long-discredited theory of how evolution works. It hypothesizes the acquisition of an immediately favourable adaptation by one creature which is then passed directly into the bodies of its offspring, in contrast to actual modes of change in established Darwinism, which describe the slow accumulation of random changes over centuries or millennia, changes that happened to survive because they were favourable. Human behaviour, however, does change itself in a 'Lamarckian' way, because societies deliberately, consciously and often very quickly alter themselves in response to changing contexts, chances and demands, at least when these are direct, perceptible and immediate, and they pass these alterations on. For example, it was the invention of hand axes and spears that turned human ancestors into fearsome predators, not millions of years evolving a physiology of deadly claws and teeth. So it is not just that tool use and the prosthetic are, paradoxically, inherent to what the human is, but that the relative speed of change in these things means that the human, although not unique as an animal possessing culture in the sense of 'socially transmitted innovation',[26] inhabits a very different time scale from the rest of the natural world.

So 'human' names here the particular site of a capitalization of information and energy far speedier than in the rest of nature, making it a capricious accelerator and changer of Earth system processes, notably in the exploitation of fire and combustion.[27] In such a bio-cybernetic conception of life, 'culture' must be seen as an emergent development in evolution, and the Anthropocene as the latest and perhaps culminating manifestation of the human as an increasingly powerful force – or effect – of a scalar disjunction in the Earth's physical, energy and biological systems.

It is not hard to see how such disjunction, an anachrony in the strict sense, may become destructive through its own success. Without following through the implications of his arguments for our own species, the palaeontologist Richard Fortey makes some very pertinent points about the evolution of ecosystems in general, in this case during the Permian period some 250 million years ago:

As was the case with [. . .] other enduring ecologies, it is difficult to avoid the language of improvement, of adaptations getting better and better still, to describe the changes that happened in the ecosystem through time; but use of such language is misleading. The fairly obvious improvements in the musculature of the jaw, or in posture, among the reptiles are not a matter for the ecology, which works rather as a system. If one of the early reptilian predators had suddenly acquired the speed and efficiency of a tiger, the whole [. . .] system might have collapsed immediately. Changes in the ecology happen by animals interacting with one another; a better and faster grazer will be balanced by a more effective hunter, but not one that is so efficient that it eliminates its own food supply, as did the seamen who once feasted on dodos.[28]

Fortey does not say it, but the implication of such an argument must be that the human would be today the ecological equivalent of that hypothetical freak reptile which suddenly 'acquired the speed and efficiency of a tiger', threatening the collapse of the whole system of planetary life. To consider the human impact over the relatively brief geological period of 20,000 years, from the exterminations of large mammal species beyond Africa at the end of the Pleistocene to the intensifying, current mass extinction, is to be convinced that Fortey's hypothetical scenario is precisely what has been playing itself out.[29]

This discrepancy of scale is crucial to defining the eventhood of the Anthropocene as a threshold concept. The predatory supremacy of global neoliberal capitalism would represent a further, exploitative intensification of this scalar disjunctiveness, the 'time–space compression' described by David Harvey,[30] as a way of gaining power over human and nonhuman others. As Rob Nixon writes: 'the exponential upsurge in indigenous resource rebellions across the globe during the high age of neoliberalism has resulted largely from a clash of temporal perspectives between the short-termers who arrive . . . to extract, despoil and depart, and the long-termers who must live alongside the ecological aftermath and must therefore weigh wealth differently in time's scales.'[31]

Like numerous other environmentalist thinkers, Nixon describes the seeming advantage of capitalistic modes of exchange in terms of a discrepancy of scale, short-term gains against longer-term exhaustions. Such a description also stresses the increasingly visible element of human self-destruction in this process. The discrepant sense of time and change that once constituted human culture to such an adaptive advantage now overshoots its own material base.

In the work of Cohen and Colebrook, a similar view of the human informs an explicitly nihilistic argument, at odds with that humanist strain in ecocriticism that sees the widespread environmental destruction as an aberration from some more truly benign human nature, located either in the past or in some possible future culture that remains to be constructed. Colebrook writes that 'the human is not so much an event within life as a rupturing in the very figure of life: not one being among others so much as a violent symbiosis (or "sym-thanatosis") (. . . a "perfect storm" of death forces).'[32] This stance also takes issue with the lingering species narcissism to be traced even in emancipationist critics like Judith Butler. Cohen takes up Butler's 2004 *Precarious Life*,[33] a defence of the humanities based on their possible ethical force. He writes of how Butler is interested in the divide across which someone being considered fully 'human' is constructed, how some entities are included, others demonised or excluded. He first quotes her:

> 'I am referring not only to humans not regarded as humans, and thus to a restrictive conception of the human that is based upon their exclusion [. . .] If the humanities has a future as cultural criticism, and cultural criticism has a task at the present moment, it is no doubt to return us to the human where we do not expect to find it, in its frailty and at the limits of its capacity to make sense.'[34]

Butler is representative here of whole generation of literary and cultural critics. Her agenda, to 'return us to the human', is exemplary of the way the humanities have defended themselves by an ethic of supposed inclusiveness, as a defence of the particular and singular, the idiosyncratic, of the excluded or unjustly denigrated. Cohen, however, suggests:

> But it may be that the humanities do not have a future (in this way). The commodity of 'cultural criticism' offers itself incoherently – and does so with the premise that its ethical value lies in a reconciliation of *peaceable* others. Yet, it is still and precisely the artificed image of a human 'other' with whom 'we' would empathically commune that involves a foreclosure in the very way the 'social' or 'we' has been fashioned.

Cohen's rebuttal of Butler's kind of emancipationist humanism exemplifies arguments that the environmental crisis undermines rather than supports forms of humanism or species narcissism. The implication is that such narcissism is better confronted directly than, as Butler does, appealing to it even in order to support arguments against social injustice. To engage global environmental violence may not be just a matter of taking up already current ideals of the cultural, the 'human', of respect, recognition and so on, and extending them to others, including future generations, and to nonhuman creatures. Colebrook offers the bleak but unavoidable alternative that what becomes visible in the Anthropocene is that our very notions of the moral and ethical are at fault, that our normative conception of the human is evasively underexamined: 'What possible future could there be for morality given that the fundamental concepts of normativity and recognition require that I maintain some commitment to being the being who I am?'[35]

What might thinking in the humanities become if human ethics as such can now come under such intense suspicion? The emergent effects of the Anthropocene may include the notion that the human is inherently parasitic and polluting, leading to calls for a drastic re-envisioning of the humanities in terms that move beyond narcissistic kinds of humanism. Colebrook argues, in a book on human extinction:

> Let us accept that humanity is and must be parasitic: it lives *only* in its robbing and destruction of life that is not its own. Our current predicament of climate change, whereby we have consumed and ingested blindly – bloating and glutting our body politic through the constant destruction of resources without recompense – would not be a late accident, nor a misjudgement of a post-industrial age. To be a body is to be a consuming body, to be in a relation of destructive consumption with what is effected as other, as resource, through consumption. Climate change would be the condition of human organicism in general.[36]

There is however an oddly exultant tone to Colebrook's work on human extinction, and it can make her reader pause a little and take stock of these attacks on the traditions of humanism whose complacency and misprisions have enabled her critique. Take the rhetoric of the passage just quoted. Some of Colebrook's language implies some firm and even rather moralistic tenets – 'robbing' other species, humanity 'bloating and glutting our body politic' – language that clearly implies a transgressed moderation as norm, even as the thrust of her argument is that no such plausible norm exists. If so, however, what *is* the basis for the violent sense of condemnation and disgust in Colebrook's account? Her term 'blindly' implies that, if people were more circumspect, the destructive syndrome might be evaded, yet this is exactly what the nihilistic argument states cannot be possible, given that parasitism and destruction are said to be fundamental.

The clash in Colebrook's language recalls the unresolved and perhaps unresolvable conflicts revealed by thinking the world of the Anthropocene at different scales. To return to the Carver example, acts of generosity and self-denial at one scale of perception feed into syndromes of destruction at a larger one, but neither frame of reference is adequate as a basis for a definitive ethics or for dismissing the importance of the other. Analogously, Colebrook's language of outraged condemnation accompanies, contradictorily and unresolved, claims about an *inevitable* disastrousness inherent to what humanity is. Colebrook's version of 'Anthropocene disorder' draws on the denunciatory force of more moralistic kinds of environmental ethic even while denying their plausibility. It gives witness to a sense of alternative norms even in denying them; for in fact it is hard to see the point of writing a book that asserts forthcoming human extinction with an odd kind of intellectual exaltation if the traditions of humanism, idealism, speciesism and so on being shown to be destructive are not being attacked in relation to some implicit sense of preferable norms.[37]

Clearly, Colebrook's language implies that it is better to live than die, that the mass destruction of other species and places is wrong and that humanity, even as it becomes the object of an ever deeper disgust, also projects in that very disgust some norm, however vague, of better ways of life, however fragile and impracticable. In this way the Anthropocene, for all the hopelessness it induces, is also a threshold at which such norms are reaffirmed, even as the destructive and illusory is purged from given traditions of humanism and progressivism.

Notes

1 'Reading and Writing the Weather: Climate Technics and the Moment of Responsibility', *Theory, Culture & Society* 27.2–3 (2010), 9–30, 11.

2 Greenpeace, *How to Save the Climate – Personal How to Guide*, http://www.greenpeace.org/international/en/publications/reports/how-to-save-the-climate-pers/

3 These examples are taken from 'Explaining Extreme Events of 2013 From a Climate Perspective', Special Supplement to the *Bulletin of the American Meteorological Society 95.9*, September 2014.

4 See, for example, 'Force of Law: The Mystical Foundation of Authority', trans. Gil Anjdar, in Gil Anjdar (ed.), *Acts of Religion* (London: Routledge, 2002), 230–98, 255.

5 According to an Australian study of 2012, awareness of climate change now informs a kind of obsessive compulsive disorder (OCD). In past decades, OCD has been fed by the public anxiety of the day; once it may have been syphilis, then cancer, then HIV; now it is climate change. The disorder is characterized; it seems by a pathological derangement of scale in the relationship of individual action and global effect:

Some [. . .] worry that rising temperatures will evaporate water they leave out for their pets, and so they check the bowls time and time again. . . . One man was obsessed with the idea that global warming would make his house fall down. He compulsively checked the skirting boards, pipes and roofs for cracks. . . .' (David Adam, 'Prisoners of Thought', *New Scientist*, 26 April 2014, 36–8, 37).

6 James Hansen, *Storms of My Grandchildren: The Truth about the Coming Climate Catastrophe and Our Last Chance to Save Humanity* (New York: Bloomsbury USA, 2009), 236. See also Lee Billings, 'Goodbye Goldilocks?', in *New Scientist* 8 June 2013, 40–3.

7 'A woman told me, still with a sense of her original horror: "I worked out that for each tonne of carbon dioxide I'm responsible for, someone elsewhere in the world loses a year of their life"' (Rosemary Randall, 'Great Expectations', in Weintrobe (ed.), *Engaging with Climate Change*, 87–102, 92).

8 Isabel Pérez Ramos, Interview with Richard Kerridge, in *Ecozon*, September 2012, www.ecozona.eu/index.php/journal/article/view/317/624

9 Heise, review of Timothy Morton, *Hyperobjects: Philosophy and Ecology after the End of the World*, in *Critical Inquiry*, http://criticalinquiry.uchicago.edu/ursula_k._heise_reviews_timothy_morton

10 Serpil Oppermann, quoting Susan Hekman, in 'Rethinking Ecocriticism in the Ecological Postmodern Framework', in *Literature, Ecology, Ethics*, 35–49, 44.

11 Levi R. Bryant, 'Black', in *Prismatic Ecology*, 290–310, 296.

12 'Brown', *Prismatic Ecology*, 193–212, 209.

13 Serenella Iovino and Serpil Oppermann (eds), *Material Ecocriticism* (Bloomington, IN: Indiana University Press, 2013).

14 'Material Ecocriticism: Matter, Text, and Posthuman Ethics', in *Literature, Ecology, Ethics*, 51–68, 58.

15 *Prismatic Ecology*, 252–69. Stacy Alaimo's essay on the deep ocean in this same collection exemplifies the difficulty that 'material ecocriticism' has in turning its ecological generalities into a specific method of reading. Her 'Violet-Black' is effectively indistinguishable from many a piece of good, popular science writing on the deep ocean, except perhaps that she adds some observations on how thinking of such a zone displaces anthropocentric attitudes.

16 However, the mechanism of influence remains extremely vague, as in Levi Bryant's simply asserting that 'Theories Too are Agents, Entities in the World' (*Prismatic Ecologies*, 301).

17 Jane Bennett, *Vibrant Matter: A Political Ecology of Things* (Durham, NC: Duke University Press, 2010), 13.

18 'Material Ecocriticism: Matter, Text, and Posthuman Ethics', 66.

19 Ibid., 68.

20 'The Theme: The Passions of the Earth', in Anna-Teresa Tymieniecka (ed.), *Passions of the Earth in Human Existence, Creativity and Literature* (Dordrecht: Kluwer Academic Publishers, 2001), 1–12, 1.

21 Ibid.

22 'Nature Post-Nature', *New Formations: A Journal of Culture/ theory/Politics* 26 (2008), 51–64, 55.

23 Quoted in Adam Robbert, 'Six Problems in Thinking Nature– Culture Interactions', http://knowledge-ecology.com/six-problems-in-nature-culture-interactions/

24 For this anti-humanist school, see work in the *Critical Climate Change* series by Cohen and Colebrook from the Open Humanities Press, http://www.openhumanitiespress.org/critical-climate-change.html

25 'Lamark Redux: Temporal Scale as the Key to the Boundary Between the Human and the Natural Worlds', in Charles S. Brown and Ted Toadvine (eds), *Nature's Edge: Boundary Explorations in Ecological Theory and Practice* (Albany, NY: SUNY Press, 2007), 19–40, 36.

26 See Helena Feder, 'Ecocriticism, Posthumanism, and the Biological Idea of Culture', *Oxford Handbooks Online, 2013*. DOI: 10.1093/ oxfordhb/9780199742929.013.006

27   See, for example, 'Stone Tools made us Human', interview with
     Timothy Taylor, *New Scientist*, 21 August 2010, 48 – 'biological
     intelligence' here means the capacities of the brain itself, separate
     from the use of technical prostheses. 'We were never fully biological
     entities. We are and always have been artificial apes' (ibid.).

28   *Life: An Unauthorized Biography* (London: Flamingo, 1998), 234.

29   It is also notable that at the time of the Permian, land on Earth
     formed essentially one gigantic continent, 'Pangea' which has since
     broken up to form the continents as they are today. However, since
     humans now dominate the Earth, the suggested analogy holds well
     between the human species and Fortey's hypothetical freak predator
     that would have destroyed the 'whole Pangean system' (234).

30   *The Condition of Postmodernity: An Enquiry into the Origins of
     Cultural Change* (Oxford: Wiley-Blackwell, 1991), 240.

31   *Slow Violence and the Environmentalism of the Poor* (Cambridge,
     MA: Harvard University Press, 2011), 17.

32   'Not Symbiosis, Not Now: Why Anthropogenic Climate Change
     is not really Human', in *Oxford Literary Review* 34.2 (2012),
     185–210, 188–9.

33   *Precarious Life: The Powers of Mourning and Violence* (London
     and New York: Verso, 2004).

34   Cohen, 'Introduction: Murmurations – "Climate Change" and
     the Defacement of Theory', in Tom Cohen (ed.), *Telemorphosis:
     Theory in the Era of Climate Change*, Vol. 1 (Michigan, MI: Open
     Humanities Press, 2012), 13–42, 22, http://quod.lib.umich.edu/o/
     ohp/10539563.0001.001/1:11/-telemorphosis-theory-in-the-era-of-
     climate-change-vol-1?rgn=div1;view=toc

35   'Not Symbiosis, Not Now', 188–9.

36   *Death of the Posthuman: Essays on Extinction*, Vol. 1 (Michigan,
     MI: Open Humanities Press, 2014), 178, http://quod.lib.umich.edu/
     cgi/p/pod/dod-idx/death-of-the-posthuman-essays-on-extinction-
     volume-one.pdf?c=ohp;idno=12329362.0001.001

37   Mick Smith traces in Ulrich Beck's work on modern society as 'risk
     society' an unresolved doubleness or irresolution similar to that in
     Colebrook's contradictory meshing of terms of inevitability with
     those of responsibility and blame. See his 'Environmental Risks and
     Ethical Responsibilities: Arendt, Beck, and the Politics of Acting
     into Nature', *Environmental Ethics* 28 (2006), 227–46, 241.

CHAPTER EIGHT

Denial: A reading

*It was as far as their imaginations would allow,
and it was too far.*[1]

More and more people in the so-called developed world do have
an environmental understanding of the situation in which they
find themselves. They are aware that, for example, 'just' driving
to work, heating a house or 'just' flying for brief trip abroad is
not the whole situation, and that the larger-scale picture implies
a re-evaluation of the significance of what they are doing. In this
way, to keep on doing the same old thing – as if it were still 'just
driving to work' and so on – shifts subtly towards the status of
being a form of denial. The word sounds like an accusation, but
in these cases 'denial' is less the assumed property of a personality
than of the encompassing condition in which it finds itself. Most
modern infrastructure in the developed world is, so to speak,
denial in concrete, for the distribution of buildings, work places,
shopping areas and roads encourages or even enforces certain ways
of life, such as private vehicle use, and makes (only temporary)
sense in a period of cheap fossil fuel use. For millions of people,
the objects and routines of normal, daily life are forms of denial
in this extended, only distantly psychological sense, a subtle
mix of knowledge, inertia, self-deception, evasion and material
entrapment.

Environmental criticism in the Anthropocene is likely to be
more and more about unacknowledged denial. An environmental

critic who still thinks it normal or even prestigious to take an international flight to attend an academic conference would be one trivial example of this.

An alarming and pervasive 'denialism', what many call 'normal life', becomes itself an enigma for environmental thinking. Yet environmental writers are often still held back by certain strategic assumptions in their work. First, as John Keen writes, 'In spite of Darwin's contribution linking mankind with its biological heritage and Freud's account of the disowned operations of the mind, our public discourse tends to follow the Enlightenment view that rational thought now predominates.'[2] Thus now innumerable popular science books on the crisis, how 'we' got here and the cultural transformations 'we' must urgently undergo to avert further disaster are all implicitly investing in the Enlightenment faith that a deficit of understanding is at the root of the issue, and that once people know and understand the insidious dangers of the Anthropocene, the appropriate individual, social and political measures will follow. Yet this is to assume a naïve model of the human mind and behaviour increasingly being refuted by reality, a model premised on

a unitary and rational self, not one that is torn, ambivalent and in two minds (or several minds, for that matter); nor one whose sense of self, other, environment and so on is governed by powerful narratives, meanings and imaginings, nor one besieged by potentially overwhelming emotions such as fear, despair, anxiety, guilt, love or hope.[3]

The widespread and increasingly disastrous 'apathy' about climate change ascribed to many people in the developed world, always more interested in debating the location of some 'much-needed' new airport or 'relief road' than doing anything to help consider the mass extinction of life, is often not apathy, in a sense of not caring, or denial in the simple, pyschic sense, but withdrawal of affect as a sort of defence. To withdraw attachment to a threatened object is a way of protecting oneself.[4]

In respect of this definitive characteristic of the Anthropocene condition, some of Lorrie Moore's literary techniques in her short fiction from 1990 are uncannily appropriate. One text in particular stands out as a study of how daily life normalizes environmental denial. The oddly named 'Joy' (1990) opens with a powerful paragraph that, on the surface, bears little or even no relation to the story that follows:

> IT WAS A FALL, Jane knew, when little things were being taken away. Fish washed ashore, and no one ate a clam to save their lives. Oystermen netted in the ocean beds, and the oysters were brought up dead. Black as rot and no one knew why. People far from either coast shuddered to think, saw the seas and then the whole planet rise in angry, inky waves of chowder the size of a bowl. It was as far as their imaginations would allow, and it was too far. Did this have anything to do with them? They flicked off the radios, left dishes in the sink, and went out. (365)

This sets up a context for the rest of the text, something for which the usual word 'background' becomes inappropriate. Never mentioned again, the simple positing of this collapse of the oceans alters, without being explicit, many features in the subsequent narrative. It is clearly something far more drastic than merely the 'drought' mentioned in Alison Kelly's reading of the story.[5]

What does follow is a mundane and even mildly facetious account of the normal, routine of Jane's bland, prosperous suburban life in the Midwestern USA. Jilted by her German boyfriend whose motto, in mangled English, was 'you only live at once', her life has become a banal scene of evasive pleasantness, of forced indulgence in small pleasures (a spoilt cat, singing to herself in her car):'She knew there were only small joys in life – the big ones were too complicated to be joys when you got all through – and once you realized that, it took a lot of pressure off' (368). So the daily life of 'Joy', framed by the much bigger questions raised in the opening paragraph and then forever deferred, is that of someone hovering indeterminately between the state of being happy and having given up.

The disjunctions in 'Joy' – between title and text, the first paragraph and the suburban routines – instantiate a characteristic feature of the modern short story more generally. Short fiction in particular has developed ever-more sophisticated ways of making its brevity an artistic resource rather than a limitation, rendering it at times a virtuoso form of writing for engaging with situations or states of mind in which something is legibly *not* mentioned, or is evaded, or repressed. Ernest Hemingway formalized this in his famous iceberg principle – that a story gains its power from material that the writer, not an editor, chooses to exclude, such that its absence determines the contours of the text that readers actually follow. So, in his 'Big Two-Hearted River' (1925) a seemingly idyllic fishing trip is also a study of war trauma.[6] What is there continually *not* being said projects itself on to, or haunts or dislocates, the slow, almost hallucinatory clarity of descriptions of the river, of casting a fishing line, or making camp. In 'Joy', this characteristic of short fiction particularly suits it as a study of environmental/contextual denial.

At first, however, the topic of denial suggests a conventionally psychological reading of the surface, breezy narrative of 'Joy' and Jane's day. This is how Alison Kelly reads it in her *Understanding Lorrie Moore* (68–70). She takes it as the study of someone living after a failed relationship but in denial of its hurt. This includes memories of violently confronting her former boyfriend in bars with other women. Such a reading would be a very plausible exercise, a character study akin, say, to Katherine Mansfield's 'Bliss' (1920).[7] The striking thing here, however, is that this reading would also be itself an exercise in containment and normalization, for the immense dislocation and future disturbance implicit in the opening paragraph is thereby evaded. Like Hemingway's 'Big Two-Hearted River', whose slow, almost hallucinatory prose is so conspicuously *not* about war, but now in a doubled virtuoso manner, 'Joy' foregrounds a narrative of someone in denial of personal hurt as itself a sort of screen, blocking off acknowledgement of a more general, social denial: 'Did this have anything to do with them? They flicked off the radios, left dishes in the sink, and went out' (365).

Jane works in a delicatessen in a shopping mall, but part of the story is set in the waiting room at a vet's where pampered cats and dogs are treated, an odd contrast to the animal deaths of the first paragraph. On a second reading, however, as with Moore's other stories, one sees that simple hierarchies between background and foreground, central and incidental, environment and character, may be breaking down.

This is expressed in the motif of 'small things' that may not be so small. Jane seems to over-interpret things in a slightly paranoid way. She is taking her cat to the vet to be groomed and cleaned of a few suspect fleas. The fleas – more small things – become the object of a bizarre, even absurd meditation that briefly suggests another deranging of scales:

> There were rumours about fleas. They could feast on you five or six times a day and never let go. You could wake up in a night sweat with a rash and your saliva gluey and white, in ligaments as you tried to speak. You could look out at your life and no longer recognize it. (365)

Such a focus on an individual life and its vicissitudes, Jane's little narratives of loss and gain, comes to form for the reader a just-glimpsed recognition of the entrapments of knowledge and action at the individual scale. Its finitude is highlighted in 'Joy' through the unresolved disjunctiveness of its title and its opening paragraph and the slight air of facetious detachment in everything. For instance, there is a pseudo-epiphany about 'nature' – a remembered moment with the former boyfriend near the Mississippi, looking at distant trees, feeling 'that at last here was a moment she could take with her into the rest of life, *unlosable*' (emphasis in original) and it seems immediately mocked ('There seemed nothing so true as a yellow tree' (378)).

The 'little things' of the opening sentence reappear as 'small things' at the end. Darkly, this is in connection with fish:

> 'Let *every heart prepare him a room*', sang Heffie, her mouth full of fish. The world was lovely, really, but it was tricky, and peevish with the small things, like a god who didn't get out much. (379; emphasis in original)

The text refers twice, inconsequentially, to the fact that a workmate, Heffie, who snacks continually and surreptitiously at the delicatessen, has thinning hair. In fact, the text ends with a moment of sinister comedy. As a joke Heffie sticks a food tag into her hair as she eats fish with Jane and Jane's old school acquaintance, Bridey: 'the hair was vanishing, and the deforested scalp shone back in surprise, pale, but constant, beneath' (379).

The word 'deforested', with its fleeting image of a denuded landscape, takes the last sentence of the text back to the opening paragraph.

MANIFEST IMAGE

A term often heard in philosophical and scientific accounts of the human mind is 'folk psychology'. It is usually mentioned in contradistinction to the scientific worldview that all human psychology and behaviour be explained naturalistically, as instantiations of physical laws and the workings of the brain. 'Folk psychology' names that common-sense philosophy of mind according to which human beings are relatively free agents and that what they do can be explained by reference to such posited entities as inner thoughts, decisions, desires, projects and intentions, each held to be directing meaningful sequences of action and goal-oriented behaviour. In other words, it names that 'manifest image' (Wilfrid Sellars)[8] that we have of ourselves as people, of what being a person means.

Bruce Hood writes, 'It is faster, more economic and more efficient to treat others as a self rather than as an extended collection of past histories, hidden agendas, unresolved conflicts and ulterior motives.'[9] This common-sense model of mind has emerged over the millennia as seeming to provide a reliable framework in which to conceive of ourselves and our interactions. One way to inflect the reading of 'Joy' (and of the texts by Carver or Lawson already discussed) would be to trace how far narrative strategies and modes of characterization either help sustain or undermine this pragmatic fiction of personhood.

Clearly, from the viewpoint of naturalistic science, the 'manifest image' can be only a surface appearance or pragmatic convenience. Nevertheless – and this is the critical point or difficulty – it, and perhaps elements of the fiction Ingold names 'inversion' – seem socially necessary. As Ray Brassier writes, the importance of the manifest image is not as a description of fact – that this is what a human being actually is. It is normative in the sense of giving the basic framework 'that allows us to make sense of ourselves as rational agents engaged in pursuing various purposes in the world. Without it, we would simply not know what to do or how to make sense of ourselves'.[10]

In the humanities, the 'manifest image' is often reinforced by forms of second-hand psychoanalysis and sociology. It dominates almost all literary criticism with its widespread use of such pseudo-explanatory notions as 'the self' or readings in terms of 'a quest for identity' or personal or social 'narratives'. Clearly, insofar as ecocriticism sees itself as appealing to the self-image and cultural attitudes and subsequent intentions of its readers, it inhabits the day-to-day functioning of the assumption of personhood. The notion of the person as a site of intentional agency is not something about which we even have that much choice – what practical difference does it make to live knowing oneself the contingent product of evolution? '[M]an is that being which conceives of itself in terms of the manifest image. To the extent that the manifest image does not survive [. . .] to that extent man himself would not survive' (Wilfrid Sellars).[11]

Contemporary ecocriticism in particular is caught in a contradiction here, keen to stress nonhuman or material agency and critical of destructive delusions of human control, yet also deeply aware of the urgency of more decisive human action to help avert environmental collapse. Kerridge sums the perplexing situation (another case of Anthropocene disorder): 'there does seem to be something paradoxical about dispersing and qualifying our notion of human agency at the very moment when we need to make an unprecedented demand upon that agency .. . . it is hard to think of the rapid transformations we need as anything but an increase in human responsibility.'[12]

Nikolas Rose takes up the issue of personhood and the notion of responsibility:

> We may, as Nietzsche predicted in 1878, have come to recognize that 'freedom of the will is an error'. But we cannot, it seems, abandon the idea of responsibility. On the contrary, within the criminal justice systems of our contemporary cultures of individual accountability, we reconceptualize offenders as creatures inescapably required to bear full responsibility for the outcomes of their actions, and deem those actions to be moral choices whatever the material causes.[13]

What, however, if one emergent effect of the Anthropocene were the severe erosion of the credibility of this image of the human, especially as modes of life taken for normality increasing enact a condition of 'denial', less as a conscious psychic characteristic than a material entrapment? This suggests also a dark hypothesis that the Anthropocene involves a threshold at which the manifest image of personhood begins to have latently destructive effects. Consider again the readings of Carver's 'Elephant' and the way that what passes as normal life on a personal or individual scale, including acts of generosity, becomes part of a barely perceived process of destruction at the larger scale. The lived illusion of an intelligible and coherent world at the personal scale, centred on individual agency, its needs and projects, along with that intuitive but contingent sense of space given in our terrestriality, must now be juxtaposed with the insidiously imperceptible nature of scale effects, both in relation to atmospheric pollution and to overpopulation. These conflicting scales of the real may now become out of kilter with each other, and the contaminated complexities of things now mean that to continue in the previous priorities of the individual scale becomes latently destructive. Yet how can the scale of individual personhood not persist? A poverty-stricken farmer who rushes to exploit the thin soil left by deforestation may simply be striving to support a family, just as, in the Carver story, a character under financial pressure is prepared to drive ever-greater distances to find work. And what on earth would it mean *not* to be treating other human beings in terms of personhood?

The society in 'Joy' can be compared with Kari Norgaard's 'Bygdaby', a pseudonym for a northern Norwegian town that was the subject of her compassionate sociological study of climate change denial.[14] 'What perplexed me was that despite the fact that people were clearly aware of global warming as a phenomenon, everyday life in Bygdaby went on as though it did not exist' (xvi). Its people live a kind of double life. In parallel with Moore's in 'Joy', where the environmental disaster of the opening paragraph is clear for all to see or hear in the mass media, the kind of denial at issue is not a repudiation of fact, as with some politicized climate change deniers, but 'integrative denial', meaning that there is a failure or inability to 'integrate this knowledge into everyday life or to transform it into social action' (Norgaard, 11).

So for Norgaard, climate change denial in 'Bygdaby' is not primarily to be traced to the propaganda of the rich and powerful intent on defending selfish short-term interests.[15] She registers how society actively if unconsciously produces various modes and strategies for managing and maintaining denial, even in Norway, a country where knowledge of global warming is prevalent. Denial inheres, rather, in the fact that so many dominant ways of making sense or ascribing importance to things in ordinary life and social interactions implicitly negate, or at least would like to negate, the thought of global environmental disaster. Norgaard writes: 'In sharp contrast to psychological approaches to denial, the notion of socially organized denial emphasizes that ignoring *occurs in response to social circumstances* and *is carried out through a process of social interaction*' (9; Norgaard's emphasis), through conversation and its norms. Climate change denial may be implicit in things as innocuous as the trivial but entrenched conventions of daily conversation, the shared respect for certain expectations of sociability and composure. Lacking an adequate integrative context, anxieties about the future are only expressed in occasional individual confidences or passing jokes about the weather, rarely in socially sanctioned contexts that lead to any form of more active engagement or political activity. Norgaard makes instead the surprising claim:

> I wish to clarify that a key point in labelling the phenomenon of no direct activity in response to climate change as *denial* is to highlight the fact that nonresponse is not a question of greed, inhumanity, or lack of intelligence. Indeed, if we see information on climate change as being *too disturbing* to be fully absorbed or integrated into daily life . . . this interpretation is the very opposite of the view that nonresponse stems from inhumanity or greed. Instead, denial can – and I believe should – be understood as testament to our human capacity for empathy, compassion, and an underlying sense of moral imperative to respond, even as we fail to do so. (61; Norgaard's emphasis)

Norgaard's study of small talk in Bygdaby can also serve as a reading of 'Joy'. Moore writes, concerning a minor gesture of reproach between Jane and her workmate Heffie: 'Pleasantness was the machismo of the Midwest. There was something athletic about it. You flexed your face into a smile and let it hover there like the dare of a cat' (371).

There is then a pervasive sense of irony in 'Joy', though it is not the kind of irony that means knowing something others do not, from a stance of superior understanding. The effect is rather of a text pervaded by a knowing form of not-knowing, or a not-knowing form of knowing. It contrasts to that mode of irony in which, when something is said that seems absurd, self-refuting or just hackneyed, and we infer what is really meant instead. In 'Joy' the disjunctiveness itself, not some specific other referent, is registered as what is (not) 'meant'. It is a matter of 'denial', but no longer in relation to the sense of knowledge that feeds into the Enlightenment principle of telling the truth to oneself being empowering and liberating, the mantra of so many self-help books or works of environmental non-fiction. In this case, denial enables normal life and its small routines to continue. Denial is empowering, at least for the time being.[16]

Denialism also needs to become an object of specific studies in environmental education and thought more generally. Greg Garrard underlines just how little research has actually been done on the efficacy of environmental teaching practices. Can one assume a simple, direct route from environmental knowledge to environmental living? After all, contrary to received ideas, people can often be fairly well informed about environmental issues on the big scale but live with the usual disregard for it in their day-to-day contexts. Garrard writes:

> there remains a widespread, untested and untheorised assumption that education *about* the environment (nature writing, ecopoetry and environmental literature) delivered *through* the environment (place-based education) will automatically be education *for* the environment ('Problems and Prospects in Ecocritical Pedagogy').[17]

Day-to-day norms of attention, conversation and feeling make up what Steven Lukes calls a 'third dimension of power' (quoted in Norgaard, 133). Unlike the large-scale reading of Lawson's 'Telling Mrs Baker', in which vast, ecological dynamics are seen to ironize a human play-acting that has no sense of them, matters in 'Joy' are semi-consciously structured by illusion, but there is no would-be heroism, only an emptily sustained normality.

At the luxury vet, Jane watches a family, the Millers, come in to deliver their cat. It needs thyroid surgery. Later, picking up her own cat, Fluffers, she sees that the Millers' cat, which died suddenly on the operating table, is also being collected in a box marked, oddly, 'DOLE PINEAPPLE'. The reaction of the two children whose pet it was is no less poignant for being ironically framed by the opening imagery of general ecological collapse. This is not a satire of the sentimental, but a disconcerting kind of tonal instability, caught between a mundane, upsetting and easily grasped bereavement and a situation too appalling to be perceived or felt directly.

Norgaard's attention is also directed towards climate change denial in the United States. She cites studies of 'individualism' as a major discourse in which Americans are accustomed to think of themselves.

Americans are so immersed in the ideology of individualism that they lack the imagination or knowledge of alternative political means of response. Because climate change requires so much more than individual action, discourses of individual responsibility, rather than enhancing agency, merely '[alert] individuals to their essential ineffectiveness in tackling complex, global, environmental issues' (Norgaard, 192).

Garrard contrasts Norgaard's subtle points about conversations in 'Bygdaby' with evolutionary explanations of climate change apathy as owing to the 'mismatch between the capacities, biases and limitations of our "paleolithic mind" and unprecedented modern conditions'. Against this, Norgaard's diagnosis is clearly that the apathy, whether in Norway or the United States, is socially constructed.[18] This would be so, however, as an effect of the deeper form of 'denial' with which this chapter opened, one in which 'denial' is less the characteristic of a person than of the assumed norms projected by an encompassing infrastructure. Norms of conversation in 'Bygdaby', Lukes's 'third dimension of power' and, in a US context, the pervasive culture of individualism, are projected daily by that deeper, unspoken denial that literally persists in concrete.

Norgaard's points about the ideology of individualism can be applied to the superficial or merely psychological reading of 'Joy'. If one focuses exclusively on its foreground psychological narrative of personal hurt, one will block out the way this is itself a screen for a more general condition of environmental denial. This can be seen in Alison Kelly's reading of 'Joy' as the study of a woman whose self-composure has been crippled by a failed affair and a certain emotional guardedness, such that she 'experienced sexual love as a threat, not only to her psychological equilibrium but also to her very sense of identity' (Kelly, 69). The implication of Kelly's reading is that Jane is struggling in vain to regain a desired, more healthy autonomy and control over her life. In fact, Kelly's mode of reading, with its methodological individualism, becomes in its own way a case of denial, exemplified by Kelly's general statement about how to read Moore's texts: 'Disease and mortality infect several of these stories *as metaphors for the fears and unsatisfied longings* that make all the lives portrayed deficient or defective in some significant, and often devastating, way' (8; emphasis added). However, to read 'Joy' as a character study, with such a conventionally individualistic focus, has the effect of blocking off in advance considerations of such issues as the wider and more disastrous context.

Take for instance the following exchange in the delicatessen between Jane and her workmate Heffie, who is snacking food:

> [Heffie] popped it into her mouth. 'You ever been surfing?' she asked Jane.
>
> 'Surfing?' Jane repeated incredulously. She would never figure out how Heffie came up with the questions she did.
>
> 'Yeah. Surfing. You know – some people have done it. The fiberglass board that you stand on in the water and then a wave comes along?' Heffie's face was a snowy moon of things never done.
>
> Jane looked away. 'Once a couple of summers ago I went waterskiing on a lake', she said. 'In Oregon'. Her lover, the daredevil toymaker, had liked to do things like that. 'Khem on, Jane', he had said to her. 'You only live at once.' Which seemed to her all the more reason to be careful, to take it easy, to have an ordinary life. She didn't like to do things where the trick was not to die. (372)

Kelly relates this fear of water-skiing to Jane's broader sense of vulnerability, a fear of sex for instance. The individual psychological reading is again convincing but limited, and again it acts to block off other considerations, such as the way the image of surfing evokes an image of the sea at its most vital, contrary to what is depicted in the opening paragraph ('People far from either coast shuddered to think, saw the seas and then the whole planet rise in an angry, inky waves of chowder the size of a bowl'). The German boyfriend's memorable (mis-) statement 'You only live at once' (presumably for 'You only live once') could also be drawn into the mildly moralistic character study that sees Jane as a self-repressed and damaged person needing to release herself. However, it also expresses a kind of narcissistic individualism, a kind of moral denial – life being seen primarily as an object of maximum extracted gratification, something to be filled with sensation-seeking activities such as water-skiing.

Strikingly, in Kelly's individualistic reading, the momentous opening paragraph on the collapse of the oceans is misread simply as a 'drought' and seen entirely in the psychological terms: 'disease, decay, and death [. . .] reflect Jane's persistent morbid anxieties' (70). This rather obtuse framing of Moore's text instantiates Norgaard's argument on individualism and denial. The challenging thing here is the extent to which a critic's dominant sense of individualism as the norm, with a focus always on the quest for self-fulfilment, is actually *disempowering* when it comes to thinking about environmental collapse, or even, in this case, to registering properly a decisive part of the text at issue.[19]

Anthropocene disorder means the seeming loss of proportion – or is it the vertiginous experience of a true or truer sense of proportion? Or is it consciously not being able to know which is which? It inhabits the weird instability of tone in Moore's text. These questions relate back to many of the issues discussed in Chapter 4 on scale framing. This time, however, they emphasize not only the permeability of the frames that help produce a sense of order, and a relative measure of control and intelligibility, but also simultaneously, their unavoidability. Framing an issue on a scale at which one feels capable of dealing with it is clearly a desirable step, however insufficient, just as Selby's conventional reading of the Snyder lyric offers its own limited kind of closure. However, the unique dilemma of the Anthropocene is this: that one needs to think in contained ways that one knows, at the same time, to be insufficient or even perhaps as yet unrecognized forms of denial. Anthropocene disorder seems always ready to break out.

Notes

1 Lorrie Moore, 'Joy', in *The Collected Stories* (London: Faber & Faber, 2008), 365–80, 365.

2 John Keene, 'Unconscious Obstacles to Carting for the Planet', in Sally Weintrobe (ed.), *Engaging with Climate Change: Psychoanalytic and Interdisciplinary Perspectives* (London: Routledge, 2013), 144–59, 144.

3 Paul Hoggett, 'Climate Change in a Perverse Culture', in *Engaging with Climate Change*, 56–70, 56.

4 Renee Aron Lertzman, 'The Myth of Apathy', in *Engaging with Climate Change*, 117–33.

5   *Understanding Lorrie Moore* (Columbia, SC: University of South Carolina Press, 2009), 70.

6   In James Fenton (ed.), *The Collected Stories* (London: Everyman, 1995), 143–62.

7   In *The Collected Stories* (London: Penguin Classics, 2001), 91–105.

8   See Sellars, 'Philosophy and the Scientific Image of Man', in Robert Colodny (ed.), *Frontiers of Science and Philosophy* (Pittsburgh, PA: University of Pittsburgh Press, 1962), 35–78.

9   Bruce Hood, *The Self Illusion: Why There is No 'You' Inside Your Head* (London: Constable, 2012), e-book, location 214.

10 Ray Brassier, *Nihil Unbound: Enlightenment and Extinction* (Basingstoke: Palgrave Macmillan, 2007), 6.

11 Quoted in Brassier, 6.

12 'Ecocritical Approaches to Literary form and Genre: Urgency, Depth, Provisionality, Temporality', in Greg Garrard (ed.), *The Oxford Handbook of Ecocriticism* (Oxford: Oxford University Press, 2014), 361–76, 367.

13 *The Politics of Life Itself: Biomedicine, Power, and Subjectivity in the Twenty-First Century* (Princeton, NJ: Princeton University Press, 2007), 236.

14 Kari Marie Norgaard, *Living in Denial: Climate Change, Emotions, and Everyday Life* (Cambridge, MA: MIT Press, 2011).

15 For that, see Peter J. Jacques, R. E. Dunlap and M. Freeman, 'The Organisation of Denial: Conservative Think Tanks and Environmental Scepticism', *Environmental Politics* 17 (2008), 349–85.

16 Compare Norgaard's observation that 'the European nation that is threatened most by sea-level rise, the Netherlands, ranks at the very bottom of level of concern regarding climate change' (76).

17 www.academia.edu/233301/Problems and Prospects in Ecocritical Pedagogy

18 'The Unbearable Lightness of Green: Air Travel, Climate Change and Literature', *Green Letters: Studies in Ecocriticism* 17 (2013), 175–88, 178–9.

19 Kelly's misreading of the 'Joy' may exemplify just how far a certain kind of liberal individualism is taken as a given norm in the modern West, especially in North America. As Robert Bishop argues of social scientists:

Liberal individualism and political liberalism figuratively are the air social scientists breathe. Just as we rarely notice air as we go about our daily life, so social scientists barely notice how liberal individualism and political liberalism come to expression in or colour their inquiry. The practising social scientist simply sees her subjects of inquiry as individuals deserving of respect, tolerance, dignity and the like, as if that objectively is the way people are (in contrast to beings finding their identity largely in their allegiance to tribe or group as in premodern societies) (*The Philosophy of the Social Sciences* (London: Continuum, 2007), 109–10).

The seemingly incontrovertible nature of the aim of seeing others as individuals deserving of respect, tolerance, dignity and the like makes Bishop's point in itself. Whether one agrees with them or not, this understanding of people projects what are really *norms* of behavior in human interaction, not pre-given facts about what human beings *are*. Yet much work in the social sciences and literary criticism effectively treats them as such. As an example, Bishop cites supposedly objective studies of marriage and of religion, both of which are unwittingly structured by individualistic assumptions, and a correspondingly instrumentalist understanding of all phenomena in human experience as either enabling or thwarting self-realization: 'observers have noted how Americans, for example, frequently report that religion is a key source of personal satisfaction, as if spirituality is a means to their end of self-fulfilment. . . . Yet how could people under the sway of liberal individualism and an instrumental picture of life see spirituality in any other way.' (111; see also 179–86)

Bishop's point might suggest a sceptical rereading of George Marshall's suggestion that campaigners against climate change look to religion as a model of effective engagement in issues that seem to escape the spheres of more immediate self-interest. Marshall cites American sources on the satisfactions and galvanizing power of religion, but does so in terms that exemplify the deeper power of liberal individualism in that culture, something that may not be so obviously transferable to other parts of the world (George Marshall, *Don't Even Think About It: Why Our Brains are Wired to Ignore Climate Change* (New York: Bloomsbury, 2014), Chapters 41 and 42).

CHAPTER NINE

The tragedy that climate change is not 'interesting'

Ecocritics have been responding to a call for humanity newly to realize itself in its role as a truly global species. It would entail a new cosmopolitanism, transcending given cultural, natural, economic and social boundaries, the accomplishment of a sort of communal super-subjectivity – a peaceful, future epoch with humanity as the mindful steward of life on Earth. What else could there be to hope and work for? At the same time, these hopes should not ignore a crucial feature of the Anthropocene. This is its growing spectacle of the human as a species in the way other animals are species, that is as the creatures of a specific and a largely but not fully determining biology that plays itself out in individual lives over and above the way specific selves may perceive themselves and their goals.

The call to kinds of global cosmopolitanism has been met by various critical readings, but even more by the new kinds of art and literature that have arisen in recent decades to respond to what is now being called the Anthropocene. The result has been a great deal of innovative work, but the challenges and difficulties faced by such art have also been striking, given that crucial forms of environmental destruction cannot immediately be seen or localized, and resist representation at the kinds of scale at which most poetry, narrative or drama operate. The question that dominates this chapter, and which can be elucidated but not resolved, is this: are the limits of imaginative engagement emerging in these novels, poems, piece of music and in painting, sculpture, cinema, art installations and so on, merely the limits of now anachronistic cultural conventions, capable of reinvention? Or, more profoundly, does the Anthropocene form a threshold at which art and literature touch limits to the human psyche and imagination themselves?

Artistic work that attempts to convey the Anthropocene at its most counter-intuitive has the challenge of somehow mapping it onto those topics and psychological and cognitive structures that constitute the 'interesting' – not just for a small number of critical specialists, but for most human beings – for art and literature are nothing without a significant audience. Yet, as a source of profound emotional engagement – even for those specialists – how feasible is such a remapping? Or is the goal of instilling a widespread, deeply internalized and consequential engagement with the Anthropocene through cultural artefacts as hopeless as, say, trying to represent to a chimp the workings of mathematical calculus through the varying patterns with which hidden or offered peanuts are made available?

The challenge can be illustrated in a novel celebrated for its comparatively successful representation of a climate change drama, Barbara Kingsolver's *Flight Behaviour* (2012).[1] Maggie Kainulainen writes: 'because climate change as a totality can only be encountered through discourse, the issue of representation is key'.[2] Kingsolver's novel chooses the strategy of focusing on a small poor community in Tennessee whose local woodland has suddenly become a winter home for migratory monarch butterflies, settling dangerously further north than usual, a disturbance of their usual behaviour caused by an unstable climate, and one which suggests the imminent extinction of the species. It seems very possible they may not survive the Tennessee winter. The plot focuses on the life of one Dellarobia, a local woman trapped in poverty and a dull marriage, who first discovers the butterflies in the woods near her home. Over the next few months, she finds that she is falling in love with the charismatic Ovid Byron, an entomologist who sets up a temporary research laboratory on her farm and where she becomes an assistant, finding unexpected fulfilment in the role. Increasingly, as the novel develops, Dellarobia's hopes for the survival of the butterflies through the Tennessee winter and for her own future personal happiness and a possible career seem to become closely intertwined.

It is this aspect of the novel that illustrates the artistic challenge, and the limits of Kingsolver's particular mode of scale framing.

Because the monarch butterflies acquire so many personal associations for Dellarobia at a crucial point in her life, their final fate becomes increasingly impossible not to be read as symbolic of her personal trajectory. At first, it looks as if not enough of the insects have survived to ensure their future when they finally continue their migration. In the final section, however, as Dellarobia tells her son (and thus the reader) of the momentous decision she and her husband have made to separate, of her moving to a nearby town so she can attend college (her admission there made possible by Ovid Byron), the butterflies reappear overhead. We read, in the very last paragraph but one, that Dellarobia looks up to see

> Not just a few, but throngs, an airborne zootic force flying out in formation, as if to war. In the middling distance and higher up they all flowed in the same direction, down-mountain, like the flood itself occurring on other levels. The highest ones were faint trails of specks, ellipses. Their numbers astonished her. Maybe a million. (433)

Here, the insects seem to have come almost entirely to symbolize a positive turning point in one character's life, a kind of visual background music for Dellarobia's story. Kingsolver's decision to engage a reader's interest in climate change in this individualizing way exemplifies some of the, possibly inevitable, pitfalls in how a novelist may negotiate a global issue opaque to immediate or empirical representation. Kingsolver's novel has been praised for representing issues connected with global warming without sensationalism or much simplification. As Patrick Murphy writes in an appreciative account, there are many pertinent climate change issues that *Flight Behaviour* covers, including the various social and economic pressures that lead to environmental damage, such as Dellarobia's father-in-law's desire to clear cut the woods because he badly needs the money, and the insensitivity of environmental organizations to the pressures of real poverty (how can you respect an admonition to 'fly less' if you have almost no money anyway?).[3] Yet the challenge of representation being met by Kingsolver's focusing almost exclusively on Dellarobia's life also highlights other challenges in the way readers respond to novels: why is the trajectory of one, individual fictional life still felt by a reader to be so much more powerful as a story than that of the natural history of the insects, whose strange behaviour would still remain a harbinger of ecosystem collapse and extinction?

Even with a focus on such spectacular insects, readers' imaginations are still so much more easily engaged and drawn in by the human drama, with its humour, suspense, love interest and psychological identification, than by the environmental one, concerned with insect behaviour, largely invisible ecological and population dynamics, climate projections and slow-motion ecocide. Is the human imagination really so depressingly enclosed, able to be captivated only by immediate images of itself?

In so complex a context as the Anthropocene, narrative closure of the kind achieved in Kingsolver's novel will always risk being evasive. One could argue that, in fact, a pointed *disjunction* between the individual character's story and the fate of the insects would have made the text more provocative as a climate change novel. Personal success would then have been presented against the discordant backdrop of a degrading biosphere. Alternatively, the survival of the butterflies could have been juxtaposed with some personal defeat or resignation.

There is a case to be made that the psychology of narrative – of what makes for people a credible or compelling story – is itself a problem for representations of the Anthropocene with its plethora of Level III events. George Marshall's study of climate change denial takes up the question. In a striking experiment, Marshall describes how both environmental campaigners and climate change deniers often deploy an exactly identical 'archetypal' narrative structure when making their cases, with only the placeholders varying according to their respective convictions. Marshall writes:

> This experiment provides strong clues about what makes a compelling narrative –cause, effect, a perpetrator, and a motive (ideally one that is consistent with our assumptions about how we believe they might act). The most compelling narratives in climate change have this structure: Governments (perpetrators) justify carbon taxes (effect) in order to extend their control over our lives (motive). Right-wing oil billionaires (perpetrators) fund climate change denial (effect) to increase their wealth (motive).[4]

Seemingly compelling stories about the real state of the world may need to be treated with caution as to the source of their compulsion. Awareness of these narrative structures, as one reads or listens to debates, can turn what present themselves as arguments into the moves of zombie choreography. Marshall also observes that Christopher Booker, a theorist of narrative and author of *The Seven Basic Plots: Why We Tell Stories* (2004),[5] is also a leading climate change denier who has written several books for that cause, even losing a case for libel against Rajendra Pachauri, then head of the UN's Intergovernmental Panel on Climate Change (IPCC).[6] Marshall's point seems to be that a strong sense of how narratives work will make someone sceptical of some dominant stories about climate change, for they seem to fit so well the templates of a psychological formalism.

Adam Trexler's extensive overview of novels that engage with climate change is effectively an exploration of the adequacy of otherwise of narrative in this context.[7] Trexler values the novel form above all for its capacity to be relatively comprehensive as a tool of intellectual enquiry: what fiction can do is to conceptualize complex, heterogeneous systems: how national pride, bioengineering, aesthetics, familial love, social resistance, species loss, job loss, changing foods and flooding might all combine to create ways of life in the future. He does not, however, really take up the thorny question of reader response, of what gives a novel emotional force for a readership, focusing instead of how far any text achieves a representationally accurate model of the multiple realities of the Anthropocene.

Take, for example, George Marshall's own novel *The Earth Party: Love and Revolution at a Time of Climate Change* (2009).[8] This can be evaluated as a kind of thought-experiment, one in which a writer strives genuinely to conceive and depict, within the conventions of empirical and psychological plausibility that constrain realist fiction, a future scenario in which governments and other bodies come together in response to radical environmental activism and effectively confront and genuinely mitigate climate change. In this respect, the very implausibility of the result has implications darker than objections that Marshall's novel is too creaky: 'Marshall's novel is something of a test case, because of the extraordinary transformations it must make to the Earth Party's political organization and environmental aims in order to make it a viable power' (Trexler, 121). Here, as with the comparable case of Robinson's Washington trilogy, discussed in Chapter 4, even the relative failure of a novel can offer insight: 'On the strength of evidence, fiction seems to have great difficulty in imagining how radical environmental politics could lead to a fundamental shift in our culture's dependence on fossil fuels' (Trexler, 135).

Nevertheless, Trexler also argues:

> Climate change is not just a 'theme' in fiction. It remakes basic narrative operations. It undermines the passivity of place, elevating it to an actor that is itself shaped by world systems. It alters the interactions between characters and introduces entirely new things to fiction. (233)

These are exciting claims, but they may also need to be qualified. Take the account of Ian McKewan's *Solar*,[9] a comic 'cli-fi' novel that Trexler claims to be innovative in the attention it devotes to the agency of material things and their effects on plot. His argument hinges around the depiction of McEwan's comic central character, Michael Beard, a corrupt, opportunistic scientist who is using the publicity surrounding climate change and his climate-related research to promote himself and his selfish and environmentally irresponsible lifestyle. The central move of the plot is that Beard has stolen a crucial invention, artificial photosynthesis, from a colleague, Aldous, who died before making it public. Trexler argues that the way this material invention is so central to the plot drives the novel beyond the conventions of 'literary realism' into something new which he nicknames 'scientific realism':

> Nor is character [in *Solar*] a stable entity on which to build a reading: it is not merely hypocrisy that transforms Beard's political self from one who sees no significant difference to the world at large if Bush or Gore finally wins the US election in 2000, to a 'lifelong Democrat' who describes the same election as a time 'when the Earth's fate hung in the balance, and Bush snatched victory from Gore to preside over the tragedy of eight wasted years' [. . .] Rather, the photosynthesis technology Beard steals from Aldous remakes his inner affections and his political alliances, forming an alliance with his brazen self-interest. *Solar* [. . .] is not an example of social, political, or human realism, but rather a network of humans and nonhumans assembled by the force of climate change. (Trexler, 68)

Trexler's argument here that nonhuman agency (the technology) undermines 'human realism' is not convincing, nor does it support the claim that climate fiction such as this is radically new. Beard's motives and alliances are of course altered by his possession of the technology, making it an agent in the plot, yet would not a character suddenly transformed by desire for some hoard of gold – not exactly an uncommon motif in literature – also be a recipient of 'nonhuman agency' in the way described? Do not innumerable novels and films, especially detective fiction or those involving court cases or reconstructions of a crime or event, almost always work through tracing the vectors of narrative projected by material things, such as a found weapon, a lost diary, a blocked door . . .? Trexler is not really describing an innovation in the novel form per se: he is describing a mode of critical reading newly sensitized by the demands of the Anthropocene, one become suspicious of readings that give exclusive primacy to pre-given psychological motives as agents of the plot. This new mode of reading is not exclusive to accounts of climate change fiction – the reading of Raymond Carver given earlier, for example, also pivots around nonhuman agency, in that case material infrastructure.

A strength of Trexler's study of climate fiction, as it traces the various failings, fallings-short and hard-won successes in representations of the Anthropocene, is that this tracing also draws a strong picture, implicit but omnipresent, of those norms of response, interest and engagement that need to be overcome. In literary representations of the Anthropocene the techniques available to engage a reader's immediate emotional interest emerge as most often at odds with the scale, complexity and the multiple and nonhuman contexts involved. Thus politically engaged novels and films almost always dramatize the issues in the form of a confrontation or conflict between the stance of characters with opposing views, so that a reader's or viewer's engagement with intellectual debate tends to become eclipsed by familiar modes of suspense and identification, which usually have more to do with the human psychology of competition or self-fulfilment (as in Dellarobia's case) than with the true complexities of the issue. The major question raised here, and by consideration of Kingsolver's novel, is suggested at the beginning of this chapter: are the limits of readers' engagement being encountered merely those of now dated cultural and artistic conventions capable of change and reinvention?

Or does the challenge of representing major ecological issues mean acknowledging the limits of the human capacity for engagement beyond certain scales in space or time, and beyond the spheres of immediate identification or empathy? This limit could be inexorable, just as we have no choice in our day-to-day interactions with each other but to let 'folk psychology', the immediate conception of oneself and others as autonomous, intention-directed 'persons', override the viewpoint of naturalistic science, even while knowing our norm of personhood to be a kind of pragmatic fiction.

Related questions are raised by so-called cli-fi novels such as *The Rapture* (2009) (Liz Jensen), or *Finitude* (2009) (Hamish MacDonald).[10] Extreme environmental scenarios unfold with a kind of remorseless logic whose effect of protest is undone by their aesthetic logic of increasing suspense, in which horror merges with a kind of gripping excitement. The more graphic the depiction of flooding or drought, the more it becomes a phantasmagoria, an unacknowledged indulgence in a pleasurable destructiveness, whose very dream-like qualities compromise its attempted status as a sort of activist fiction, making it another case of Anthropocene disorder. This syndrome clearly affects projections of actual global warming in the media: to cite again the Australian journalist Philip Adams quoted in Chapter 1, 'the more the scientists predicted a catastrophe, the more the audiences seemed to like it'.

William Flesch, while arguing against that 'armchair evolutionary psychology' that sees human psychology as 'hard-wired' to a very specialized level, nevertheless makes a very convincing case that human interest in narratives stems from our evolution as social creatures, endlessly monitoring each other in the contexts of living in tightly cooperative and/or competitive groups, extraordinarily sensitive to issues of fairness, favouritism, just deserts and blame. Consequently, the human interest in narrative will 'always depend on our emotional recognition of motive and desert among characters'.[11] In this respect, it is chastening that the end of *Flight Behaviour* so closely matches this theory of the primary appeal of narrative – its sense of closure for the reader is less about the butterflies, or about the environment, but the performance of a sense of 'poetic justice' among the human protagonists.[12]

What is often perceived as the 'boring' quality of environmental issues bears out the problem. In mass media and other representations there seems inevitably always a more immediate interest in interactions between human beings, with issues of cooperation, fairness, cheating, deception, attraction/repulsion and justice, than with the possible workings of some physical or meteorological system. Thus, debate about climate change becomes soon a scene of accusations and counter-accusations, and less about the meteorological claims being made than those making them and their alleged interests. The tendency in literary and cultural criticism over the past generation to make any issue in life exclusively into a function of cultural politics enacts a comparable syndrome – the deeper interest of an issue is held to lie in competition for power, authority or recognition between humans in the present. Such criticism may – in part at least – be walking into a kind of anthropological and anthropocentric trap.

The Anthropocene as threshold to a new phase of art?

Timothy Morton suggests that the art of the Anthropocene, meaning in this case art roughly post-1945, represents a new phase of art history previously unrecognized. Using G. W. F. Hegel's philosophy of art as a foil, Morton defines the new phase as arising in a rejection of the phase which, he argues, has dominated since Hegel defined it in the early nineteenth century, the 'romantic' phase. This is used to describe the understanding of art as a privileged means of human expressiveness. Now, however, the emerging awareness of effects of nonhuman agency sidelines theories of art that see it solely as an instrument of human self-expression, whether individual or social, with the object world taken as only being of interest when reflecting human interiority or in some way (see *Hyperobjects*, 161ff). With the paintings of Jackson Pollock in the 1940 and 1950s, for example, 'Paint and brushes and drips started to set themselves free from the inner space whose representation they were supposed to be, in some ironic, half-failed way.'[13] Morton also refers to other works in which the materiality and formal qualities of a piece come to displace or overwhelm the kinds of cognitive, representational, intentional or expressive elements that they might have been supposed to convey, as in kinds of expressionist painting that abolish 'the play between background and foreground' (*Hyperobjects*, 76). Consequently, the putative new phase of art that Morton suggests is one which stresses disjunctiveness, a being-overwhelmed by contexts in which the human perceiver is deeply implicated but cannot hope to command or sometimes even to comprehend. Morton talks of art that evokes 'in its very form' his conception of hyperobjects, that is, 'massively distributed objects that can thought and computed, but not directly touched or seen'.[14] For instance, he refers to John F. Simon's *Every Icon*, a piece of algorithmic software art, easily found online, where we read

> The piece consists of a 32 × 32 square grid where every square can be colored black or white. *Every Icon* starts with an image where every square is white and progresses through combinations of black and white squares until every square is black. The piece will show every possible image. Although it takes only 1.36 years to display all of the variations along the first line, it takes an exponentially longer 5.85 billion years to complete the second line.[15]

Morton's 'new phase of art' would best be thought 'as a strange asymmetry between equally matched forces: the human capacity for knowledge and computation on the one hand, and the gigantic and withdrawn hyperobjects on the other'.[16] For instance, 'the gigantic billowing waves of plastic cups created by Tara Donovan in *Untitled (Plastic Cups) (2006)*' reveal 'properties hidden from the view of a person who uses a single cup at a time' (*Hyperobjects*, 114). Also, 'Felix Hess allows us to hear the sound of air pressure fluctuations over the Atlantic by recording sounds from microphones placed on a window, then speeding up the recording to a more-than-human speed' (*Hyperobjects*, 175). Morton also affirms art-forms or scenes from TV programmes that convey some experience of the seeming paradox of something being itself and not-itself at the same time, both container and contained, implicated abyssally in modes of space and time beyond perception and so on. 'Art can now only be an uneasy collaboration between humans and nonhumans, not a purely human exploration of access to nonhumans, or the lack thereof' (*Hyperobjects*, 50).

Morton's proposed new phase of art history is representative of a recent critical trend among thinkers engaged with art and climate change. Colebook's arguments are similar. She writes that 'there is something interesting, at the very least, in visual productions that short-circuit recognition', citing in this respect the Dadaist Marcel Duchamp's so-called readymades (indifferent everyday objects disconcertingly presented as having the dignity of works of art).[17] Maggie Kainulainen draws on the old category of 'the sublime' and applies it to the Anthropocene. She writes that 'the sublime, in all its theorizations, is marked by an event or encounter with something so vast that it escapes all attempts to apprehend it fully' and she finds 'sublime potential' in the challenges of representing climate change with works such as John Quigley's 'Melting Vitruvian Man'.[18] In a recent essay, Bernd Herzogenrath draws readers' attention to the 'sound art practice' of the environmental activist John Luther Adams in Alaska.[19] This is music that does not try to imitate or evoke natural scenes or processes but which sets up technical means by which those processes themselves can be made to generate sound. Using information from weather stations and collaboration with scientists, as Adams describes in his *The Place Where You Go To Listen* (2004),[20] soundscapes can be made out of the rhythms of day and night, weather, seismic data and changes in the Earth's magnetic field.

As a posited geological epoch in which humanity will have affected the planet to such a degree as still to be visible in the geological strata in millions of years' time, the more strictly geological concept of the Anthropocene entails the chastening projection of future human extinction. In this respect, Colebrook turns to modes of art that attempt a nonhuman or inhuman vision of phenomena: 'one might say that climate change should not require us to return to modes of reading, comprehension and narrative communication but should awaken us from our human-all-too-human narrative slumbers.'[21] Jonathan Bate misread Keats's 'To Autumn' as not human-centred, but Colebrook affirms more convincingly kinds of art that effectively short-circuit or resist the human brain's drive to process sensuous percepts into familiar norms and meanings. She refers to some recent films by Danny Boyle, 'The figure of a frozen Sydney opera house, a London where Trafalgar Square is desolate, layers of rock distorted through a camera lens that is not a point of view for anybody, an underwater Manhattan, or a sunlight so bright that it would destroy the eye.'[22] An art correlated to the Anthropocene is one that, however momentarily, dispels the phantasm of human normality.

Ecocritical work on art like this is effectively offering a new theory of the avant garde, reaffirming the still prevalent idea of art as a cultural vanguard. The term 'avant garde' is especially appropriate here if one takes it in the contentious sense of that phrase argued in Peter Bürger's *Theory of the Avant Garde* (1974).[23] Bürger saw the essence of the avant garde as being an attack on art itself *as a cultural institution*, as distinct from it being a matter of the content of individual works. By 'institution' here is meant that act of framing whereby something is taken as demanding attention '*as art*', so that even a piece of random prose or an everyday object can become so-called found art. The institution of art involves not just a host of cultural assumptions and beliefs, but also galleries, publishers, publicity mechanisms, laws of property and copyright, reviewers, systems of education and notions of cultural and social status. Bürger identifies the avant garde above all with the anti-art of the 'Dadaist' movement of the early twentieth century:

> with the historical avant-garde movements, the social subsystem that is art enters the stage of self-criticism. Dadaism, the most radical movement within the European avant garde, no longer criticizes schools that preceded it, but criticizes art as an institution, and the course its development took in bourgeois society. The concept 'art as institution' as used here refers to the productive and distributive apparatus and also to the ideas about art that prevail at a given time and that determine the reception of works. (Bürger, 22)

Avant garde works like Duchamp's readymades were mocking art as a bourgeois institution that can make anything the object of a mode of attention that relishes the supposed refinement of its own stance – the aesthetic realm functioning as an institution of social hierarchy.

The hypothetical new phase of Anthropocene art is seen to do something comparable. In this new context, the interest is still in works that question the institution of art. Clearly, relations of cultural, social and even military power are there to be unmasked in works such as Donovan's plastic bottles, as they would be in earlier sorts of avant-garde art, let alone in the sound of an atomic explosion (Morton, 'Poisoned Ground', 37). However, unlike the avant garde that is Bürger's focus, we are also engaged in these works with the recalcitrance of human terrestriality and scale, and the illusions of autonomous personhood. So, underlining the presence or intervention of the nonhuman in the human field of perception, or highlighting the finitude and thingness of the human itself, what this art uncovers is not just a cultural issue but a more intractable, less decidable hybrid of the cultural and the biological or anthropological. The realms of human intentions, expressiveness and the aesthetic give way to a new sense of finitude and participation in materiality: 'It's not reality but the subject that dissolves, the very capacity to "mirror" things, to be separate from the world' (*Hyperobjects*, 35).

This putative avant garde also concerns real phenomena re-framed as a kind of installation art – as in the sound-art already mentioned by John Luther Adams or Hess's *Air Pressure Fluctuations* ('when I hear *Air Pressure Fluctuations*, I am hearing the standing wave caused by pressure changes over the Atlantic Ocean' (Morton, *Hyperobjects*, 56)). At the same time, one notes the almost complete absence of literature or the arts of language from the discussion, something surprising given that Morton, Colebrook, Herzogenrath and Kainulainen are all literary critics. Linguistic narrative in particular seems at issue solely as that mode which, by implication, fits least well the demands of the Anthropocene, seemingly more allied with forms of anthropocentric thinking to be overcome, or as an art of sequences of human action or attention geared to a definite significant end in some fulfilled or unfulfilled intention. 'Narrative' here always names something to be interrupted, broken or questioned. Even Morton's reference to J. G. Ballard's *Empire of the Sun* (1984) and a quotation about the atom bomb dropped on Japan cites Steven Spielberg's 1987 film of the novel, not the book itself ('It was a white light in the sky. Like god taking a photograph') (*Hyperobjects*, 50). If Morton makes a reference to poetry in *Hyperobjects* it is to heightened episodes that interrupt the would-be narrative continuity of purposive perception, such as the quasi-traumatic breakdowns of normal perceptual categories that William Wordsworth labelled 'spots of time' (*Hyperobjects*, 51, 72).

Some questions

Duchamp's readymades now fetch high prices in auctions, precisely as novel works of art. The original avant garde became quickly assimilated into the very institution it sought to undermine. Is a comparable danger lurking for the putative environmental avant garde described by Morton and others?

This putative movement, such as it is, comprises works that strive to shake human cultural frames and scales of perception, revealing our own implication in material dynamics we cannot command and the illusoriness of any would-be sovereign overview. Morton relates such environmental anti-art to his notion of hyperobjects, whose effects he wishes to assimilate to the intellectual tradition of post-enlightenment, would-be liberatory critique: 'The panic and denial and right-wing absurdity about global warming are understandable. Hyperobjects pose numerous threats to individualism, racism, speciesism, anthropocentrism, you name it. Possibly even capitalism itself' (*Hyperobjects*, 21). This seems attractive, if tentative.

However, the new avant garde is also being recuperated too hastily into ethical and cultural agendas one would have expected it to question. Even as some of the artworks are acknowledged as producing disgust and pain, Morton's position on them becomes an underdefined and mildly sentimental ethic of care arising from the knowledge of interconnection and interdependence. He writes that our obligation to others is due to 'the simple fact that existence is coexistence' (*Hyperobjects*, 125), which is 'after all what ecology profoundly means' (*Hyperobjects*, 128). Hyperobjects, as known through such art, are said to intervene positively in prisoner dilemma/tragedy-of-the-commons type situations by bringing others nearer into a recognizably shared space, 'an already-existing intimacy with all lifeforms, knowledge of which is now thrust on us whether we like it or not' (*Hyperobjects*, 124). However, Morton does not engage with an issue all too relevant to many of the works he celebrates, that human beings often find spectacles of violence and abjection pleasing and enjoyable, whatever the concomitant sense of fear or horror. So, artworks whose implications seem so clearly anti-humanist are still being framed by humanist readings that implicitly depend on the hope that a prompted knowledge of interdependency is also the awakening of an 'ethics of the other', 'beyond any meaningful limit of self-interest' (*Hyperobjects*, 124).[24]

Kainulainen observes similarly 'the profound meaning that climate change can reveal: interconnection, and its ethical implications'. Art of the kind celebrated by Kainulainen, as well as by Morton, and Herzogenrath, is held to make spectators newly aware of interrelatedness, to weaken fantasies of appropriation and to help them take responsibility for their existing modes of life. It is hard, however, to endorse here the assumption that knowledge of interconnection must somehow lead to an ethic of care. Morton acknowledges the 'weakness' or lack of compulsion of this ethic, for 'the other' at issue may be distant or in the future (*Hyperobjects*, 123). Would not equally plausible alternative responses be that the effect of much of this art could be to strengthen fear and disgust, reinforce a heightened anxiety about protecting one's own future interests or produce support for the 'Voluntary Human Extinction Movement', VEHEMENT?[25] Rather than foreclose the kind of cultural work done by this vague and emerging avant garde, is it not better to step back a little from imposing too hasty readings upon it, let alone slightly moralizing ones?

Discussions of art, literature and the Anthropocene are at an extremely early stage. However, it seems worth suggesting some further implications of the work surveyed in this chapter.

The first implication concerns the nature and limits of climate change fiction. Trexler offers an insightful overview of the intellectual challenges of this material. Nevertheless, he does not touch on an issue which must severely qualify even the relative successes in some of the more recent novels he analyses. This is the issue of the mode of readers' engagement and, above all, the obvious but important fact that the work at issue is being read *as a novel*, as a work of imaginative fiction that a reader will always know as such, however achieved its representation of some of the more elusive aspects of the Anthropocene. If avant-garde art, in both its old and revisionist guises, faces the paradoxical need of resisting the very institution of art, then that subset of it which might be called the 'institution of the novel' is always a latent neutralization of its content. Thus, inevitably, many of the reviews of Paolo Bacigalupi's *The Windup Girl* (2010),[26] an SF novel Trexler deems successful in capturing some aspects at least of climate change, remain primarily an appreciation of Bacigalupi's performance of his art, as in the promises of consumer pleasure quoted on the book's back cover: 'One of the finest SF novels of the year'; '. . . enjoy the darkly complex pleasures of *The Windup Girl*'. The institution of the novel forms a limit both to the possible impact of climate change fiction and to the hope of ecocriticism that the informed reading of it can take on a crucial role of political and social leadership. After all, a specific work of environmental criticism can only ever have a *derivative* impact, as a function, that is, of the social status and force already granted literature, criticism and the realm of cultural representations more generally. This suggests that thinkers working to build on Trexler's project would need to take up broader questions such as the social–political functions of literature and its reception, its imbrication in education systems and the entertainment industries and the dominant valorization of the reading experience as a kind of consumer commodity.

This point also suggests a revaluation of one of the most noted supposed weaknesses of early ecocriticism in the 1990s, namely its focus on kinds of environmental non-fiction and 'nature writing', and correspondingly, its awkward discomfort with the very category of fiction. At the time, a certain narrowness of generic focus seemed a limitation for a thinking striving for acceptance as a form of literary criticism. Yet, a more generous, retrospective hypothesis about that awkwardness with fiction suggests itself. Larry Shiner's *The Invention of Art* (2001) traces from the late eighteenth to the nineteenth century the rise of the category of the aesthetic as a supposedly fully autonomous realm of value. Correlative with this was the rise of a specific ideal of the 'literary' as high linguistic art, an ideal of the imaginative that implicitly denigrated many non-fictional forms as not to be regarded true 'literature'. Shiner writes: 'The idea of literature underwent a similar transformation as one after another of the older components of literature in general began to drop out, first scientific writing, then history, and finally the sermon and the letter.'[27]

The discomfort with the very category of fiction in early ecocriticism and its attention instead to demoted non-fiction genres appears, in retrospect, as a partial reversal of the trend Shiner describes, even a latent 'avant-garde' gesture. Efforts to re-evaluate non-fictional modes of representation, in early work like Lawrence Buell's *The Environmental Imagination* (1995), were a rejection of certain aestheticizing conventions of reading, of the overvaluation of imaginative fiction and the tendency to value literature in terms of the savoured performance of individual artistic virtuosity. However, arguments in the 1990s that environmental issues and the novel were ill-suited to each other – with the novel being traditionally and predominantly concerned with matters of individual development and social questions as opposed to nonhuman contexts – were taken at that time largely as outlining a problem which ecocriticism needed to confront and overcome, moving beyond its supposed fetishization of the wild: 'if ecocriticism is to realize its full potential, it will need to find a way of appropriating novelistic form' (Dominic Head).[28] Yet, the newly counter-intuitive demands on representation being made by issues such as climate change mean that, ultimately, the deeper challenge may be the other round: that still-dominant conventions of plotting, characterization and setting in the novel need to be openly acknowledged as pervaded by anthropocentric delusion, and that environmental thinking would be stronger if it explored more directly and aggressively the drastic nature of the cultural break that recognizing this may entail.

Looking back over the sample of literary texts considered in this study, it is striking how far the exercise of reading on several different scales at once entails uncovering deep or structural forms of illusion or delusion. It remains to be seen how deeply emerging fractures in former continuities between past and present will run, and to what effect. For example, is to celebrate the natural wisdom of Keats's 'To Autumn' without awareness of questions of scale and the contingency of the seasons now to perpetuate a damagingly false conception of human reality? Canonical works such as this must become rather more deeply historicized, less amenable of being celebrated in terms of immediate contemporary relevance. For instance, Shakespeare's plays should not be presented as a model for analysing notions of ecophobia without some sense of how, since the seventeenth century, the Anthropocene has altered the whole context for understanding what may be environmentally destructive or not.

A further implication of the putative avant garde is this: that the very perceived *need* for such scalar art, along with the fact that even the most devoted person can only allow it so much time outside routines of work and daily life, still highlights how little it may alter the given terrestriality of day-to-day perception or its overwhelming power in human thought. The kind of scalar art celebrated by Kainulainen, Morton and others can be read as liberating, a release from false modes of reality taken as a norm. Alternatively, it could be read as highlighting our normal entrapment in the delusory and potentially destructive projections of the personal scale. Again, as with the novel and the category of fiction, the Anthropocene forms an indeterminate threshold: how far is it a liberating or a paralyzing thing for new art and criticism to encounter and highlight those structural and embodied limits and stupidities in which even the most intelligent are caught?

Notes

1 *Flight Behaviour* (London: HarperCollins, 2012).

2 'Saying Climate Change: Ethics of the Sublime and Problems of Representation', *Symplokē* 21 (2013), 109–23, 111.

3 'Pessimism, Optimism, Human Interim, and Anthropogenic Climate Change', *ISLE* 21.1 (Winter 2014), 149–63.

4 Marshall, *Don't Even Think about It*, 106.

5 *The Seven Basic Plots: Why We Tell Stories* (London: Continuum, 2004).

6 Marshall, *Don't Even Think about It*, 107.

7 *Anthropocene Fictions*, XX.

8 *The Earth Party: Love and Revolution at a Time of Climate Change* (Brighton: Pen Press, 2009).

9 *Solar* (London: Jonathan Cape, 2010).

10 Liz Jensen, *The Rapture* (London: Bloomsbury, 2010); Hamish MacDonald, *Finitude* (DIY Book podcast, 2009).

11 William Flesch, *Comeuppance: Costly Signaling, Altruistic Punishment, and Other Biological Components of Fiction* (Cambridge, MA: Harvard University Press, 2007), 73.

12 Some theorists of narrative argue that folk psychology, the capability of interacting with and understanding others by the ascription to them to beliefs and intentions, is not only bolstered by the universal human practice of story-telling, but that acquiring narrative competence in childhood is the major mechanism for the emergence of folk psychology in the first place. D. D. Hutto argues that there is a feedback loop between narrative and folk-psychological competence; that storytelling exercises and strengthens folk psychology, which in turns enables more subtle understanding and production of narrative, which in turn further strengthens the capacity to understand others through ascribing to them beliefs and intentions at increasing levels of complexity, especially the ability to

track false beliefs or deceptive behaviours (thus 'narratives the world over are replete with trickster stories, which emphasize and warn of the dangers of free-riders and the fact that taking what others say at face value can have heavy consequences'). (D. D. Hutto, 'Folk Psychology as Narrative Practice', *Journal of Consciousness Studies* 16.6–8 (2009), 9–39, 24)

13 'Poisoned Ground: Art and Philosophy in the Time of Hyperobjects' *Symplokē* 21 (2013), 37–50, 47.

14 Ibid., 37.

15 http://numeral.com/panels/everyicon.html

16 'Poisoned Ground', 7.

17 *The Death of the Posthuman*, 25.

18 'Saying Climate Change', 111, 120. In Kainulainen's account: 'Quigley recreated da Vinci's Vitruvian Man on a piece of Arctic sea ice using the copper strips normally used in solar panels. One edge of the sketch disintegrates into the ocean as the sea ice melts' (120). It is a mode of allusive art whose significance lies almost entirely in the kinds of reading or framing brought to it.

19 'White', in *Prismatic Ecology* 1–21, 11.

20 *The Place Where You Go To Listen: In Search of an Ecology of Music* (Middletown, CT: Wesleyan University Press, 2004).

21 'Framing the End of the Species: Images without Bodies', *Symplokē*, 21 (2013), 51–63, 60.

22 *Death of the Posthuman: Essays on Extinction*, Vol. 1 (Michigan, MI: Open Humanities Press, 2014), 24.

23 *Theory of the Avant Garde*, trans. Michael Shaw (Minneapolis, MN: University of Minnesota, 1984). Bürger's identification of the avant garde has been criticized. Morton for instance reads twentieth-century avant-garde art as a only new form of romanticism ('Poisoned Ground', 46).

24 Likewise, 'By embracing the hyperobjects that loom in our social space, and dropping Nature, *world*, and so on, we have a chance to create more democratic modes of coexistence between humans and with nonhumans' (*Hyperobjects*, 121).
At times, Morton's list of the kinds of art supposed to this new phase drifts dangerously close to being the consumerist celebration of any aesthetic object that offers a very intense personal experience. 'When I listen to My Bloody Valentine . . . a physical force . . . almost lifts me off the floor. Keven Shields's guitar sears into me like an x-ray . . .' (*Hyperobjects*, 29).

25   For VEHEMENT, in the interests of future life surviving on Earth, the human species should refrain from reproducing itself, bringing its numbers down, ultimately to zero. 'Even if our chances of succeeding were only one in a hundred, we would have to try. Giving up and allowing humanity to take its course is unconscionable. There is far too much at stake.' www.vhemt.org/aboutvhemt.htm#serious

26   *The Windup Girl* (London: Orbit, 2010).

27   *The Invention of Art: A Cultural History* (Chicago, IL: University of Chicago Press, 2001), 191.

28   'Ecocriticism and the Novel', in Laurence Coupe (ed.), *The Green Studies Reader: From Romanticism to Ecocriticism* (London: Routledge, 2000), 235–41, 236.

Conclusion

Anthropocene disorder – the intellectual, moral and political insecurity that accompanies the derangement of given norms – is latent in the question that has recurred in this book: at what point does continuing in activities that were once merely normal or even admirable turn, despite itself, into intellectual evasion? For the regional field of literary and cultural criticism, there is the mess and excitement of a phase of transition, with old notions and procedures coming to seem empty and formulaic, but as yet with little that seems sufficient in their place.

At the same time, the stakes of the Anthropocene are so extraordinarily high – a sixth mass extinction event that, over the very brief geological timespan, could well see the extinction of a large percentage of life on Earth – that any text which simply perpetuates long-dominant assumptions about humanity and human society (and which do not?) must come to seem suspect. Imagine the current canon of literature being read in some future urban wasteland, genuinely akin, say, to the fictional dystopias of the Los Angeles of Ridley Scott's *Blade Runner* (1982) or Neill Blomkamp's *Elysium* (2013), an Earth with no forests and in which no animal larger than a dog exists outside of factory farms or wildlife parks. Would not the kinds of uncertain irony and instability of judgement we have encountered in trying to reread and evaluate Snyder's 'Late August' with a changed, retrospective understanding not affect almost every text?

Anthropocene disorder also inheres in the institutional predicament of environmental critics. As the degradation of the planet intensifies, the tension must increase between thinking in ecocriticism and its institutional context in an educational system still largely bound to the reproduction and legitimation of the status quo. Environmental criticism currently straddles a knife-edge between being a privileged and minority area of activism, involved in the education of students that may include future leaders, and being a force of intellectual and political containment. An observer might ask: if you are really *so* concerned with an encroaching disaster on the monstrous scale described, why is there never any commitment at your conferences to such measures as civil disobedience, the withholding of taxes, or judicious, non-violent environmental sabotage?

In such a situation an overinvestment in the power of cultural representations, of the social importance of art and literature, becomes an understandable ethical temptation. It may be a kind of 'reaction-formation', that is, the psychic defence mechanism of reacting to an unacknowledged anxiety by an exaggerated espousal of an opposing factor. Hence the mildly disingenuous over-exaggeration by critics of the power and centrality of the cultural and of cultural change per se as a determiner of history.[1] This finds form in kinds of escapist fantasies about ecocriticism's own centrality and power, as in Jonathan Bate's bizarre talk of poetry saving the planet (*Song of the Earth* 283), or Jeffrey R. Di Leo's almost equally incredible claim that 'theory' and work in the 'humanities' faculty 'gives us our best chance to save the planet'.[2] The extreme implausibility of such rhetoric, together with the rather brittle, not-quite-full seriousness with which it is offered, testifies again to the destabilization of norms in the Anthropocene, the general loss of ethical and political coordinates because no-one can conceive a likely practicable response proportionate to the threats.

An emergent intellectual effect of the Anthropocene is a general contamination and expansion of previously focused contexts of understanding and evaluation. For the work of criticism this calls for kinds of '*overreading*' in the positive sense discussed by Colin Davis in his *Critical Excess* (2010). Davis cites a debate of the early 1990s between Umberto Eco, Jonathan Culler and Richard Rorty, on the nature and limits of interpretation, or reading and *over*-interpretation. The environmental tragedy was not an issue in the controversy, but Culler's response is still suggestive. Davis writes

> Culler . . . accepts that there may be such a practise as overinterpretation, and he sets out to defend it. Moderate interpretation, guided by the widely accepted principles and

yielding widely accepted results, articulates a consensus which is of little interest. Culler insists that 'interpretation is interesting only when it is extreme' . . . Extreme interpretation may of course be as dull and ineffective as its moderate counterpart; but, if successful it pushes thinking as far as it can go, puts pressure on its objects in order to uncover things which might have remained hidden, and gives fresh insights into language, literature, and ourselves.[3]

The kinds of interpretative dilemma faced by new readings engaged with questions of what may or may not be environmentally significant in a past text mean that ecocriticism at its best must be 'overreading', even beyond the sense sketched by Culler: for the issues to consider overspill the traditional parameters of critical judgement, abandon the guard-rails of given borders between the humanities and the sciences, render anachronistic previous notions of a text's 'original context', and refute would-be explanations of issues by reference to limited and anthropocentric models of cultural politics. As a consequence, however, the excitement of intellectual novelty is also accompanied by a crisis of critical competence and, inevitably, of intellectual standards. Environmental criticism now finds itself having to break down intellectual barriers that in the past gave its own procedures and objects relative separateness and coherence.

The hope in environmental criticism has been that cultural change can form a kind of inverse of the tragedy of the commons, a self-multiplying social and psychic force strong enough to prevail against free-loaders or non-participants. *The Live Earth Global Warming Survival Handbook,* official companion volume to the Live Earth concerts, exemplifies the hope often expressed that cultural change will be a kind of multiplier:

> Live Earth is the start of a global environmental movement, one that harnesses the power of everyone working together. So let us not be overwhelmed by the size of the problem. The positive sum of small actions, multiplied by millions of people, can lead to dramatic effects. You are part of this movement and the small changes you make will add up.[4]

However, the impersonal game space of the Anthropocene, its relentlessness intensified by the large numbers involved, is reducing the scope for the likely significance or effect of any one action by any single group, or the likely effect of some green cultural change in any one place or group. The capricious, emergent nature of scale effects implicates the cultural in kinds of statistical, physical and non-intentional dynamics and complexities that can only weaken the hope for the 'communal imaginary' to work as a decisive, easily identifiable and malleable agent.

Ecocritics have been responding to the call for a hypothetical future phase of the Anthropocene, that of an epoch of humanity as the just and responsible steward of the Earth. What else is there to hope or work for? Yet the Anthropocene entails effects that touch on the viability of ecocriticism itself as a possible force of significant change. Environmental readings of literature and culture may need to engage more directly with delusions of self-importance in their practice, keeping alert to the need for more direct kinds of activism. The more complex and even opaque the overall context, then the more any specific framing of it must drift towards simplification. This is a challenge for any sort of activism, but especially for one that limits itself to the realm of cultural representations.

Notes

1 Wojciech Malecki writes of this in 'Save the Planet in Your Own Time? Ecocriticism and Political Practice', *The Journal of Ecocriticism* 4.2, July 2012, 48–55, 49.

2 'Can Theory Save the Planet?', *Symplokē* 21 (2013), 27–36, 35.

3 *Critical Excess* (Stanford, CA: Stanford University Press, 2010), x–xi.

4 Rob Reiner, Foreword to David de Rosthchild, *The Live Earth Global Warming Survival Handbook* (London: Virgin Books, 2007), 6.

BIBLIOGRAPHY

Adam, D. (2014), 'Prisoners of Thought', *New Scientist*, 26 April 2014, 36–8.

Adams, J. Luther (2004), *The Place Where You Go to Listen: In Search of an Ecology of Music*, Middletown, CT: Wesleyan University Press.

Agamben, G. (2004), *The Open. Man and Animal*, trans. Kevin Attel, Stanford, CA: Stanford University Press.

Alaimo, S. (2010), *Bodily Natures: Science, Environment, and the Material Self*, Bloomington, IN: Indiana University Press.

Alberts, P. (2011), 'Responsibility Towards Life in the Early Anthropocene', *Anglelaki* 16 (4), 5–16.

Allenby, B. R. and Sarewitz, D. (2011), *The Techno-Human Condition*, Cambridge, MA: MIT Press.

Anderson, I. (1995), 'Australia's Growing Disaster', *New Scientist*, 29 July 1995, 12–13.

Atwood, M. (2003), *Oryx and Crake*, Toronto: McClelland and Stewart.

Bach, R. A. (2013), Review of '*Ecocriticism and Shakespeare: Reading Ecophobia* by Simon C. Estok, and of Dan Brayton and Lynne Bruckner' (eds), *Ecocritical Shakespeare*, *Shakespeare Quarterly* 64 (1), 110–13.

Bacigalupi, P. (2010), *The Windup Girl*, London: Orbit, 2010.

Bartlett, A. A. (2000), 'Democracy Cannot Survive Overpopulation', *Population and Environment* 22 (1), 63–71, 66–7.

Bate, J. (2000), *Song of the Earth*, London: Picador, 2000.

Beck, H. and Kolankiewicz, L. J. (2000), 'The Environmental Movement's Retreat from Advocating U.S. Population Stabilization (1970–1998): A First Draft of History', *Journal of Policy History* 12 (1), 123–56.

Beck, U. (1999), *World Risk Society*, London: Polity.

Behringer, W. (2010), *A Cultural History of Climate*, trans. Patrick Camiller, Cambridge: Polity, 2010.

Bennett, J. (2010), *Vibrant Matter: A Political Ecology of Things*, Durham, NC: Duke University Press.

Bergthaller, H. (2010), 'Housebreaking the Human Animal: Humanism and the Problem of Sustainability in Margaret Atwood's *Oryx and Crake* and *The Year of the Flood*', *English Studies* 91, 728–42.

Billings, L. (2013), 'Goodbye Goldilocks?', *New Scientist*, 8 June 2013, 40–3.

Bishop, R. (2007), *The Philosophy of the Social Sciences*, London: Continuum.

Blanchot, M. (1993), *The Infinite Conversation*, trans. Susan Hanson, Minneapolis: Minnesota University Press.

Booker, C. (2004), *The Seven Basic Plots: Why We Tell Stories*, London: Continuum.

Boyle, T. C. (2000), *A Friend of the Earth*, New York: Viking.

Brassier, R. (2007), *Nihil Unbound: Enlightenment and Extinction*, Basingstoke: Palgrave Macmillan.

Braun, B. and Whatmore, S. J. (eds) (2010), *Political Matter: Technoscience, Democracy, and Public Life*, Minneapolis: University of Minnesota Press.

Brin, D. (1990), *Earth*, London: Orbit.

Brunner, J. (1968), *Stand on Zanzibar*, London: Doubleday.

Bruns, G. (1982), *Inventions: Writing, Textuality and Understanding in Literary History*, New Haven: Yale University Press.

Buell, L. (1995), *The Environmental Imagination: Thoreau, Nature Writing and the Formation of American Culture*, Cambridge, MA: Harvard University Press.

Bürger, P. (1984), *Theory of the Avant Garde*, trans. Michael Shaw, Minneapolis, MN: University of Minnesota.

Butler, J. (2004), *Precarious Life: The Powers of Mourning and Violence*, London and New York: Verso.

Cafaro, P. and Crist, E. (2012), 'Human Population Growth as If the Rest of Life Mattered', in P. Cafaro, and E. Crist (eds), *Life on the Brink*, Athens, GA: University of Georgia Press, 3–15.

— (eds) (2012), *Life on the Brink: Environmentalists Confront Overpopulation*, Athens, GA: University of Georgia Press.

Cage, J. (1994), 'Overpopulation and Art', in M. Perloff and C. Junkermann (eds), *John Cage: Composed in America*, Chicago, IL: University of Chicago Press, 14–38.

Callicot, B. (2007), 'Lamark Redux: Temporal Scale as the Key to the Boundary between the Human and the Natural Worlds', in C. S. Brown and T. Toadvine (eds), *Nature's Edge: Boundary Explorations in Ecological Theory and Practice*, Albany, NY: SUNY Press, 19–40.

Carter, A. (1999), *A Radical Green Political Theory*, London: Routledge.

Carver, R. (1990), *Conversations with Raymond Carver*, B. G. Gentry and W. L. Stull (eds), Jackson, MS: University Press of Mississippi.

— (1993), *Where I'm Calling From: The Selected Stories*, London: Harvill Press.

Castree, N. (2014), 'The Anthropocene and the Environmental Humanities: Extending the Conversation', *Environmental Humanities* 5, 233–60.

Chakravarty, D. (2009), 'The Climate of History: Four Theses', *Critical Inquiry* 35, 197–222.

— (2012), 'Postcolonial Studies and the Challenge of Climate Change', *NLH* 43, 1–18.

Chew, S. C. (2001), *World Ecological Degradation: Accumulation, Urbanization, and Deforestation 3000 BC-AD 2000*, Walnut Creek, CA: Altamira Press, 2001.

Clark, N. (2010), 'Volatile Worlds: Confronting Abrupt Climate Change', *Theory Culture and Society* 27, 31–53.

Clark, T. (2005), *The Poetics of Singularity: The Counter-Culturalist Turn in Heidegger, Derrida, Blanchot and the Later Gadamer*, Edinburgh: Edinburgh University Press.

— (2011), *The Cambridge Introduction to Literature and the Environment*, Cambridge: Cambridge University Press.

Coghan, A. (2014), 'Africa's Road to Riches', *New Scientist*, 11 January 2014, 8–9.

Cohen, J. J. (ed.), *Prismatic Ecology: Ecotheory beyond Green*, Minneapolis, MN: University of Minnesota, 1–21.

Cohen, T. (2012), 'Introduction: Murmurations – "Climate Change" and the Defacement of Theory', in T. Cohen (ed.), *Telemorphosis: Theory in the Era of Climate Change*, Vol. 1, Michigan, MI: Open Humanities Press, 13–42.

Cohen, T., Colebrook, C. and Miller, J. H. (2012), *Theory and the Disappearing Future*, London: Routledge.

Colebrook, C. (2012), 'Not Symbiosis, Not Now: Why Anthropogenic Climate Change Is Not Really Human', in T. Clark (ed.), 'Deconstruction in the Anthropocene', *Oxford Literary Review* 34 (2), 185–210.

— (2013), 'Framing the End of Species: Images without Bodies', in *Symplokē* 21, 51–63.

— (2014), *Death of the Posthuman: Essays on Extinction*, Vol. 1, Open Humanities Press, http://quod.lib.umich.edu/cgi/p/pod/dod-idx/death-of-the-posthuman-essays-on-extinction-volume-one.pdf?c=ohp;idno=12329362.0001.001

Coole, D. (2013), 'Too Many Bodies? The Return and Disavowal of the Population Question', *Environmental Politics* 22, 195–215.

Coronil, F. (1997), *The Magical State: Nature, Money, and Modernity in Venezuela*, Chicago, IL: University of Chicago Press.

Cosgrove, D. (1994), 'Contested Global Visions: One-World, Whole-Earth and the Apollo Space Photographs', in *Annals of the Association of American Geographers* 84, 270–94.

Crist, E. (2012), 'Abundant Earth and the Population Question', in P. Cafaro and E. Crist (eds), *Life on the Brink*, 141–53.

Crosby, A. W. (1986), *Ecological Imperialism: The Biological Expansion of Europe, 900–1900*, Cambridge: Cambridge University Press, 1986.

Curry, P. (2008), 'Nature Post-Nature', in *New Formations: A Journal of Culture/Theory/Politics* 26, 51–64.

D'Arcy, G. W. (ed.) (2008), 'Eco-Historicism', special issue of *The Journal for Early Modern Cultural Studies* 8 (2), Fall/Winter.

David, W. (2005), 'What Is Eco-Phenomenology?', *The Step Back: Ethics and Politics after Deconstruction*, Albany: SUNY, 149–68.

Dean, T. (1991), *Gary Snyder and the American Unconscious: Inhabiting the Ground*, New York: St Martin's Press.

Derrida, J. (1976), *Of Grammatology*, trans. G. C. Spivak, Baltimore, MD: Johns Hopkins University Press.

— (2000), 'The Deconstruction of Actuality', in M. McQuillan (ed.), *Deconstruction: A Reader*, Edinburgh: Edinburgh University Press, 527–53.

— (2000), *On Hospitality: Anne Dufourmantelle Invites Jacques Derrida to Respond*, trans. Rachel Bowlby, Stanford, CA: Stanford University Press.

— (2002), 'Force of Law: The Mystical Foundation of Authority', in *Acts of Religion*, trans. G. Anjdar, London: Routledge, 230–98.

— (2012), *The Beast and the Sovereign II*, trans. G. Bennington, Chicago: University of Chicago Press.

Di Leo, J. (2013), 'Can Theory Save the Planet?' in *Symplokē* 21, 27–36.

Diamond, J. (2000), *Guns, Germs and Steel: A Short History of Everybody for the Last 13,000 Years* (1997), London: Vintage Books.

— (2006), *Collapse: How Societies Choose to Fail or Survive*, London: Penguin.

Dimock, W. C. (2006), *Through Other Continents: American Literature Across Deep Time*, Princeton: Princeton University Press.

Domingo, A. (2008), '"Demodystopias": Prospects of Demographic Hell', in *Population and Development Review* 34, 725–45.

Ehrlich, P. (1968), *The Population Bomb*, New York: Ballantine Books.

Ellis, E. (2011), 'The Planet of No Return: Human Resilience on an Artificial Earth', in Ted T. Nordhaus and M. Shellenberger (eds), *Love Your Monsters: Postenvironmentalism and the Anthropocene*, E-book, np: The Breakthrough Institute.

Estok, S. C. (2011), *Ecocriticism and Shakespeare: Reading Ecophobia*, Basingstoke: Palgrave.

Evernden, N. (1996), 'Beyond Ecology: Self, Place, and the Pathetic Fallacy', in C. Glotfelty and H. Fromm (eds), *The Ecocriticism Reader: Landmarks in Literary Ecology*, Athens, GA: University of Georgia Press, 92–104.

Feder, H. (2013), 'Ecocriticism, Posthumanism, and the Biological Idea of Culture', *Oxford Handbooks Online*, DOI: 10.1093/oxfordhb/9780199742929.013.006.

Fetzer, J. H. (1996), 'Methodological Individualism: Singular Causal Systems and their Population Manifestations', *Synthese* 68 (1), 99–128.

Fischlin, D. and Nandorfy, M. (2012), *The Community of Rights: The Rights of Community*, Montreal: Black Rose Publishing.

Flesch, W. (2007), *Comeuppance: Costly Signaling, Altruistic Punishment, and Other Biological Components of Fiction*, Cambridge, MA: Harvard University Press.

Ford, T. H. (2013), 'Aura in the Anthropocene', *Symplokē* 21, 65–82.

Fortey, R. (1998), *Life: An Unauthorized Biography*, London: Flamingo.

Franklin, A. (2004), *Animal Nation: The True Story of Animals and Australia*, Sydney: University of New South Wales Press.

Fraser, R. (2002), *Ben Okri*, Tavistock: Northcote House.

Garb, Y. J. (1990), 'Perspective or Escape? Ecofeminist Musings on Contemporary Earth Imagery', in I. Diamond and G. F. Orenstein (eds), *Reweaving the World: The Emergence of Ecofeminism*, San Francisco: Sierra Club, 264–78.

Gardiner, S. M. (2005), 'The Real Tragedy of the Commons', *Philosophy and Public Affairs* 30, 387–416.

— (2011), *The Perfect Moral Storm: The Ethical Tragedy of Climate Change*, Oxford: Oxford University Press.

Garrard, G. (2010), 'Problems and Prospects in Ecocritcal Pedagogy', http://www.academia.edu/233301/Problems and Prospects in Ecocritical Pedagogy

— (2013), 'The Unbearable Lightness of Green: Air Travel, Climate Change and Literature', *Green Letters: Studies in Ecocriticism* 17, 175–88, 178–9.

Gidal, E. (2008), '"O Happy Earth Reality of Heaven!" Melancholy and Utopia in Romantic Climatography', in *Journal for Early Modern Cultural Studies* 8 (2), 74–101.

Gonzalez, G. A. (2009), *Urban Sprawl, Global Warming, and the Empire of Capital*, Albany, NY: SUNY Press.

Gosine, A. (2012), 'Non-White Reproduction and Same-Sex Eroticism: Queer Acts against Nature', in C. M. Sandilands and B. Erickson (eds), *Queer Ecologies: Sex, Nature, Politics, Desire*, Bloomington: Indiana Press, 149–72.

Gray, T. (2006), *Gary Snyder and the Pacific Rim. Creating Countercultural Community*, Iowa City, IA: University of Iowa Press.

Grewe-Volpp, C. (2012), 'No Environmental Justice without Social Justice: A Green Postcolonialist Reading of Paule Marshall's *The Chosen Place, the Timeless People*', in T. Müller and M. Sauter (eds), *Literature, Ecology, Ethics: Recent Trends in Ecocriticism*, Heidelberg: Winter, 227–37.

Griffiths, T. (1997), 'Introduction' to *Ecology and Empire: Environmental History of Settler Societies*, in T. Griffiths and L. Robin (eds), Edinburgh: Keele University Press, 1–16.

Hansen, J. (2009), *Storms of My Grandchildren: The Truth about the Coming Climate Catastrophe and Our Last Chance to Save Humanity*, New York: Bloomsbury USA.

Hardin, G. (1968), 'The Tragedy of the Commons', in *Science* 162, 1243–8.

Harvey, D. (1991), *The Condition of Postmodernity: An Enquiry into the Origins of Cultural Change*, Oxford: Wiley-Blackwell.

Hawkins, R. (2012), 'Perceiving Overpopulation: Can't We See What We're Doing?', in P. Cafaro and E. Crist (eds), *Life on the Brink*, 202–13.

Head, D. (2000), 'Ecocriticism and the Novel', in L. Coupe (ed.), *The Green Studies Reader: From Romanticism to Ecocriticism*, London: Routledge, 235–41.

Heise, U. (2008), *Sense of Place and Sense of Planet: The Environmental Imagination of the Global*, Oxford: Oxford University Press.

— (2010), 'Afterword: Postcolonial Ecocriticism and the Question of Literature', in B. Roos and A. Hunt (eds), *A Postcolonial Green: Environmental Politics and World Narratives*, Charlottesville, VA: University of Virginia Press, 251–8.

— (2014), Review of *Hyperobjects* in *Critical Inquiry*, 4 June 2014, http://criticalinquiry.uchicago.edu/book_review/

Herzogenrath, B. (2013), 'White', in J. J. Cohen (ed.), *Prismatic Ecology: Ecotheory beyond Green*, Minneapolis, MN: University of Minnesota, 1–21.

Hiltner, K. (2009), 'Renaissance Literature and Our Contemporary Attitude to Global Warming', *ISLE* 13, 429–42.

Hoggett, P. (2013), 'Climate Change in a Perverse Culture', in S. Weintrobe (ed.), *Engaging with Climate Change*, 56–70.

Hood, B. (2012), *The Self Illusion: Why There is No 'You' Inside Your Head*, London: Constable.

Huggan, G. (2007), *Australian Literature: Postcolonialism, Racism, Transnationalism*, Oxford: Oxford University Press.

Huggan, G. and Tiffin, H. (eds) (2007), 'Green Postcolonialism', *Interventions* 9 (1).

Hughes, E. (2007), 'Dissolving the Nation: Self-deception and Symbolic Inversion in the GM Debate', *Environmental Politics* 16, 318–36.

Hutto, D. D. (2009), 'Folk Psychology as Narrative Practice', *Journal of Consciousness Studies* 16 (6–8), 9–39.

Ingold, T. (2011), *Being Alive: Essays on Movement, Knowledge and Description*, London: Routledge.

Iovino, S. (2012), 'Material Ecocriticism: Matter, Text, and Posthuman Ethics', in T. Müller and M. Sauter (eds), *Literature, Ecology, Ethics: Recent Trends in Ecocriticism*, 51–68.

IPCC (2014), Fifth Assessment Synthesis Report, http://www.ipcc.ch/pdf/assessment-report/ar5/syr/SYR_AR5_LONGERREPORT.pdf

Jacques, P. J., Dunlap, R. E. and Freeman, M. (2008), 'The Organisation of Denial: Conservative Think Tanks and Environmental Scepticism', *Environmental Politics* 17, 349–85.

Jay, M. (2011), 'Historical Explanation and the Event: Reflections on the Limits of Contextualization', *NLH* 42, 557–71.

Jensen, L. (2009), *The Rapture*, London: Bloomsbury.

Jonas, H. (1984), *The Imperative of Responsibility: In Search of an Ethics for the Technological Age*, Chicago: University of Chicago Press.

Kainulainen, M. (2013), 'Saying Climate Change: Ethics of the Sublime and Problems of Representation', *Symplokē* 21, 109–23.

Keene, J. (2013), 'Unconscious Obstacles to Caring for the Planet', in S. Weintrobe (ed.), *Engaging with Climate Change*, 144–59.

Kelly, A. (2009), *Understanding Lorrie Moore*, Columbia: University of South Carolina Press.

Kerridge, R. (2012), Isabel Pérez Ramos, Interview with Richard Kerridge, *Ecozon Sept 2012*, http://www.ecozona.eu/index.php/journal/article/view/317/624

— (2013), 'Ecocriticism' in *The Year's Work in Critical and Cultural Theory* 21, chapter 18, 1–30, The English Association.

King, Y. (2013), 'The Ecophobia Hypothesis: Re-membering the Feminist Body of Ecocriticism', in G. Gaard, S. C. Estok and S. Oppermann (eds), *International Perspectives in Feminist Ecocriticism*, London: Routledge, 70–84.

Kingsolver, B. (2012), *Flight Behaviour*, London: HarperCollins, 2012.

Kolankiewicz, L. J. (2012), 'Overpopulation versus Biodiversity: How a Plethora of People Produces a Paucity of Wildlife', in P. Cafaro and E. Crist (eds), *Life on the Brink,* 75–90.

Latour, B. (2011), 'Waiting for Gaia: Composing the Common World through Arts and Politics', np, http://www.bruno-latour.fr/sites/default/files/124-GAIA-LONDON-SPEAP_0.pdf

Lawson, H. (1996), *The Penguin Henry Lawson Short Stories*, in J. Barnes (ed.), London: Penguin.

Lertzman, R. A. (2013), 'The Myth of Apathy', in S. Weintrobe (ed.), *Engaging with Climate Change*, 117–33.

Lévi-Strauss, C. (1966), *The Savage Mind*, Chicago, IL: University of Chicago Press.

Levin, S. A. (1992), 'The Problem and Pattern of Scale in Ecology: The Robert H. MacArthur Award Lecture', *Ecology* 73, 1943–67.

Levitin, D. (2014), *The Organized Mind: Thinking Straight in the Age of Information Overload*, New York: Dutton.

— (2014), 'It's All too much', *New Scientist*, 16 August 2014, 26–27.

Lincoln, S. L. (2008), *Expensive Shit: Aesthetic Economies of Waste in Postcolonial Africa*, Ph.D. thesis, Duke University.

MacDonald, H. (2009), *Finitude* DIY Book podcast.

McGurl, M. (2012), 'The Posthuman Comedy', *Critical Inquiry* 38, 533–53.

MacKenzie, D. (2008), 'Are We Doomed?', *New Scientist*, 5 April 2008, 33–5.

McKewan, I. (2010), *Solar*, London: Jonathan Cape.

McKibben, B. (1989), *The End of Nature*, New York: Random House.

McNeill, J. R. (2000), *Something New Under the Sun*, New York: Norton.

Malecki, W. (2012), 'Save the Planet in Your Own Time? Ecocriticism and Political Practice', *The Journal of Ecocriticism* 4 (2), 48–55.

Mansfield, B. and Haas, J. (2006), 'Scale Framing of Scientific Uncertainty in Controversy Over the Endangered Steller Sea Lion', *Environmental Politics* 15, 78–94.

Marshall, G. (2009), *The Earth Party: Love and Revolution at a Time of Climate Change*, Brighton: Pen Press.

— (2014), *Don't Even Think about it: Why Our Brains Are Wired to Ignore Climate Change*, New York: Bloomsbury.

Meadows, D. H., Meadows, D. L., Randers, J. and Behrens III, W. W. (1972), *Limits to Growth*, New York: New American Library.

Menely, T. and Ronda, M. (2013), 'Red', in J. J. Cohen (ed.), *Prismatic Ecology: Ecotheory beyond Green*, Minneapolis, MN: University of Minnesota, 22–41.

Merleau-Ponty, M. (1962), *Phenomenology of Perception*, trans. Colin Smith, London: Routledge and Kegan Paul.

Michaud, M. A. G. (2007), *Contact with Alien Civilizations: Our Hopes and Fears about Encountering Extra-terrestrials*, New York: Copernicus Books.

Miller, J. H. (2010), 'Anachronistic Reading', *Derrida Today* 3, 75–91.

— (2013), 'Biodiversity and the Abyssal Limits of the Human', *Symplokē* 21, 207–20.

Moore, L. (2008), 'Joy', in *The Collected Stories*, London: Faber and Faber, 365–80.

Morton, T. (2010), *The Ecological Thought*, Cambridge, MA: Harvard University Press.

— (2012), 'The Oedipal Logic of Environmental Awareness', in *Environmental Humanities* 1, 7–21.

— (2013), *Hyperobjects: Philosophy and Ecology after the End of the World*, Minneapolis, MN: University of Minnesota Press.

— (2013), 'Poisoned Ground: Art and Philosophy in the Time of Hyperobjects', *Symplokē* 21, 37–50.

Müller, T. and Sauter, M. (eds) (2012), *Literature, Ecology, Ethics: Recent Trends in Ecocriticism*, Heidelberg: Winter, 227–37.

Murphy, P. (2014), 'Pessimism, Optimism, Human Interim, and Anthropogenic Climate Change', *ISLE* 21, 149–63.

Nessset, K. (1995), *The Stories of Raymond Carver: A Critical Study*, Athens: Ohio University Press.

Nikolas, N. (2007), *The Politics of Life Itself: Biomedicine, Power, and Subjectivity in the Twenty-First Century*, Princeton, NJ: Princeton University Press.

Nixon, R. (2011), *Slow Violence and the Environmentalism of the Poor*, Cambridge, MA: Harvard University Press.

— (2012), 'Neoliberalism, Genre, and "The Tragedy of the Commons"', *PMLA* 127, 593–9.

Norgaard, K. M. (2011), *Living in Denial: Climate Change, Emotions, and Everyday Life*, Cambridge, MA: MIT Press.

Northcott, M. S. (2007), *A Moral Climate: The Ethics of Global Warming*, London: Dartman, Longman and Todd, 215–16.

Norton, B. G. (2000), 'Population and Consumption: Environmental Problems as Problems of Scale', *Ethics and the Environment* 5, 23–45.

Ophuls, W. (1997), *Requiem for Modern Politics: The Tragedy of the Enlightenment and the Challenge of the New Millennium*, Boulder, CO: Westview Press.

Oventile, R. S. (2013), 'Paul de Man Now, or, Nihilisms in the Right Company', *Symplokē* 21, 325–39.

Pick, A. (2011), *Creaturely Ethics: Animality and Vulnerability in Literature and Film*, New York: Columbia University Press.

Plumwood, V. (2008), 'Shadow Places and the Politics of Dwelling', *Australian Humanities Review* 44, np.

Ponting, C. (1991), *A Green History of the World*, New York: St Martin's Press.

Prieto, E. (2005), 'The Use of Landscape: Ecocriticism and Martinican Cultural Theory', in E. M. DeLoughrey, R. K. Gosson and G. B. Handley (eds), *Caribbean Literature and the Environment: Between*

Nature and Culture, Charlottesville, VA: University of Virginia Press, 236–46.

Prosser, S. (2013), 'Emergent Causation', *Philosophical Studies* 159, 21–39.

Pule, P. (1993), 'Epidemics and Revolutions: The Rinderpest Epidemic in Late Nineteenth-Century Southern Africa', *Past & Present* 138, 112–43.

Pyne, S. J. (2011), *Fire: A Brief History*, Seattle, WA: University of Washington Press.

Rampal, P., Weiss, J., Dubois, C. and Campin, J.-M. (2011), 'IPCC Climate Models Do Not Capture Arctic Sea Ice Drift Acceleration: Consequences in Terms of Projected Sea Ice Thinning and Decline', *Journal of Geophysical Research* 116 (August 2011).

Rapaport, H. (2011), *The Literary Theory Toolkit: A Compendium of Concepts and Methods*, Oxford: Wiley-Blackwell.

Reiner, R. (2007), Foreword to David de Rosthchild, *The Live Earth Global Warming Survival Handbook*, London: Virgin Books.

Rigby, K. (2009), 'Writing in the Anthropocene: Idle Chatter or Ecoprophetic Witness?', in *Australian Humanities Review*, http://www.australianhumanitiesreview.org/archive/Issue-November-2009/rigby.html

Robbert, A. (2004), 'Six Problems in Thinking Nature-Culture Interactions', http://knowledge-ecology.com/six-problems-in-nature-culture-interactions/

Robinson, K. S. (2004), *Forty Signs of Rain*, New York: HarperCollins.

— (2005), *Fifty Degrees Below*, New York: HarperCollins.

— (2007), *Sixty Days and Counting*, New York: HarperCollins.

Rolls, E. (1981), *A Million Wild Acres*, Ringwood, Victoria: Penguin Australia.

Rose, D. B. (2004), *Reports from a Wild Country: Ethics for Decolonization*, Sydney: University of New South Wales Press.

Rosemary, R. (2013), 'Great Expectations', in S. Weintrobe (ed.), *Engaging with Climate Change*, 87–102.

Roszak, T., Gomes, M. E. and Kanner, A. D. (eds) (1995), *Ecopsychology: Restoring the Earth, Healing the Mind*, San Francisco, CA: Sierra Club Books.

Ruddiman, W. S. (2005), *Plows, Plagues, and Petroleum: How Humans Took Control of Climate*, Princeton, NJ: Princeton University Press.

Ruddiman, W. S., Vavrus, S., Kutzbach, J. and He, F. (2014), 'The Real Debate about Anthropogenic Global Warming', *The Anthropocene Review Blog*, 10 May 2014, http://anthropocenerev.blogspot.co.uk/

Rukeyser, M. (2000), *The Book of the Dead*, in K. Daniel (ed.), *Out of Silence: Selected Poems*, Evanston, IL: Northwestern University Press, 37–40.

Sagan, C. (1997), *Pale Blue Dot: A Vision of the Human Future in Space*, New York: Random House.

Sekeris, P. G. (2014), 'The Tragedy of the Commons in a Violent World', *RAND Journal of Economics* 45, 521–32.

Selby, N. (2000), '"Coming Back to Oneself / Coming Back to the Land": Gary Snyder's Poetics', in J. Tallmadge and H. Harrington (eds), *Reading under the Sign of Nature: New Essays in Ecocriticism*, Salt Lake City, UT: University of Utah Press, 179–97.

Sellars, W. (1962), 'Philosophy and the Scientific Image of Man', in R. Colodny (ed.), *Frontiers of Science and Philosophy*, Pittsburgh, PA: University of Pittsburgh Press, 35–78.

Serres, M. (1995), *The Natural Contract*, trans. E. MacArthur and W. Paulson, Ann Arbor, MI: University of Michigan Press.

Shiner, L. (2001), *The Invention of Art: A Cultural History*, Chicago, IL: University of Chicago Press.

Simon, J. F. (1996), http://numeral.com/panels/everyicon.html.

Small, H. (2013), *The Value of the Humanities*, Oxford: Oxford University Press.

Smith, M. (2006), 'Environmental Risks and Ethical Responsibilities: Arendt, Beck, and the Politics of Acting into Nature', *Environmental Ethics* 28, 227–46.

Snyder, G. (1999), *The Gary Snyder Reader: Prose, Poetry, and Translations*, Washington, DC: Counterpoint.

— (2007), *Back on the Fire: Essays*, Emeryville, CA: Avalon.

'Sourdough Mountain Fire Lookout' (2010), http://www.youtube.com/watch?v=Y2UbkRI6vXg

Spinage, C. A. (2003), *Cattle Plague: A History*, New York: Springer Science & Business Media.

Steffen, W., Crutzen, P. J. and McNeill, J. R. (2007), 'The Anthropocene: Are Humans Now Overwhelming the Great Forces of Nature?', *Ambio* 38, 614–21.

Steinberg, T. (2009), *Down to Earth: Nature's Role in American History*, New York: Oxford University Press.

Szerszynski, B. (2010), 'Reading and Writing the Weather: Climate Technics and the Moment of Responsibility', *Theory, Culture & Society* 27 (2–3), 9–30.

— (2012), 'The End of the End of Nature: The Anthropocene and the Fate of the Human', *Oxford Literary Review* 34 (2), 165–84.

Taylor, T. (2010), 'Stone Tools Made Us Human', interview with Timothy Taylor, *New Scientist*, 21 August 2010, 48.

Thomashow, M. (2002), *Bringing the Biosphere Home: Learning to Perceive Global Environmental Change*, Cambridge, MA: MIT Press.

Toadvine, T. (2006), 'Scholar's Session on David Wood', Society for Phenomenological and Existential Philosophy, Philadelphia, 14 October 2006, http://pages.uoregon.edu/toadvine/Toadvine%20 and%20Wood%20Scholar's%20Session.pdf

— (2012), 'Novel Climes: Anthropocene Histories, Hans-Jörg Rheinberger's *Trace*, and Clive Cussler's *Arctic Drift*', *Oxford Literary Review* 34 (2), 295–314.

Trexler, A. (2015), *Anthropocene Fictions: The Novel in a Time of Climate Change*, Charlottesville, VA: University of Virginia Press.

Turnbull, N. (2006), 'The Ontological Consequences of Copernicus: Global Being in the Planetary World', *Theory Culture and Society* 23, 125–39.

UN (1987), The World Commission on Environment and Development, *Our Common Future*, Oxford: Oxford University Press.

— (2012), 'A New UN Report on Our Impending Overpopulation' (February 2012) http://www.mercatornet.com/demography/ view/10244#sthash.8G3Mv3ml.dpuf VEHEMENT, http://www. vhemt.org/aboutvhemt.htm#serious

Ward, R. (1966), *The Australian Legend*, 2nd ed., Melbourne: Oxford University Press.

Weeden, D. and Paloma, C. (2012), 'A Post-Cairo Paradigm: Both Numbers and Women Matter', in P. Cafaro and E. Crist (eds), *Life on the Brink*, 255–73.

Weintrobe, S. (ed.) (2013), *Engaging with Climate Change: Psychoanalytic and Interdisciplinary Perspectives*, London: Routledge.

Welzer, H. (2012), *Climate Wars: Why People Will Be Killed in the 21st Century*, Cambridge: Polity Press.

Wenzel, J. (2006), 'Petro-Magic-Realism: Toward a Political Ecology of Nigerian Literature', *Postcolonial Studies* 9, 449–64.

Whalen, P. (1999), *Overtime: Selected Poems*, London: Penguin.

Williams, A. (2014), 'California Burning', *New Scientist*, 16 August 2014.

Williams, W. C. (1963), *Paterson*, New York: New Directions.

Wilson, E. O. (2008), Foreword to J. Sachs, *Common Wealth: Economics for a Crowded Planet*, New York: Penguin, vi–xiii.

Zalasiewicz, J. et al. (2012), 'Response to Austin and Holbrook, "Is the Anthropocene an Issue of Stratigraphy or Pop Culture?"' *GSA Today*, v. 22. http://www.geosociety.org/gsatoday/comment-reply/pdf/i1052-5173-22-10-e21.pdf

Žižek, S. (2010), *Living in the End Times*, London: Verso.

INDEX